Counsels of Religion

Counsels of Religion

by
Imām ʿAbdallāh al-Haddād

Translated by
Moṣṭafā al-Badawī

FONS VITAE

First published in 2010 by
Fons Vitae
49 Mockingbird Valley Drive
Louisville, KY 40207
http://www.fonsvitae.com
Email: fonsvitaeky@aol.com

Library of Congress Control Number: 2010935424
ISBN 9781891785405

The author of this book, Imām 'Abdallāh Alawī al-Haddād (died, 1720), was one of the most illustrious masters of the house of Banī 'Alawī, the descendants of Imām Husayn who settled in Hadramawt, and is widely held to have been the spiritual "renewer" of the twelfth Islāmic century. That Imām al-Haddād was the ultimate authority of his time, especially as concerns questions of method and gnosis, is substantiated by the statements of the saints of his time. A direct descendant of the Prophet, his sanctity and direct experience of God are clearly reflected in his writings.

Other Fons Vitae titles in the
Imām al-Haddād Spiritual Master series include:

The Lives of Man (1991)
The Book of Assistance (2003)
Gifts for the Seeker (2003)
The Sufī Sage of Arabia (2005)
The Sublime Treasures (2008)

This book was typeset by Neville Blakemore, Jr.

Printed in South Korea

CONTENTS

Translator's Introduction

In the Name of God, All-Merciful and Compassionate

This work by Imām al-Ḥaddād, his largest, was completed in 1089 A.H. He had written nearly half of it prior to his departure for *Ḥajj*, and these chapters were read in his presence in both Makka and Madina, where he had been received with enthusiasm and acknowledged as the foremost scholar of his time. He later told his student and servant, Shaykh Aḥmad al-Shajjār, "Our aim in the Book of Counsels was that it be easy, clear, intelligible to the reader possessed of understanding, and sufficient. Should he not find it sufficient, then it would prepare him for more elaborate works.[1] Someone once called it the "*ḥ*" of the *Iḥyā'*..." He also said, "A scholar in the Two Sanctuaries said to us: 'This book is nothing but the *Iḥyā*''. We replied: 'It is as you say'."

The contents of the book are indeed in many ways similar to those of the *Iḥyā'*, despite the fact that the latter is made of four large volumes. The book opens with a discourse on *taqwā* or God-fearing, leading up to the role of *taqwā* in attaining to a good ending to life, which means passing into the next life as a Muslim, thereby making certain of reaching paradise. As parts of *taqwā* are discussed such outward endeavors as unity among Muslims, the avoidance of division and discord, and the duty to enjoin good and forbid evil. *Taqwā* also comprises inward things such as contentment with God and His decrees, avoiding distraction and illusory hopes, fear of God, the remembrance of death, avoiding hoping for forgiveness without working for it, while using predestination as a justification. The essential role of knowledge in Islam is discussed next, followed by four of the five pillars of Islam. The fifth, which in the usual order comes first, the testimony of *Lā ilāha illa'llāh, Muḥammadun Rasūlu'llāh* is left till the end, where it is explained as the Creed of *Ahl al-Sunna wa'l-Jamā'a*. This statement of belief, suitably concise, yet very clear, was later printed separately many times, both in Arabic and in English translation, distributed widely in the Islamic world, and included by *Ḥabīb* Aḥmad Mashhūr al-Ḥaddād in his widely read *Key to the Garden*. The four other pillars, the ritual

1. More detailed works of the same quality or with the same properties can only be the works of Imām al-Ghazālī; which explains the next remarks by the Imām.

prayer, *zakāt*, fasting, and pilgrimage, are discussed not in regard with their outward legal aspect, but rather their dimension of *iḥsān*, which is what one ought to do and what pitfalls to avoid in order to render the act of worship outwardly and inwardly sound and thus acceptable to God. Among the most important things which make an act of worship acceptable is the degree to which one's heart is present with God, and to this and to reciting the Qur'ān a chapter is devoted. The eighth and ninth chapters are related, since enjoining good and forbidding evil constitute a major part of *Jihād*. The tenth relates to the rights and duties of people toward each other, such as the duties of political leaders towards their communities, those of judges, those of children toward their parents, parents toward their children, spouses toward each other, relatives, and other such matters with which those who enjoin good and forbid evil should be well acquainted. Then come two chapters which in the *Iḥyā'* constitute two of its largest sections and so to speak its heart, "Ruinous Things" which are those deeds, emotions, and characters which ruin one's heart by darkening it, and "Saving Things" which, being their opposites, lead to the heart's purification and enlightenment. Ruinous things include everything that is legally forbidden, as well as the crimes of the tongue and ailments of the heart such as arrogance, resentful envy, avarice, and so on. Saving things include repentance, the nine stations of certainty mentioned in the *Book of Assistance*, in addition to sincerity, reflection, and short hopes.

That section of the *Iḥyā'* relating to death and what comes after it has no counterpart here, but forms a major part of another of Imām al-Ḥaddād's books, *The Lives of Man.*

Imām al-Ḥaddād's intention was never to summarize the work of Ghazālī, rather he was so familiar with them and had practiced what they teach so thoroughly that spontaneously he could produce the essence of them in his well known style, joining both concision and clarity, the two qualities necessary for the readership of these times. He once wrote to an Egyptian scholar, Shaykh Yūsuf al-Azharī, counseling him to read the *Iḥyā'* repeatedly, "They said that Imām al-Ghazālī—may God have mercy on him—disciplines with his books[2], because of what he entrusted to them of the realities

2. This was written six hundred years after Imām al-Ghazālī's death. The intended meaning is evidently that he still disciplined students with his books and was likely to continue doing so as long as there remains someone who reads them.

of things concerning the Sacred Law as well as spiritual method." The Imām said on other occasions, "*Subḥān'Allāh*! The writings of Imām al-Ghazālī can make you do without any others, while others cannot make you do without him." And, "The books of Imām al-Ghazālī have a special quality which is that they draw hearts to be present with God, by this quality, not by mere knowledge." All this might also be said with total confidence about the works of Imām al-Haddād, for soon after one starts perusing one of these, the spiritual secret within them makes itself felt and the heart flies to the higher worlds, yearning for its Lord.

The correct manner in which to make use of both Imām al-Haddād's and Imām al-Ghazālī's books, as proved by experience, is to return to them every few months and read them again. With each reading meanings that are new appear and others that have already been grasped become more deeply ingrained in one's psyche, until such time as one begins automatically to produce answers to existential questions and solutions to ever changing situations that are in conformity with that pattern, which is none other than the *Sunna* of the Prophet-may God's blessings and peace be upon him and his family.

May God reward both Imāms as befits His generosity for their immensely influential role in guiding thousands of souls thirsty for their Lord along the royal path of self-purification and love that leads to His Presence.

Counsels of Religion

Al-Naṣā'iḥ al-Dīniyya wa'l-Waṣāyā'l-Īmāniyya

In the Name of God, All-Merciful and Compassionate

Prologue

There is neither power nor ability
save by God the High, the Formidable.

Transcendent are You! We have no knowledge save
what You taught us; You are the Knowing, the Wise.

Praise belongs to God, Lord of the worlds, who caused summoning to guidance, showing where the good lies, and counseling Muslims, to be one of the best acts of worship and of the highest degrees, and the most important of things religious. This is the way of God's Prophets and Messengers, His virtuous saints, and those scholars who practice what they know[1] and are firmly rooted in knowledge and certainty. And May God's blessings and peace be upon our master and patron Muḥammad, the trustworthy Messenger, the high ranking Beloved, the leader of the God-fearing, the master of the ancients and the latecomers, upon his sincere and truthful family and Companions, and upon those who follow them with excellence till Judgment Day.

To proceed: The Messenger of God—may God's blessings and peace be upon him—said, *Actions are but by intentions, to each person what he intended. He whose emigration was to God and His Messenger, his emigration is to God and His Messenger. He whose emigration is to something of the world he desires or a woman he wishes to marry, his emigration is to that which he has emigrated to.*[2] And he has said—may God's blessings and peace be upon him, *Religion is but good counsel.* They asked, "For whom, O Messenger

1. As opposed to those who are learned but lack the sincerity and spiritual resolution to put what they know into practice so as to purify and illuminate their hearts. Great is the difference between scholars who have attained to sanctity and the profound wisdom that comes with it, and those who possess of knowledge only the outward shell.
2. Bukhārī, *Ṣaḥīḥ*, (1); and Muslim, *Ṣaḥīḥ*, (3530).

of God?" He said, *For God, His Book, and His Messenger; for the leaders of the Muslims and their common people.*[3]

This is a book we have authored, compiling therein some counsels of religion and exhortations of faith. Our intention was to make it of benefit to ourselves and others, and to be a reminder for ourselves and our brother Muslims. We have written it in an easy accessible style, using ordinary understandable expressions, that it may be understood by both the elite and the common people among those who are people of *Īmān* and *Islām*. We have called it: The Book of Counsels of Religion and Exhortations of Faith. We ask God the Exalted to cause it to be purely for the sake of His Noble Countenance, to draw us near to His proximity in the Gardens of Bliss, and to make great its benefit both to us and all our brother believers, for He is Worthy of this and Capable of it. God suffices us and He is the Best of Guardians. My success is but by God, upon Him do I rely and to Him do I return.

3. Meaning that counsel is given for God's sake, in a manner that pleases Him, according to the knowledge in the Qur'ān and that bequeathed by the Messenger of God. Those qualified to counsel others will have counsels specific to leaders and others more appropriate for the people, since the order of priorities varies according to the function, as Imām al-Ḥaddād explains in a book devoted entirely to this subject, *al-Da'wa al-Tāmma*. The *ḥadīth* is in Muslim, *Ṣaḥīḥ*, (55); Tirmidhī, *Sunan*, (1926); Nasā'ī, *Sunan,* (4197); and Abū Dāwūd, *Sunan,* (4945).

Chapter One: On *Taqwā*

God the Exalted says, *And whose speech is more truthful than God's?* [4:87] *O Believers, fear God as He should be feared, and die only as Muslims; and hold firmly to God's rope and do not disperse. And remember God's favor upon you, that you were enemies and He caused harmony between your hearts, so that you became brothers by His favor. And that you were on the brink of an abyss of fire and He saved you from it. Thus does God make plain His signs, that you may be rightly-guided. Let there be from you a group who invite to goodness, enjoin good, and forbid evil. Those are the successful. And do not be like those who fell into division and discord after the clear proofs had come to them. For those there is a formidable torment.* [3:102 to 105]

His saying—Exalted is He, *O believers, fear God as He should be feared,* is a command from Him—August and Majestic is He—to His believing servants to fear Him. It is as if He had gathered in the fear of Him—Transcendent is He—everything good, both immediate and delayed, then enjoined it upon His believing servants, that they may succeed and gain all the goodness and merits in it, as well as happiness and success. This He did in compassion for His believing servants, *for He is ever Compassionate to the believers.* [33:43]

Taqwā is the counsel that the Lord of the Worlds gave both the ancients and the latecomers. He says—Exalted is He—*We have counseled those who were given the Book before you and yourselves to fear God.* [4:131] For there is no good, immediate or remote, outward or inward, but that the fear of God is the path leading to it and the means to reach it. And there is no evil, immediate or remote, outward or inward, but that the fear of God is the strongest protection and most powerful defence against it, to escape its harm. How numerous are the major benefactions and immense good fortunes said to depend on it by God the Formidable in His August Book.

Among these are:

Being with God, which is the gentle protective togetherness: God—Exalted is He—says, *Fear God and know that God is with the God-fearing.* [2:194] *"Fear God and God will teach you.* [2:282]

Discernment at times of confusion, requital of bad acts, and forgiveness of sins: God—Exalted is He—says, *O Believ-*

> *ers, if you fear God, He will give you discernment, requite your bad deeds, and forgive you. God's favor is immense.* [8:29]
>
> Safety from the Fire: God—Exalted is He—says: *There is not one of you who shall not come to it. This is the inevitable decree of your Lord. Then We shall save those who feared [their Lord] and abandon the unjust therein on their knees.* [19:71-72] And He says, *And God shall save those who feared [Him] by their gains, evil shall not touch them, neither will they grieve.* [39:61]
>
> A way out of difficulties, provision from whence it is not expected, ease in life, and a great reward: God—Exalted is He—says, *He who fears God, He will make a way out for him and provide for him from whence he did not expect. And he who fears God, He will make his affairs easy. And he who fears God, He will requite his bad deeds and make his reward immense.* [65:2,3,4,5]
>
> The promise of the Garden: God—Exalted is He—says, *This is the Garden that We give those of Our servants who were God-fearing.* [19:63] And He says—Exalted is He, *The likeness of the Garden that the God-fearing are promised...* [13:35] *And the Garden was brought near for the God-fearing.* [26:90] *For the God-fearing are Gardens of bliss at their Lord's.* [68:34] *The God-fearing are in gardens and rivers, in seats of truth near a powerful King.* [54:545]
>
> Honor in this world and the next: God—Exalted is He—says, *The most honorable of you in the sight of God are those who fear [Him] most.* [49:13] Thus did He make honor in His sight conditional upon *taqwā,* not upon lineage, wealth, or any other thing. How often have God and His Messenger promised the God fearing goodness, happiness, degrees, rewards, well-being, success, gifts, and gains the mention of which would be too lengthy and the enumeration of which impossible.

How excellent in this context is the following verse:

> He who fears God is one to whom profitable commerce
> has been granted.

As also the following verses:

He who knows God but finds not in this knowledge
all that he needs, he indeed is wretched.

He who serves God is never injured
by what he may suffer in His service

What gains a servant from the eminence of wealth
since all eminence belongs to the God-fearing

Certain scholars—may God be pleased with them—have said, "*Taqwā* is to obey God the Exalted's injunctions, and avoid what He has prohibited, outwardly and inwardly, together with feeling how formidable He is and being in fear, awe, and dread of Him. Certain commentators [of the Qur'ān]—may God have mercy on them—said that His saying—Exalted is He, *Fear God as He should rightly be feared,* [3:102] means that He should be ever obeyed, never disobeyed; ever remembered, never forgotten; and ever thanked, never [have His favors] denied.

No servant [of God] will ever be able to fear God as He rightly should be feared, even were he to have a thousand thousand souls added to his and a thousand thousand lifetimes added to his; and were he to spend all of them in serving God and doing what pleases Him. This is because of the immensity of God's rights upon His servants, His awesome greatness, His lofty degree, and His sublime glory. The best and most perfect of all who have ever acquitted themselves of God's rights upon them, Muḥammad,—may God's blessings and peace be upon him—confessing his inability to praise God as He should be praised, said in his prayers, *I seek refuge in Your satisfaction from Your wrath, in Your safeguard from Your punishment, and in You from You. I cannot exhaust Your praises, You are as You have praised Yourself.*[1]

We have been informed that God has angels whose state, since they were created, is to remain constantly bowing or prostrating, extolling and sanctifying God, never slackening, never attending to other than He. Yet, come Judgment Day, they will say, "Transcendent are You! Yours are all praises and thanks! We have not known You as You should be known, neither have we worshipped You as You should be worshipped."

1. Muslim, *Ṣaḥīḥ*, (751); Abū Dāwūd, *Sunan*, (745, 1215); Tirmidhī, *Sunan*, (3415, 3489).

Other scholars have said that His saying—Exalted is He, *Fear God as He should rightly be feared.* [3:102] was abrogated by His saying, *so fear God as best you can.* [64:16] Others still said that the second verse merely explains the meaning of the first, but does not abrogate it. This last opinion is the correct one, God willing, for God—Exalted is He and to Him all praises—imposes upon a soul only that which it is capable of. It is His by right to impose more should He so wish and command, for it is His to do what He will in His kingdom, His domain. But He has lightened the burden—Transcended is He—and made things easy. As He says—Exalted is He, *God wished to lighten your burden, for Man was created weak.* [4:28] *God desires ease for you and does not desire hardship for you.* [2:185]

Imām al-Ghazālī—may God have mercy on him—says in his *Iḥyā'*: When this saying of His was revealed—Exalted is He, *To God belongs what is in the heavens and what is in the earth. Whether you reveal what is in yourselves or conceal it, God will ask you to account for it.* [2:284] the Companions of the Messenger of God were distraught—may God's blessings and peace be upon him and may He be pleased with them. They came to him saying, "O Messenger of God, we cannot possibly bear what has been imposed upon us." For they understood from the verse that they would be brought to account for every incidental thought. He said to them—may peace be upon him, *Do you wish to say, as the Israelites said: We hear and disobey? Rather say: We hear and obey, Your forgiveness, O our Lord; to You is the destination.* When they repeated this, God revealed, *The Messenger believes in what was sent down to him by his Lord, and so do the believers. They all believe in God and His angels, and His books, and His Messengers. And they say, 'We hear and obey. Your forgiveness, O our Lord; to You is the destination'.* [2:285] [2] Thus did God recount [in the Qur'ān] what they said, as well as the rest of their prayers to Him, that He brings them not to account for acts done in forgetfulness or by mistake, that He does not impose hard rules upon them, and so on. He responded to them, made things lighter and easier for them, and relieved them of hardship. May He be praised and thanked in abundance. The Prophet—may peace be upon him—confirmed it by saying, *That shall be overlooked for my Nation which is committed by mistake, in forget-*

2. Muslim, *Ṣaḥīḥ*, (179); Aḥmad, *Musnad*, (8976).

fulness, or under duress[3]*; as well as that which crosses their minds, so long as they neither utter nor do it.*[4]

His saying—Exalted is He, *Die not except as Muslims.* [3:102] is a command from Him—Transcendent is He—to die adhering to Islam, God's religion, of which He informed us in His Book that it is the only Religion in His sight and that He will accept none other, that it is the religion He found pleasing for His Messenger and His believing servants. He says—Exalted is He, *Religion in the sight of God is but Islam.* [3:19] And He says, Exalted is He, *And he who wishes for other than Islam as a religion, it will not be accepted from him, and in the hereafter he will be among the losers.* [3:85] And He says—Exalted is He, *Today I have perfected your religion for you, and completed My favor upon you, and was satisfied with Islam as your religion.* [5:3]

A human being lacks the power to force himself to die as a Muslim, but God has granted him the means to attain to that. When he makes use of the means he would have done what is his to do and obeyed what he was commanded to do, namely to intend to die a Muslim, love this, wish for it, resolve to do it, and loathe to die on any other religion. He should persist in praying for this, imploring God and beseeching Him to take him to Him as a Muslim. Thus did God describe His Prophets and the virtuous among His servants. He said in mentioning Joseph son of Jacob—may peace be upon them, *You are my ally in this world and the next, take me as a Muslim and make me join the virtuous.* [12:101] And in mentioning Pharaoh's magicians when they became believers and were threatened chastisement by Pharaoh, *Our Lord, give us fortitude in abundance and take us as Muslims.* [7:126] And He informed us—Exalted is He—that Abraham—may peace be upon him—exhorted his sons, and so did Jacob—may peace be upon them—to die on Islam. He says—Exalted is He, *Thus did Abraham exhort his sons and also Jacob, O my sons, God has chosen the best religion for you, so die only as Muslims.* [2:132][5]

---

3. Ibn Māja, *Sunan*, (2033, 2035); Al-Ḥākim, *Mustadrak*, (2752).

4. Bukhārī, *Ṣaḥīḥ*, (2343).

5. The word Islam in this context refers to its original meaning of submission to God, which is the primordial religion of Adam and his descendants which came naturally to early mankind, and which the Prophet aimed to restore. Islam is the essence and spirit of all true religions. This is why the Qur'ān calls all previous Prophets Muslims and their religions Islam,

A person should strive to guard his Islam and strengthen it by accomplishing those acts of obedience to God—Exalted is He—which he is commanded to do. He who neglects God's commands exposes himself to die on other than Islam; for his being neglectful is evidence that he cares little for his religion and takes it lightly. Let every Muslim beware of this to the extreme. He should also avoid sins and evil deeds, for they weaken Islam, render it feeble, shake its foundations, and make it liable to be wrested away at the time of death, as has actually happened—may God protect us—to many who persistently committed such acts. There is an indication to this in His saying—Exalted is He, *then evil was the consequence to those who dealt in evil, because they denied the signs of God and mocked them.* [30:10] So reflect on this and impose upon yourself obedience to the injunctions of God the Exalted, and avoidance of what He has prohibited. Should you slip into any of these, repent to God—Exalted is He—and beware to the extreme to persist. And constantly ask God for a good ending [to your life]. It has reached us that the Devil—may God curse him—says, "He has broken my back who asks God for a good ending. I then say: when will this one become proud of his deeds? I fear that he may have understood!"

Praise and thank God abundantly for the grace of Islam, for it is the greatest and most immense of graces. Were God to give this world and all that is in it to one of His servants, but withhold Islam, it would be a catastrophe for him. But were He to grant another of His servants Islam and withhold the whole world, it would not harm him. For when the first dies he will end up in the Fire, while the second, when he dies, will end up in the Garden. You must maintain yourself in a state of fear and anxiety of a bad ending, for God is He who turns hearts, He guides whom He will, and leads astray whom He will. An authentic *ḥadīth* states, *By He with whom there is no other God, one of you will keep doing the works of the people of the Garden until he is one cubit away from it, then the record overtakes him, he will then behave as the people of the Fire do until he enters it. And one of you will keep doing the works of the people of the Fire until he is one cubit away from it, then the record overtakes him, he*

---

despite the differences in formulation and practical details necessitated by differences of time, location, ethnic character, and so on. Only after the final revelation did the term Islam come to indicate the religion revealed to Muḥammad-May God's blessings and peace be upon him.

will then behave as the people of the Garden do until he enters it.[6] In this is a terrifying threat for people possessed of God-fearing and rectitude, let alone people of neglect and confusion. One of our virtuous predecessors used to say, "By God! None has ever felt secure from being dispossessed of his religion but that he was." Our virtuous predecessors, may God have mercy on them, were all extremely apprehensive of an evil conclusion to their lives, despite their good works and scarcity of sins, to the extent that one of them said, "Were I to be given a choice between dying as a Muslim at the door of my room or as a martyr at the door of the house, I would choose to die as a Muslim at the door of my room, for I know not what will happen to my heart in the distance between the door of my room and the door of the house." Another said to one of his brothers, "When I am about to die, sit near my head and watch: If you see that I have died a Muslim, take all my possessions, sell them, buy sugar and almonds, and distribute it among the children. But if you see that I have died on other than that, then let the people know, so that those who wish to pray my funeral prayer would do so in full awareness. Then he told him of a sign by which he would know whether he had died a Muslim or not. His brother later on recounted how he had seen that he had died a Muslim and had distributed his donation to the children as instructed. Such stories of theirs abound."

Know that those who neglect their obligatory prayers often suffer a bad ending to their lives, and so do those who neglect obligatory *zakāt*, pry upon other Muslims' privacy, cheat in weights and measures, deceive Muslims and delude them by causing them confusion, whether in religious or worldly matters, and those who belie God's saints and disparage them unjustly, as well as those who falsely pretend they possess the states of the saints and their stations, and other such loathsome things.

Other things that threaten their perpetrators most seriously with a bad ending are innovation in religion (*bid'a*), and harboring doubts concerning God, His Messenger, and the last Day. So let every Muslim beware of these to the extreme. None is protected from God's decree except those He has mercy on.

O Most Merciful of all, we ask You by the light of Your Noble Countenance to take us to you as Muslims and make us join the virtuous, in wellbeing, O Lord of the Worlds.

---

6. Bukhārī, *Ṣaḥīḥ*, (2969, 3085); Muslim, *Ṣaḥīḥ*, (4781).

His saying—Exalted is He, *And hold firmly to God's rope and do not divide.* [3:103] is a command to take refuge in God's religion, which is to uphold and conform to it steadfastly, and be united in so doing. It is a command not to be divided in matters of religion, for union is a mercy, whereas division is hardship. God's hand is with those who are united, as the Prophet has said—may God's blessings and peace be upon him.[7]

This noble religion's rise was based on cohesion, mutual support, and united intentions. Therefore, disunity and lack of cohesion in upholding it lead to its enfeeblement and weakness. It is thus clear that cohesion in religion is the basis of all good and success, whereas division is that of all evil and hardship.

His saying—Exalted is He, *And remember the favor of God upon you: how you were enemies and He made harmony between your hearts, so that you became brothers by His grace, and how you were on the brink of an abyss of fire and He saved you from it. Thus does God clearly show His signs to you, that you may be rightly-guided.* [3:103] is a command to thank Him for the favor of harmony that God bestowed upon them, particularly after the ferocious hostility that had existed between the [two tribes of] Aws and Khazraj, who subsequently became the Helpers of God and His Messenger; and that which had existed between the Arabs in general. They had been fighting and looting each other, in constant strife, until God raised His Messenger among them, sent down His Book upon him, thereby uniting them and weaving bonds of friendship between their hearts, removing the enmity and rancor and the seditions and discords that had previously existed between them, so that they became, by His favor, brothers in His religion, in supporting His Messenger, and revering His rites. God—Exalted is He—mentions this in the context of pointing out His favors upon His Messenger—may peace be upon him—when He says—Exalted is He, *He it is Who strengthened you with His support and with the believers, and made harmony between their hearts...* [8:62,63] For before He sent His Messenger to them they had been on the brink of an abyss of fire, because of their disbelief in God and worshipping of idols. God saved them from these by prescribing *Tawḥīd* and acts of obedience. Then God bid them thank Him for these [graces], recognize how they were saved from error by His favor and how, having been so divided, they became united. He also warned them against everything that may lead to division

7. Tirmidhī, *Sunan*, (2092); Ibn Ḥibbān, *Ṣaḥīḥ,* (4660).

and discord after union and harmony had been achieved. *Thus does God clearly show His signs to you, that you may be rightly-guided.* [3:103] Meaning that it will make you even more rightly-guided. As He says—Exalted is He, *And those who were rightly-guided, He increased them in guidance and bestowed upon them their* taqwā. [47:17]

And His saying—Exalted is He, *Let there be a group from among you, inviting to goodness,* [3:104] Goodness is faith and obedience. Inviting others to this is a lofty rank in the sight of God and a powerful means to draw nearer to Him. He said—may God's blessings and peace be upon him—, *He who invites to right guidance will be recompensed as much as those who respond to him, without this diminishing their recompense in any way; and he who invites to error will be burdened with as much sin as those who respond to him, without this diminishing their sins in any way.*[8] And he said—may blessings and peace be upon him, *He who guides to a good is equal to him who does it.*[9] Thus, he who makes enjoining goodness his habit and main preoccupation, he has taken an ample share of the heritage of the Messenger of God—may God's blessings and peace be upon him—and treaded his path, about which God—Exalted is He—says, *Say: This is my way, I summon to God, clear-sightedly, I and those who follow me; and Transcendent is God and I am not one of those who associate [others with Him].* [12:108] For he was only preoccupied—may blessings and peace be upon him—at all times with summoning to God, both with his words and his deeds. This is why God had sent him and this is what He commanded him to do. As He says—Exalted is He, *Say: I have been commanded to worship God and not associate with Him. To Him do I summon and to him is my return.* [13:36] Thus, the people nearest to the Messenger of God—may God's blessings and peace be upon him—those who are most closely connected with him in this world and the next, are those who are most concerned with this matter, most preoccupied with it, and most actively engaged in it. By "this matter" I mean enjoining good, which is faith and obedience, and forbidding their opposites, which are disbelief and sin. He says—Exalted is He, *And they enjoin good and forbid evil; and those are they who will be successful.* [3:104] Success in this context being the attainment of

8. Muslim, *Ṣaḥīḥ*, (4831); Abū Dāwūd, *Sunan*, (3993); Tirmidhī, *Sunan*, (2598).

9. Tirmidhī, *Sunan*, (2594); Aḥmad, *Musnad*, (21949).

happiness in both this world and the next. As for enjoining good and forbidding evil, they are among the greatest of religious activities, the strongest of Islam's foundations, and the most important function of Muslims. By them affairs are straightened and everything runs in a goodly manner. By neglecting them people's rights are lost, boundaries transgressed, truth disappears, and falsehood appears. Good in this context is everything that God has enjoined upon His servants and likes them to do, while evil is everything that God dislikes them to do and likes them to avoid. Enjoining good and forbidding evil is an obligation and there can be no excuse for abandoning it. The Prophet has said—may blessings and peace be upon him, *He who notices something reprehensible, let him change it with his hand; if he cannot then with his words; if he cannot then with his heart, and this would be the weakest degree of faith.*[10] Another version says, *there is beyond this*- i.e. beyond disapproving with the heart—*not a mustard seed of faith.*[11] And he said- may blessings and peace be upon him, *He is not one of us who shows no compassion to our little ones, nor reverence for our elders, who neither enjoins good, nor forbids evil.*[12] And he said—may blessings and peace be upon him, *By He in Whose Hand my soul is, you will enjoin good and forbid evil, or God will soon send upon you a chastisement from Him, then you will pray Him but He will not respond.*[13] And he said—may blessings and peace be upon him, *When my community begins to fear saying to the unjust that he is unjust, then it is farewell to them.*[14] Meaning that the good in his community will have gone and the time for it to perish has drawn near.

God—Exalted is He—does not accept fatuous excuses and false justifications such as the people of this time offer for abandoning enjoining good and forbidding evil. They sometimes say, for example, "No one will accept this from us, whether we enjoin or forbid." Or, "Unbearable harm will come to us should we enjoin or forbid."

---

10. Muslim, *Ṣaḥīḥ*, (70); Abū Dāwūd, *Sunan*, (963); Tirmidhī, *Sunan*, (2098); Nasā'ī, *Sunan*, (4922); Ibn Māja, *Sunan*, (1265, 4003).

11. Muslim, *Ṣaḥīḥ*, (71). This was said in the context of those who would create sedition and discord after the Prophet's death, disrupting religion by claiming one thing while doing its opposite, and taking initiatives based on their whims rather than on a sound understanding of the Law.

12. Tirmidhī, *Sunan*, (1844); Bayhaqī, *Shu'ab al-Īmān*, (10544).

13. Aḥmad, *Musnad*, (22212).

14. Al-Ḥākim, *Mustadrak*, (7136).

As well as other such things which are the illusory anxieties of those who have neither insight, nor concern for God's religion. Silence is indeed permitted when the occurrence of major harm or rejection is certain beyond doubt. But even under such circumstances, enjoining and forbidding is better and more appropriate, the difference being that it becomes no longer obligatory. The strange thing is that if one of them is insulted, or dispossessed of his money, even of a little sum, he becomes distressed and unable to keep quiet. At such a time he produces none of those excuses which he uses at other times to justify keeping silent when faced with reprehensible things. Can this be explained or understood as other than that their selves and their possessions are dearer to them than their religion? Even should we concede that were they to enjoin and forbid they would not be heard, then what is it that drives them to mix with corrupt people and socialize with them, when God has commanded them to avoid and shun them so long as they are not responding to God and His Messenger? It is known beyond doubt that those who witness reprehensible things without disapproving of them when able to share the sin of those who approve of them, even if not present at the time, even were there as much distance between where they are and where these acts take place as between the East and the West. He who mixes and socializes with corrupt people, even if he refrains from joining in what they do, is considered by God to be one of them. Should punishment befall them, he will be afflicted along with them. The only route to safety is for him to disapprove of what they do and exhort them to desist, then, should they fail to respond and accept the truth, move away and avoid them altogether.

To love, for God's sake, those who obey Him, and to detest, for God's sake, those who disobey Him, are two of the strongest knots of faith. The Messenger of God—may God's blessings and peace be upon him—has said, as has reached us, *When the Israelites began to do wrong their scholars rebuked them, but they did not respond. Yet they [the scholars] continued to socialize with them and share their meals. When they did, God cast hostility between their hearts and cursed them by the tongues of David and Jesus son of Mary.*[15] And in the story of the village that was by the sea, when they took to fishing on the Sabbath when it was forbidden, they divided into three groups. One group fished, doing did what God had forbidden, another refrained from fishing and rebuked them, but did

15. Tirmidhī, *Sunan*, (2974); Abū Ya'lā, *Musnad*, (4905, 4963).

not leave them, and a third having rebuked them, left them, moving away from them. When punishment came down, it befell the first two groups, the second for not having forsaken the first, even though they had not shared in the same wrong. Only the third group escaped punishment. This is His saying—Exalted is He, *We saved those who forbade wrong and [We] took the unjust with a severe torment for the corruption they had wrought.* [7:165] God turned them into monkeys and cursed them, as in the other verse, *or that We curse them as We cursed those of the Sabbath.* [4:47] Shunning and avoiding sinful people should come only after having despaired of their accepting the truth.

Know that it is not necessary for anyone to search for hidden reprehensible things so that he may forbid them, rather this is forbidden, for He says—Exalted is He, *Do not spy.* [49:12] And the Prophet—may God's blessings and peace be upon him—said, *He who seeks to expose his brother's shameful secrets, God will expose his shameful secrets …*[16] What is obligatory is to enjoin good when one sees those who do wrong. Understand this, for we have seen many people erring in this matter.

It is important that you neither believe nor accept everything that is reported to you concerning reprehensible deeds or words till you witness them yourself or a God-fearing, circumspect, truthful believer recounts them to you. For thinking well of Muslims is necessary and people's reporting each others' misdeeds have become excessive. Carelessness and lack of concern in doing so has become the rule, honesty has disappeared, and he is considered worthy of gratitude who approves of others' desires, even when contrary to rectitude with God; while he is considered blameworthy who disagrees with them, even were he to be a virtuous man. Thus you see them praising those who do not deserve it but who approve of their behavior and keep silent about their wrongdoing, but disparaging those who disapprove of their behavior and counsel them to improve their religion. This is the condition of the majority, except those whom God protects. It is important to be circumspect, reserved, and careful in all things, for the times are times of sedition and its people have turned away from the truth, save those whom God will, and a minority they are.

---

16. Tirmidhī, *Sunan*, (1955); Aḥmad, Musnad, (18963, 21368); Bayhaqī, *Shu'ab al-Īmān*, (9331, 10748).

Know that keeping to gentleness and gracious manners, as well as avoiding coarse and aggressive manners, are a major factor leading to others accepting the truth and submitting to it. Adhere to this with any Muslim you exhort [to good] or discourage [from evil] or counsel [in any other way]. Do it with tact, in private, gently, affectionately, for, as he said—may blessings and peace be upon him; *Gentleness is never mixed with anything without embellishing it, nor is it ever taken away from anything without disfiguring it,*[17] and as God—Exalted is He—said to His Messenger, *It was by a mercy from God that you were lenient with them. Had you been stern and hard hearted they would have dispersed from around you.* [3:159]

His saying—Exalted is He, *Be not like those who fell into division and discord after the clear signs had come to them.* [3:105] is an interdiction from God to His believing servants to imitate those People of the Book who fell into division and discord concerning their religion. *And those* who fell into discord concerning their religion *will suffer a formidable torment.* It behooves you—may God have mercy upon you—to fear to the extreme a torment that God the Formidable calls *formidable*. Reflect upon it and save yourself from it by conforming to the Book and *Sunna*, avoiding errors, heresies, diverging opinions and whimsical inclinations.

Know that just as the People of the Book have divided and disagreed about their religion, so has this nation divided and disagreed, as the Messenger of God—may God's blessings and peace be upon him—had foretold when he said, *The Jews divided into seventy one or seventy two sects, the Christians divided into seventy one or seventy two sects, and my community will divide into seventy three sects,*[18] *all of them in the Fire except one.*[19] This community has indeed divided into the said number a long time ago and what the Truthful, the Trustee of God's revelation said would happen has already come to pass. When he was asked—may blessings and peace be upon him—about the one group destined to be saved, he replied, *Those who will conform with how I and my Companions are.*[20] When disagreement happens, his instructions—may blessings and peace be upon him—are to keep with the great majority of Muslims. The People of the *Sunna*—may God the Exalted be praised—

17. Muslim, *Ṣaḥīḥ*, (4698); Abū Dāwūd, *Sunan*, (2119).
18. Abū Dāwūd, *Sunan*, (3980); Tirmidhī, *Sunan*, (2564).
19. Ibn Māja, *Sunan*, (3983); Aḥmad, *Musnad*, (11763).
20. Tirmidhī, *Sunan*, (2565); Ṭabarānī, *Kabīr*, (7553).

have remained the great majority of Muslims from the earliest days up to now. This is why it is well known that they are the "Group to be Saved" by the grace of God, for their adherence to the Book and *Sunna* and pattern of the virtuous predecessors who are the Companions and the Followers—may God be pleased with them all.

To proceed: We—may God be praised and thanked—are satisfied with God as Lord, with Islam as religion, with Muḥammad as Prophet and Messenger, with the Qur'ān as leader, with the Ka'ba as *Qibla*, and with the believers as brothers. We renounce every religion that differs from the religion of Islam. We believe in every Book that God ever revealed, every Messenger He ever sent, His angels, destiny, whether good or evil, the Last Day, and everything conveyed to us from God the Exalted by Muḥammad, the Messenger of God—may God's blessings and peace be upon him. Upon this do we live and upon this shall we die and be resurrected-God willing-among those who will be secure, who will fear not, neither will they grieve, by Your favor O Lord of the Worlds! The Messenger of God—may God's blessings and peace be upon him—said, *He has experienced the taste of faith who is satisfied with God as Lord, Islam as religion, and Muḥammad as Prophet.*[21] And he said—may blessings and peace be upon him, *He who says every morning and evening three times: 'I am satisfied with God as Lord, Islam as religion, and Muḥammad as Prophet', God-without doubt-will satisfy him on Resurrection Day.*[22]

Know, O brothers, that he who is satisfied with God as Lord should of necessity be satisfied with His management of his affairs and the choices He makes for him, including the bitter things He may ordain. He should be content with whatever provision He allots him, remain obedient to Him, careful to perform what He made obligatory upon him and avoid what He forbade him. He should be patient when enduring His tests, thankful for His favors, desirous to meet Him, satisfied with Him as Patron, Ally, and Guardian, sincere in His worship, relying on Him in both that which he can observe and that which is hidden from his view. He should seek no other help but His in times of difficulty and rely on none other than Him—Transcendent and Exalted is He—for the fulfillment of his needs.

He who is satisfied with Islam as religion will revere its rites and sacrosanct things and will persistently strive to acquire the kinds

21. Tirmidhī, *Sunan*, (2547); Aḥmad, *Musnad*, (1683).
22. Aḥmad, *Musnad*, (18199).

of knowledge and perform the kinds of works which confirm it and increase it in stability and steadfastness. He should be happy with it, anxious for it not to be taken away from him, respectful of its people, and averse to those who deny or antagonize it.

He who is satisfied with Muḥammad as Prophet should emulate him, follow his guidance, adhere to his law, uphold his *Sunna*, magnify his rights [upon him], and abundantly invoke blessings and peace upon him. He should love his family and Companions, invoke [God's] mercy and satisfaction upon them, and be concerned for the Prophet's community and of good counsel to them.

O believer, you should impose upon yourself to realize all the above in full, for these meanings are all included in your saying, "I am satisfied with God as Lord, with Islam as religion and with Muḥammad as Prophet." You should strive to acquire those attributes and not be content with merely mouthing them, for this is of little benefit, although not entirely devoid of it.

You must do the same for all other invocations and supplications that you use. Impose upon yourself to realize their meanings and acquire them so as to make them your own attributes. For example, when you say, "Transcendent is God!" [*Subḥān' Allāh*] your heart should be full with the magnification of God and awareness of His Transcendence. And when you say, "Praise belongs to God," [*Al-Ḥamdu lil'llāh*] your heart should be full of praises and thanks for God—Exalted is He. And when you say, "I ask God to forgive me," [*Astaghfiru'llāh*] it should be at the same time full of hope for God's forgiveness, yet fearful of His not granting it; and so on.

Strive for presence with God, reflect on the meanings of what you say, and do your best to acquire the behavior He likes and avoid that which He dislikes.

Concentrate on your inward aspect, your heart, for the Prophet has said—may blessings and peace be upon him, *God looks not at your outward forms or your wealth, but He looks at your hearts and your works.*[23] So confirm your words with your acts, your acts with your intentions and your sincerity, and your intentions and sincerity by purifying your inward and reforming your heart. For the heart is the essential thing upon which everything else depends. A *ḥadīth* says, *There is in the body a lump of flesh, when it is good the whole body is good, but when it is corrupt, the whole body is corrupt. This*

23. Muslim, *Ṣaḥīḥ*, (4651); Aḥmad, *Musnad*, (7493).

is the heart.[24] Therefore it is a duty to attend to it and concentrate on making it sound and upright. The heart is quick to turn around, excessively restless, to the extent that the Prophet said—may blessings and peace be upon him—*that it is quicker to turn around than a boiling pot.*[25] He often prayed—may blessings and peace be upon him, *O You Who turns hearts around, make my heart steadfast in Your religion.*[26] And he said, *Each heart is held between two of the All-Merciful's fingers. He keeps them upright when He so wills and He makes them swerve when He so wills.*[27] And when he wished to give force to an oath he said, *No, by He Who turns hearts around*![28]

God—Exalted is He—says that Abraham—may peace be upon him, His Intimate Friend, said, *And do not humiliate me on the day they are resurrected; a day when wealth and children avail nothing, except that one comes to God with a sound heart.* [26:87-89] So do your very best—may God have mercy on you—to come to your Lord with a heart that is free of idolatry, hypocrisy, heresy, and reprehensible traits of character such as arrogance, ostentation, jealousy, deceitful behavior toward Muslims, and so on. Seek God's help and be patient. Strive in earnest and repeat often, *Our Lord, do not cause our hearts to swerve after You have guided us; and bestow upon us a mercy from You, for You are the Bestower.* [3:8] For this is how God has described those of His believing servants who are firmly steeped in knowledge.

Beware of hardness, which is for the heart to become so coarse and callous that it is no longer affected by counseling, and neither softens nor is sensitive to the mention of death, of promises and threats, or of the events of the hereafter. He said—may blessings and peace be upon him, *The thing most remote from God—Exalted is He—is a heart that is hard.*[29] Our predecessors have said, "Four things are signs of wretchedness: hardness of the heart, dryness of the eye, avarice, and long hopes." So beware of these four. And he

24. Bukhārī, *Ṣaḥīḥ*, (50); Muslim, *Ṣaḥīḥ*, (2996).

25. Ṭabarānī, *Kabīr*, (16987); Aḥmad, *Musnad*, (22699); Al-Ḥākim, *Mustadrak*, (3098).

26. Tirmidhī, *Sunan*, (2066, 3444,3511); Aḥmad, *Musnad*, (11664, 13200).

27. Tirmidhī, *Sunan*, (3444); Aḥmad, *Musnad*, (16972).

28. Bukhārī, *Ṣaḥīḥ*, (6842).

29. Tirmidhī, *Sunan*, (2335); Bayhaqī, *Shu'ab al-Īmān*, (4745).

said—may blessings and peace be upon him, *and know that God accepts not the prayer of a distracted and heedless heart.*[30]

Distraction is of lesser importance than hardness. It is nevertheless blameworthy and may induce extreme harm. The distracted heart is that which does not awaken and become attentive when exposed to counsels or rebukes. It does not take them seriously, being so distracted and forgetful, so engrossed in its playthings and trivia, in the attractions of his worldly life and the pursuit of his passions. God—Exalted is He—said to His Messenger—may blessings and peace be upon him, *And remember your Lord within yourself, imploringly, fearfully, without raising your voice, in the mornings and the evenings, and be not one of the distracted.* [7:205] He thus forbade him to be one of the distracted. He also forbade him to obey or even listen to them, *And obey not he whose heart We distract away from Our remembrance, who follows his passions, and whose affairs are in disarray.* [18:28]

It is to be distracted to read or listen to the Noble Qur'ān, but neither reflect upon it, nor attempt to understand its meanings, neither obey its injunctions, nor its prohibitions, and neither accept its counsels, nor it rebukes. The same applies for the traditions of the Messenger of God—may blessings and peace be upon him—and the discourses of the virtuous predecessors—may God be pleased with them.

It is to be distracted not to remember death often, as well as what comes after it, the conditions of the blessed and those of the wretched, and not to dwell on these at length.

It is to be distracted not assiduously to keep company with those who know God and His religion, who remind of His days, His graces, His promises, and His threats, who exhort, with both words and deeds, to His obedience and to avoiding disobedience. Those who are unable to find such people should make up for that by reading their books. However-God willing—the earth will never be entirely devoid of them, even when corruption is rife and falsehood and its champions dominate, when everyone has turned away from God and from supporting the truth, except those whom God wills, and a very few are they. The Prophet—may blessings and peace be upon him—has said, *There shall remain a group in my nation, successfully upholding the truth, unharmed by those who oppose them, till*

30. Tirmidhī, *Sunan*, (3401); Aḥmad, *Musnad*, (6368); Al-Ḥākim, *Mustadrak*, (1771).

Resurrection Day.[31] There are more Prophetic and other traditions indicating that the earth will never be without a group of the people of truth, upholding the Book of God the Exalted and the *Sunna* of His Messenger—may God's blessings and peace be upon him—and exhorting others to do so. But their numbers will dwindle to the extreme at the End of Time. Furthermore, they may hide their status so as to remain unknown and unreachable, except for true seekers and sincere devotees. And God—Exalted is He—knows best.

Know—O brother—may God confirm us and you—that the best of hearts, the most loved by God, is that which is clean and pure of falsehoods, doubts, and all other evils, and receptive to the truth, right guidance, and all that is good and correct. A *ḥadīth* says, *Four are the hearts: A heart that is smooth, containing a luminous lamp, this is the heart of the believer and the lamp within is its light. A heart that is black, turned upside down, this is the heart of the disbeliever. And a heart made of layers, containing both faith and hypocrisy; the likeness of faith in it is that of a plant fed by sweet water, while the likeness of hypocrisy in it is that of an ulcer, fed by discharge and pus; whichever substance overcomes the other takes it over*.[32] I say: it appears that this last kind of hearts is that of those common Muslims who are neglectful and mix good with evil behavior. 'Alī, may God honor his countenance, said, "Faith appears in the heart like a shiny white spot which enlarges until the whole heart becomes white. Hypocrisy appears in the heart as a black spot which enlarges until the whole heart becomes black." We ask God for safety and, for us and all Muslims, to die as Muslims.

Faith increases by persevering in good works in abundance and with sincerity. As for hypocrisy, it increases by evil works such as abandoning duties and committing prohibited acts. As the Prophet—may blessings and peace be upon him—has said, *He who commits a sin, a black spot is inscribed in his heart. If he repents, his heart is re-burnished, but if he does not, it spreads until it covers the whole the heart*.[33] This is the veil about which God—Exalted is He—says, *No, but a veil has covered their hearts for that they had been doing.* [83:14]

31. Muslim, *Ṣaḥīḥ*, (3549).

32. Ṭabarānī, *Saghīr*, (1071); Aḥmad, *Musnad*, (10705).

33. Tirmidhī, *Sunan*, (3257); Ibn Māja, *Sunan*, (4234); Aḥmad, *Musnad*, (7611).

Nothing is more harmful to mankind, in this world and the next, than sins. Almost no evil nor harm befall them except due to these. God—Exalted is He—says, *Whatever misfortune befalls you is for that your hands have earned…* [42:30] Therefore, a believer should be wary of sins to the extreme and ever remain as far away from them as possible. Should he commit one, he must hasten to repent to God, for He accepts—Exalted is He—the repentance of His servants, pardons evil deeds, and knows what you do. Those who do not repent, they are the unjust. They have done themselves an injustice by falling into sin, then persisting in it by not repenting as God has commanded them, while promising them to accept it.

For God—Exalted is He—describes Himself thus, *Forgiver of sin, He Who accepts repentance, Whose punishment is severe, the Generous, there is no god other than He; to Him is the final end.* [40:3] Reflect on this verse—may God have mercy on you—the noble meanings and subtle secrets it contains, which arouse fear and hope, desire and awe, among other things. *Only those remember who turn [to God] repentant. Therefore, pray to God with sincerity, even though the disbelievers may detest it.* [40:13,14]

ʿAlī ibn Abī Ṭālib—may God honor his countenance—has said, "God possesses receptacles in the earth, these are the hearts. The best are the purest, firmest and gentlest." Then he explained this by saying, "The purest in certainty, the firmest in religion, and the gentlest toward other believers."

I say: Certainty is for faith to take over the heart with firmness, it is the tranquility that Abraham—may peace be upon him—asked of his Lord, *He said are you not a believer? He said, Indeed, but so that my heart becomes tranquil.* [2:260] Thus, it is clear that certainty is the goal and final result of faith. Ibn Masʿūd said, "Certainty is the whole of faith." Nothing was sent down from heaven more noble than certainty. Certainty is sufficient to make one independent. A *hadith* says, *Ask God for pardon and safety, for, after certainty, no one is ever given anything better than safety.*[34]

As for firmness in religion, it is strength therein, steadfastness, and being so concerned about it as to always speak the truth even when bitter and never fear to be blamed when acting for the sake of God. This is how God describes those He loves, *Then the believers will say: Are these they who swore by God their most solemn oaths*

34. Tirmidhī, *Sunan*, (3481; Bayhaqī, *Shuʿab al-Īmān*, (4595); Abū Yaʿlā. *Musnad*, (114, 117, 125).

that they were with you? Their works have failed and they have become the losers. O believers, those of you who retreat from their religion, God will bring people whom He loves and who love Him, humble before Muslims, proud toward disbelievers, striving for the sake of God and fearing not the blame of those who will blame them. This is God's favor which He gives whom He will; and God is Vast, Knowing. [5:53,54] And this is how the Messenger of God—may God's blessings and peace be upon him—describes 'Umar ibn al-Khattāb—may God be pleased with Him—saying, *The firmest among you in God's religion is 'Umar.*[35] *He speaks the truth even when bitter, and the truth has left him with no friends among people.*[36] Among believers, he was—may God be pleased with him—one of the staunchest as concerns God's religion, one of the strictest in applying it to himself and others, so much so that he became an example in justice, enjoining good, forbidding evil, and imposing the truth upon the near and far. May God be pleased with him and with every other Companion of the Messenger of God—may God's blessings and peace be upon him.

As for gentleness toward believers it is to show compassion and solicitude for them. This is one of the noblest characters and most superior attributes. Thus did God describe His Messenger, saying, *There has come to you a Messenger from among yourselves, grievous to whom is your suffering, solicitous for you, to the believers gentle and compassionate.* [9:128] And the Messenger of God—may God's blessings and peace be upon him—said, *Those who have mercy, the All-Merciful will have mercy on them, have mercy on those on earth and those in heaven will have mercy on you.*[37] And, *Those who have no mercy, receive no mercy.*[38] And, *The* Abdāl *in my community will not enter the Garden by their works, but by God's mercy, clean breasts, generous souls, and compassion for all Muslims.*[39] I say: It should not be understood from this that the *Abdāl* are not praying and fasting in abundance, nor performing all other kinds of good works in abundance, but that these attributes with which the Prophet of God—may God's blessings and peace be upon him—described them qualified them for being the foremost

35. Ibn Māja, *Sunan*, (151); Aḥmad, *Musnad*, (12437, 13479).
36. Ṭabarānī, *Saghīr*, (6068).
37. Abū Dāwūd, *Sunan*, (4290); Tirmidhī, *Sunan*, (1847).
38. Bukhārī, *Ṣaḥīḥ*, (5538, 5554); Muslim, *Ṣaḥīḥ*, (4282).
39. Bayhaqī, *Shu'ab al-Īmān*, (10468).

in approaching God and the nearest to Him, because of the nobility and superiority of these attributes over the other kinds of good works they perform, for these are acts of the hearts and qualities of the secrets, so understand!

Know that no act of the heart was ever weighed against a physical act, whether good or evil, without the act of the heart clearly outweighing it. It is through this that the Sufis acquire their superiority, for they are more intent on purifying their hearts and more concerned with the attributes and good works of the heart, whereas other Muslim worshippers and scholars are not as intently concerned with the inward. Favors are in God's Hand, He bestows them upon whom He will, and God is Vast, Knowing.

Compassion for Muslims is a duty and an incumbent right, but for the weak, the destitute, and the afflicted it is even more of a duty and a priority. He who does not find in himself pity and compassion when faced with the weak and the afflicted among Muslims, his heart is hard, overcome with callousness, deprived of compassion. Only he who is wretched is deprived of compassion, as the Prophet has said—may blessings and peace be upon him. If such a callous man is also arrogant, haughty, and disdainful of the weak and the destitute among Muslims, then may he be crushed, expelled, and loathed by God! For he harbors that which will inevitably have him expelled from God's doorstep and will be one of the arrogant who oppose God—Exalted is He. He has said—may blessings and peace be upon him, *He whose heart contains as much as a mustard seed of arrogance will not enter the Garden.*[40]

It is part of being gentle and soft hearted to feel humility in the heart and weep abundantly in fear of God. This is a noble attribute and praiseworthy endeavor. Thus has God described His Prophets and the virtuous among His servants. He says—Exalted is He, *When the signs of the All-Merciful are recited to them, they fall prostrate, weeping.* [19:58] *And they throw themselves down to their chins, weeping, and it increases them in humility.* [17:109]

The Prophet—may blessings and peace be upon him—mentioned among the seven [kinds of people] that will be shaded by God in His shade on the day when there will be no other shade, *A man who remembers God when alone and his eyes overflow* [with

40. Muslim, *Ṣaḥīḥ*, (131, 133); Abū Dāwūd, *Sunan*, (3568); Tirmidhī, *Sunan*, (1921, 1922).

tears].[41] He said—may blessings and peace be upon him, *Two eyes will not be touched by the Fire, one that has wept for the fear of God and one that has spent the night standing guard in the way of God,*[42] which means during *jihād*. Weeping solely from the fear of God is so precious as to have this rank in the sight of God, even though so many people weep. To the extent that he said—may blessings and peace be upon him, *He who weeps for the fear of God will never enter the Fire unless milk shall return back into the udder.*[43] Another *ḥadīth* says, *All eyes shall weep on Resurrection day except three: An eye that was restrained from what God has forbidden, an eye who spent the night standing guard in the way of God, and an eye from which tears as small as the heads of flies came out for the fear of God.*[44] He even made weeping for the fear of God equal to blood being spilt in the way of God. It has been transmitted, *Were one weeper to weep in a community, God would have mercy on them,* [45] because of his weeping. From the foregoing it is clear that weeping is a frequent occurrence, but that which is solely for the sake of God is scarce. So weep for the fear of God, and, if you are unable to weep, make as if you do. But beware of ostentation, affectation, and showing off before created beings, you will thus fall from consideration in the sight of the Lord of the Worlds. If you find it difficult to weep, remember what awaits you of the terrors of the life to come, which you will unavoidably, without any doubt, encounter. Without any doubt that is if you believe in God and what Muḥammad, the Messenger of God—may God's blessings and peace be upon him—has brought. Inevitably you shall weep if you have a heart that understands and a mind that is intelligent. If you possess neither of those then count yourself among the cattle roaming their pastures and enjoying their fodder. For God—Exalted is He—addresses only those possessed of hearts and reminds them when He says, *Surely in this is a reminder for he who has a heart or who listens attentively.* [50:37] And He says—Exalted is He, *A Book We sent down to you, blessed, that they may reflect upon its signs, that those possessed of intelligence may take heed.* [38:29] Elsewhere the August Book

41. Bukhārī, *Ṣaḥīḥ*, (620, 1334); Muslim, *Ṣaḥīḥ*, (1712).
42. Tirmidhī, *Sunan*, (1563).
43. Tirmidhī, *Sunan*, (1557, 2233); Nasā'ī, *Sunan*, (3056, 3057).
44. Ibn Abī 'Āsim, *al-Jihād*, (116).
45. 'Abdal-Razzāq, *Muṣannaf*, (20292); Bayhaqī, *Shu'ab al-Īmān*, (824).

says, *Only those take heed who are intelligent.* [2:269] See how He denies others the ability to take heed.

God—Exalted is He—also attributes the ability to take heed to those who are ever turning to Him, those who fear Him, and those who believe in Him, in His Messenger, His promises, and His threats. Thus He says—Exalted is He, *He it is Who shows you His signs and sends down from the sky provision for you. Only those take heed who turn to Him.* [40:13] And He says—Exalted is He, *Remind, for reminding is of benefit. He will take heed who fears.* [87:9,10] And He says—Exalted is He, *And remind, for reminding profits believers.* [51:55]

God prescribed reminding, commanding His Messenger to remind all people, but restricted its benefits to the believers among His servants, making it a proof in their favor before Him and a road to approach Him. As for others it will be proof against them, destroying their false arguments. For they turned away after knowledge had come to them, denied after being made aware [of the truth], and failed to respond to God and His Messenger. *And they say: Our hearts are shielded against that to which you are inviting us; our ears have become deaf, and between you and us is a veil, so do as you will; we, too, shall do as we will.* [41:5] *And they swore their solemn oaths by God that if a warner came to them, they would be better guided than any other nation. But when the warner came to them, it increased them only in aversion.* [35:42] This is the description of he who was called upon by his Lord, through His Messenger, to ascribe oneness to Him and obey Him, but he refused arrogantly, denied, and disbelieved.

He who believes outwardly and verbally, but denies inwardly, he is a hypocrite. He deserves as much wrath and cursing from God as the open disbeliever.

He who believes outwardly and with his heart, but neglects what God has imposed upon him in the way of obedience, and commits what He has forbidden him, he is in extreme danger. If God does not save him by granting him to repent sincerely before death, he is at risk of joining the ranks of the hypocrites and disbelievers, and becoming their companion in *God's blazing Fire, which rises up to the hearts. It is closed upon them, in outstretched pillars.* [104:6, 7, 8, 9]

Be steadfast, O believer, in obeying your Lord. Make your acts of obedience frequent, patiently persevere and be sincere in doing so, then persist until you meet Him—Majestic and High is He—at which time He will satisfy you, be pleased with you, and admit you to His abode of honor. *The likeness of the Garden that the God-fearing have been promised is that rivers flow beneath it, its food is permanent and so is its shade. This is the consequence for those who were God-fearing, and the consequence for the disbelievers is the Fire.* [13:35]

Desist, O believer, from disobedience. Repent to your Lord from it before death overtakes you and you meet your Lord in a filthy and vile condition. Then you will be as God says, *He who comes to his Lord a criminal, his is Hell, wherein he will neither die nor live.* [20:74] Never feel secure, should you not hasten to repent from your disobedience, for God may send down some punishment upon you, for the disobedient to their Lord are ever exposed to that. Have you not heard God's saying—Exalted is He, *Do those who plot evil feel secure that God will not cause the earth to swallow them, or that the torment will not come upon them from whence they are not aware? Or that He will not seize them in their movements, then they will not be able to escape? Or that he will not seize them even as they are afraid? For your Lord is Kind, Compassionate.* [16:45 to 47]

O God, O Generous One, cause us to benefit from Your reminding, to follow You and Your Messenger, to unite in obeying You, to die as Muslims, and to join the virtuous, and grant the same to our two parents and all our loved ones, by Your mercy, O Most Merciful!

Know, O brothers—may God awaken our hearts and yours from the slumber of distraction and grant us all success in preparing for the passage from the ephemeral to the permanent abode—that long hopes are among the most noxious things to man. The meaning of long hopes is to think that residence in this world will be so prolonged that this feeling overcomes the heart, which responds by behaving accordingly. The virtuous predecessors—may God have mercy on them—have said, "He whose hopes are long, his works will be wrong." This is because long hopes lead to over-preoccupation with this world and strenuous efforts to improve one's lot in it, until the point is reached when a person spends his whole time, night and day, thinking on how to improve it and acquire more. He will pursue this, now inwardly within his heart, and now outwardly by physical action, till both his heart and body become totally involved in this. Then he will forget the life-to-come, being occupied elsewhere, and will postpone doing anything for it. He will thus be diligent and earnest in worldly matters, and neglectful and procrastinating in what concerns his life to come. The correct thing would have been for him do the opposite and strive in earnest for his life to come, which is the abode of permanence, the place of residence, and God- Exalted is He—and His Messenger—may God's blessings and peace be upon him—have informed him that he will not attain to it without effort and persistence in deadly earnest. As for this world, it is a place of change and perishing. Soon he will leave it for the hereafter, abandoning it behind him. He is not commanded to desire and work for it, on the contrary, he is told not to in the Book of God the Exalted and the *Sunna* of His Messenger—may God's blessings and peace be upon him. His appointed share of it will not miss him, even were he not to work for it. However, when his hopes become long they lead him to concentrate on this world and neglect the next. Whenever the thought of death occurs to him, or that he ought to be preparing himself for it with good works, he resolves to do so sometimes in the future, once he can free himself from working for this world, as if it was his to decide when to die. This is the evil consequence of long hopes, so beware of them—may God have mercy on you—and shift delays and procrastination to worldly matters, while dealing with those of the hereafter immediately and resolutely. As the Prophet said—may blessings and peace be upon him, *Behave as one you think will never to die, but be as careful as one who fears he will die tomorrow.*[46]

Feel the imminence of death, for it is "the nearest hidden thing lying in wait". A human being does not know, it may be that only very little of his lifetime remains, yet he is attending to this world and forgetful of the hereafter. Should he die in this state, he will return to God unprepared to meet him. He might then wish to be reprieved, but will never be granted that. As He says—Exalted is He, *Until when death comes to one of them he says: My Lord, send me back, that I may do the good works I had left undone! It is but a word he speaks, and behind them is a barrier till the day they will be resurrected.* [23:99,100]

Only a fool who is prey to illusion harbors long hopes, procrastinates, and neglects preparing for death. The Messenger of God—may God's blessings and peace be upon him—has said, *He is sagacious who brings his soul to reckoning and works for what comes after death; and he is inadequate who follows his passions and har-*

46. Bayhaqī, *Shu'ab al-Īmān*, (3729).

bors [illusory] *hopes in God.*[47] Long hopes are but part of following the passions of one's soul and being deceived by its false hopes.

One of the virtuous predecessors—may God be pleased with them—has said, "Were you to witness the end and how it approaches, you would detest hope and its deceptions." Another said, "How many a man began his day but never ended it, or hoped in a morrow he never saw." Yet another said, "A man may be laughing heartily, yet his shroud has already left the bleacher's shop." A *ḥadīth* says, *The first among this nation will succeed by detachment and certainty, while the last will perish through greed and* (long) *hopes*.[48] 'Alī—may God be pleased with him—said, "The thing I fear most for you is that you follow passions and have long hopes. As for following passions, it repels one from the truth; and as for long hopes, they make one forget the hereafter. He who forgets the hereafter does not work for it, he who does not work for it reaches it bankrupt of good works, and there is neither salvation nor gain in the hereafter without them. Should he seek to be returned to this world at that time to do these good works, he will be prevented from doing so. Then his remorse and sorrow will be immense, at a time when remorse will avail nothing."

When the Messenger of God—may God's blessings and peace be upon him—counseled Ibn 'Umar—may God be pleased with him—he said, *Be in this world as if you were a stranger or a passer by*.[49] This is powerful exhortation indeed to shorten one's hopes and curb one's desire for this world. Ibn 'Umar used to say, "When you wake up in the morning do not expect the evening, and when evening comes do not expect morning; and take from your life for your death and from your good health for your sickness."

Know that as concerns hope people may be divided into three categories:

The first consists of the Foremost, namely the Prophets and the *Ṣiddīqūn*. They harbor no hopes at all, for they are ever aware of the imminence of death, being ever prepared for it by their unbroken concentration on God and obedience to Him. They are utterly unconcerned with worldly matters except that which is strictly nec-

47. Tirmidhī, *Sunan*, (2383); Ibn Māja, *Sunan*, (4250).
48. Bayhaqī, *Shu'ab al-Īmān*, (10134, 10430), Aḥmad ibn Ḥanbal, *Kitāb al-Zuhd* (52).
49. Bukhārī, *Ṣaḥīḥ*, (5837); Tirmidhī, *Sunan*, (2255); Ibn Māja, *Sunan*, (4104).

essary, whether for their own selves or those of their followers for whom they are responsible. They are so intent on God and the Last Abode that were one of them to be told: "You are to die tomorrow!" he would be unable to increase his good works, for he would already have reached the maximum possible in these; he would also need to refrain from nothing, since he long since would have abandoned everything that he would have disliked death to find him doing. To such a noble state does the Prophet's saying refer—may God's blessings and peace be upon him, *By He in whose hand my soul is, never when my eyes blink do I think they will be able to close again before I die, never when I lift my gaze up do I think I will be able to lower it again, and never do I eat a morsel of food thinking I will be able to swallow it before death makes me choke on it.*[50] Sometimes he purified himself with *tayammum* (earth purification)—may blessings and peace be upon him—when water was not far away from him. When he was asked about it he said, *I do not know, I may never reach it.*[51]

The second category consists of those superior and righteous people who are frugal, harbor short hopes which do not distract them from God and His remembrance, and do not make them forget the Final Abode, be too occupied to be able to prepare for death, be too engaged in improving and embellishing their worldly things, or be deceived by whatever ephemeral blemished beauty or pleasures it has to offer. However, they are not given as much strength as the first category in uninterruptedly feeling the imminence of death. Were this state to persist with them some of the necessary requirements of their worldly life may be compromised. They may even see some of their next world's exigencies compromised as well, so overcome by the awesomeness of this may they become, for constant awareness of the imminence of death is a formidable matter that only the strength of Prophethood or perfect *Ṣiddīqiyya* can sustain. It is because of this that it is sometimes said that, "some hopes are a mercy." These are the hopes without which the affairs of both this world and the next would be disturbed. This refers to that which has reached us concerning the progeny of Adam—may peace be upon him—when God brought them out of his loins on the Day of the Pact and the angels, seeing how numerous they were, said, "Our

50. Bayhaqī, *Shu'ab al-Īmān*, (10168); Ṭabarānī, *Musnad al-Shāmiyyīn*, (1476).

51. Aḥmad, *Musnad*, (2483, 2628), Ṭabarānī, *Kabīr*, (12812).

Lord, the world will not accommodate them." He said—Exalted is He, "I intend to create death." They said, "They will never live happily." He said, "I intend to create hope." And the Prophet—may blessings and peace be upon him—said, *The angels say to the relatives of the dead person as they walk away from his grave, 'Return to your worldly affairs that God may cause you to forget your dead!'* The Angels—may peace be upon them—are not asking for evil to befall the believers, namely blameworthy long hopes, but good, namely short hopes of the kind that do not distract from the hereafter, yet are sufficient for the fulfillment of the exigencies of life. And God knows best.

The third category consists of those people laboring under illusions and other fools who harbor such long hopes that they make them forget the hereafter, distract them from the remembrance of death, and make their hearts love this world, intent on making it prosper and amassing its debris, deceived by its beauties and ornaments, gazing at its attractiveness, which thing God forbade His Prophet—may blessings and peace be upon him—when He said—Exalted is He, *Do not gaze long at what we gave pairs of them to enjoy, the attractiveness of the life of this world, that we may try them with. The provision of your Lord is better and more permanent.* [20:131] You will see how such a person seldom remembers the hereafter or reflects on it, nor does death and the imminence of his end ever occur to him. On the rare occasions when they do, they have no effect on his heart, and when he fears that they will, he drives them away and replaces them with whatever may help him forget them, so as not to disturb his avidity for this world and enjoyment of its pleasures and appetites. This kind of hope is the kind that is unconditionally blameworthy. He who harbors such hopes is one of the losers who have been distracted by their possessions and children from the remembrance of God. When death comes and he beholds the hereafter he will say, *My Lord, if only You would reprieve me a little.* As God—Exalted is He—informs us in His Book, *O believers, let not your possessions nor your children distract you from the remembrance of God. Those who do so, they are the losers. Expend of what We have provided you before death comes to one of you and he says, 'My Lord, if only You would reprieve me a little, that I may give charity and be one of the virtuous. God will not reprieve a soul whose term has come; and God is aware of all that you do.* [63:9 to 11]

It is said that the Angel of Death—may peace be upon him—appears to the person whose time is near to inform him that this is so. When the person says, "O Angel of Death, reprieve me a little that I may repent to my Lord and ask His forgiveness!" He replies, "You have been left and granted to live for so long, yet you never repented nor turned back to your Lord till now. Now the time is over and you have reached your appointment that God has ordained for you, it is no longer possible further to reprieve you." Scholars—may God have mercy on them—have said, "Should this person own the whole world, and were it possible for him to buy one extra hour in exchange for it to prolong his life sufficiently to be able to make amends with his Lord, he would do so."

Forgetfulness of the hereafter and attending entirely to this world to the exclusion of the next may be due to long hopes, as we have mentioned before, or it may be because one doubts the hereafter and hesitates to accept that it is true—may God protect us from this, for it is disbelief in God and His Messenger. The sign that distinguishes he who is forgetful of the hereafter because of long hopes from he who is doubtful of its existence is that, when he falls ill or something else happens to him that may lead to death, the first remembers the hereafter all the time, experiences remorse for not having worked for it, and wishes to recover to be able to do some good works. As for the one whose forgetfulness of the hereafter is due to doubt, none of this will show on him when he falls ill, he will only feel sorrow for leaving his worldly life, anxiety for the fate of his children and wealth after him, and other such things indicating short sightedness and desire for this world. Watch for signs of this—may God have mercy on you—in yourself. Also watch for them in others so that if you notice evidence of their doubting the hereafter you may counsel and advise them. For although long hopes are reprehensible enough, doubting the hereafter is even more reprehensible and more dangerous.

Know that the frequent remembrance of death is a good thing and to be encouraged. It brings important benefits and profits, among which are short hopes, detachment from the world, contentment with little, and desire for the hereafter accompanied by gathering provision of good works in preparation for it. The Messenger of God—may God's blessings and peace be upon him—said, *Re-*

member often the 'defeater of pleasures,'[52] meaning death. He used to rise at night—may blessings and peace be upon him—and call out to the people, *Death has come with what it carries in its train. The first blast shivers, to be followed by the second.*[53] And when he was asked—may God's blessings and peace be upon him—about who the perspicacious among people were, he said, *Those who remember death most often and who prepare for it best. Those are the perspicacious. Theirs is honor in this world and a noble rank in the next.*[54]

I say: To be beneficial, the remembrance of death should not be for a person to repeat, 'Death, death!' for this is of little benefit, even if abundant, rather this should be accompanied by presence of the heart and reflection on what will one's state be when death comes with its terror and throes, when one begins to see the things of the hereafter? How long is one to live yet and how will one's life be concluded? How did one's peers and those of his companions who preceded him do at the moment of death? To which condition have they gone? And other similar reflections and reminders which are likely to influence the heart in a profitable way. One of our ancestors said, "Consider, anything that you do and would be pleased for death to come to you while doing it, keep to it; but anything that you do and would detest death to find you doing it, avoid it!" Reflect on these words—may God have mercy on you—for they are of immense benefit for he who would act accordingly. Success and Help are from God, there is no other Lord than He.

As for disliking death, it is a normal thing that almost no human being can be free of. This is because death is painful in itself and separates a person from everything he loves or is familiar with in this world. When the Messenger of God—may God's blessings and peace be upon him—said, *He who loves to meet God, God loves to meet him, and he who detests to meet God, God detests to meet him.* 'Ā'isha—may God be pleased with her—said to him, "O Messenger of God, but we all dislike death." He said—may blessings and peace be upon him, *It is not that, but when death comes to the believer*

52. Tirmidhī, *Sunan*, (2229); Nasā'ī, *Sunan*, (1801); Ibn Māja, *Sunan*, (4248).

53. Tirmidhī, *Sunan*, (2381); Bayhaqī, *Shu'ab al-Īmān*, (546, 1473, 10183). The first blast of the Horn is that of the Hour, when all living creatures will die. The second blast is that of the Resurrection.

54. Ṭabarānī, *Kabīr*, (63, 139, 696).

he is given glad tidings of his Lord's mercy, good pleasure, and garden, he thus loves to meet God and therefore God loves to meet him. And when death comes to the disbeliever, he is given tidings of God's torment and wrath, he thus detests to meet God and therefore God detests to meet him.[55] Also in the description of the beloved believer mentioned in the *ḥadīth qudsī* beginning with, *"My servant draws nearer to Me ... "* He says—Exalted is He, *"Never do I hesitate in doing anything more than My hesitation in taking the soul of My believing servant, for he dislikes death, and I dislike to displease him."*[56] See how He describes him as disliking death although his faith is complete and his rank with Him—Exalted is He—high, you will then grasp the truth of what we said earlier. There is also the episode in the story of Moses—may peace be upon him—where he strikes the Angel of Death who had come to take his soul, knocking his eye out.

But yes it may happen that the dawning of the lights of gnosis and certainty may overflow upon the feeling of dislike of death so that it is not felt. This occurs to those who are qualified at certain times, but not at others. As for the general rule for all believers it is that they like death because it leads to their meeting with God and journeying to the abode of permanence, having left this world which is the place of temptations and hardships; yet they dislike death because it is in the nature of the soul to do so, because of the pain that accompanies it and the separation from loved things. However, the stronger one's faith is, the less this dislike will be and the less allowance will be given to the nature of the soul, and *vice versa*. Be aware of this! May God Himself be your guide!

A long life in the service of God is to be desired, for when asked—may blessings and peace be upon him—who the best of people were? He replied, *He whose life is long and whose works are good.*[57] The longer a lifetime is in the service of God, the more good works are accumulated, and the higher the degree. On the other hand, a long life in disobedience is a calamity and an evil, for the bad deeds will abound and sins will multiply.

Should someone claim that he wishes to live long in this world that he may increase the good deeds that will draw him nearer to

55. Bukhārī, *Ṣaḥīḥ*, (6026); Muslim, *Ṣaḥīḥ*, (4845).

56. Bukhārī, *Ṣaḥīḥ*, (6021).

57. Tirmidhī, *Sunan*, (2251, 2252); Aḥmad, *Musnad*, (17020, 17037, 19519).

God—Exalted is He—then if he is careful not to neglect them, eager to pursue them and to avoid those worldly things which may distract him from them, he is probably truthful in his claim. But if he is lazy in pursuing good works and given to postponing them, he is a liar who will keep producing false excuses that will avail him nothing, for he who wishes to live for a certain purpose is expected to be most careful never to miss any of it or allow himself to be prevented from fulfilling it. This is especially so since good works are only possible in this world and are inconceivable elsewhere. The hereafter is a place of reward, not of action. Reflect well upon this, that God may make you benefit from it. Ask for God's help and be patient, strive earnestly, hasten to good works before there comes a time when you are incapable of performing them, make the best you can of your time before the end overtakes you unaware! You are prone to ailments, a target for the arrows of death. Your capital, with which you can buy perpetual happiness from God, is but your lifetime. Beware of spending your moments, days, hours, and breaths in that which is of no benefit, devoid of good, for your regrets will be prolonged and your grief after death immense, once you realize with certainty how much you have missed.

It is said that in the hereafter each human being is shown the hours of his days and nights in the form of closets, each day and night made of twenty four closets. Those hours which were occupied with service to God will be seen to be filled with light, those which were occupied with disobedience will be filled with darkness, while those where neither obedience not disobedience took place will be empty. When he will look at the empty closets he will become filled with regrets for not having filled them with light by acts of obedience. But when he will look at those which are filled with darkness, at that moment were it possible for him to die of regret and grief he would have died, but there is no death in the hereafter. He who has acted in obedience to God will constantly be joyous and satisfied, his joy and happiness increasing as days go by. But he who has disobeyed God will be distressed and aggrieved; his distress and grief increasing endlessly. So choose for yourself—may God have mercy on you—since you are still in the place of choice, that which will benefit and elevate you, for once you die you lose all choice.

Make haste, postpone not, for procrastination is an evil, since human beings are liable to suffer from various problems and become occupied with numerous things. The Prophet has said—may

God's blessings and peace be upon him, *Make the best of five before five: of your youth before your senility, of your health before your illness, of your free time before you become occupied, of your affluence before you become poor, and of your life before you die.*[58] And he said—may blessings and peace be upon him, *Hasten to good works before you become too occupied, and strengthen the bond between you and your Lord by abundantly remembering Him.*[59] And he said—may blessings and peace be upon him, *Two graces that many people are deprived of are good health and free time.*[60] I say: Deprivation here means they are given these two things, are healthy and free, yet use these in distractions and idle endeavors, or in struggling for worldly things that distract them from remembering God and from good works. They only realize they have been deprived once they die and witness the high degrees they could have attained had they expended of their health and free time to reach them.

'Alī said—may God honor his countenance, "People are asleep, once they die they awaken." And God—Exalted is He—says, *The day He assembles you for the Day of Assembly, this will be the day of deprivation.* [64:9] The Prophet—may blessings and peace be upon him—said, *The only regrets the people of the Garden shall experience shall be those for each moment they had spent* [in the world] *without remembering God.*[61] This will be when they witness how much proximity and bliss they have missed because of that moment's distraction.

As for he who uses his health and free time in sinful activities and things which attract God's wrath, he is a loathsome loser, not merely one who has been deprived. The latter is one who was deprived because he used these graces in idle rather than forbidden activities.

Deprivation in the context of good health and free time may also mean that one is not granted them to begin with, either because one is afflicted with illness, or weakness, or because of his too many occupations. Because of this he is unable to perform the good works that the healthy and free are capable of. Understand here the meaning of His saying—Exalted is He, *And God has preferred those who*

---

58. Bayhaqī, *Shu'ab al-Īmān*, (9884); Al-Ḥākim, *Mustadrak*, (7957).
59. Ibn Māja, *Sunan*, (1071); Bayhaqī, *Shu'ab al-Īmān*, (2879).
60. Bukhārī, *Ṣaḥīḥ*, (5933); Tirmidhī, *Sunan*, (2226); Aḥmad, *Musnad*, (3038).
61. Bayhaqī, *Shu'ab al-Īmān*, (541, 542); Ṭabarānī, *Kabīr*, (16608).

fight over those who stay with a formidable reward. [4:95] And his saying—may blessings and peace be upon him, *The strong believer is better and more liked by God the Exalted than the weak believer, and in each there is good. So pursue with care that which will profit you and do not be feeble. If you are overcome by something say, 'God has ordained, and what He wishes He does.' Beware of 'if only' for 'if only' allows in the work of the devil.*[62] I say: This is because "if only" is usually said by an indolent feeble person who, because of his indolence and feebleness, misses good works when they are within his grasp. It is also said by he who depends on his own power and ability, his own effort and planning, thinking that by his alertness and caution he will escape what God has decreed is to happen to him. He has said—may blessings and peace be upon him, *No amount of caution will avail against destiny.*[63] Reflect on this and meditate on it thoroughly for it has a profound meaning and underneath it is abundant knowledge. To God do all things return.

As for hopes of forgiveness and admission to the Garden without having done anything for it, namely doing what one was commanded to do, hastening to good works, avoiding forbidden things, and refraining from evil deeds, such hopes are but foolishness, self deceit, and alliance with the Devil—May God curse him!—by accepting his fraudulent and deceitful incitements, his peddling to people evil disguised as good. God—Exalted is He—says, *He who takes the Devil as an ally rather than God, he has suffered a manifest loss. He promises them and gives them hopes, but the Devil promises nothing but illusion.* [4:119, 120] Thus he who thinks that he may sin, not repent to God with a sound repentance, yet that He—Exalted is He—will forgive him, and he who neglects acts of obedience and is too occupied with worldly affairs to attend to them, yet imagines that nevertheless God will honor him and raise him in degree in the Garden along with those whose behavior was superior, he is a self deluded incapable fool. For God—Exalted is He—says, and his words are the truth, *To God belongs what is in the heavens and what is in the earth; that He may reward those who do wrong for what they did and reward those who did well with goodness.* [53:31] Then God—Exalted is He—describes those who did well by saying, *Those who avoid major sins and indecencies, save lesser things. In-*

62. Ibn Māja, *Sunan*, (4158); Aḥmad, *Musnad*, (8436, 8473).

63. Aḥmad, *Musnad*, (21033); Al-Ḥākim, *Mustadrak*, (1767); Ṭabarānī, *Kabīr,* (16627).

deed your Lord is vast in forgiveness. [53:32] *Lesser things* are the minor sins that almost no human being can be entirely free of. God also says—Exalted is He, *Or shall We make those who believe and do good equal to those who cause corruption in the earth? Or shall We make the God-fearing equal to the dissolute?* [38:28] Meaning: We shall never make them equal in Our sight, neither in this world nor the next. As He also says—Exalted is He *Do those who commit sins think that We shall make them equal to those who believe and do good, equal in their life and their death? How ill they judge!* [45:21] Here He declares false their calculations and illusions, and blames them for thinking that they and those who do good might ever be considered equal in the sight of their Lord.

In His Book God attributes to His angels and His Prophets—may peace be upon them—and His believing servants the qualities of performing good works, persevering in them, and hastening to them, together with fearfulness, awe, and anxiety. He says—Exalted is He—concerning His angels, *No, but they are honored servants, who precede Him not in speech and do as He commands them. He knows what is before and behind them. They intercede only for those whom He pleases and are anxious in the awe of Him.* [21:26,27,28] And He says—Exalted is He—concerning the Prophets, *Those whom they call upon themselves seek the means to their Lord, which of them will draw nearer* [to Him]*? They hope for His mercy and fear His torment. Indeed the torment of your Lord is a thing to beware of.* [17:57] He also says concerning them, *They used to hasten to acts of goodness, pray to Us hopefully and fearfully, and before Us they were humble.* [21:90] And He says—Exalted is He—concerning the believers, *We gave Moses and Aaron the Criterion, and a radiance and a reminder to the God-fearing who fear their Lord Whom they have not seen and are anxious of the Hour.* [21:48,49] He also says concerning them, *Those who tremble in fear of their Lord, who believe in the signs of their Lord, who ascribe no partners to their Lord, and who do what they do with hearts trembling that they are returning to their Lord, those hasten to acts of goodness and are the first to them.* [23:57 to 61]

When 'Ā'isha- may God be pleased with her—questioned the Messenger of God—may God's blessings and peace be upon him—concerning His saying—Exalted is He, *and who do what they do with hearts trembling,* whether the reference was to someone committing adultery or stealing, then being afraid? He replied, *No, daughter of Abū Bakr, it is the man who prays and fasts and gives charity, then fears it will not be accepted of him.*[64]

As for His enemies, God attributes to some of them self deceit and illusory hopes when He says, *And were I to be returned to my Lord, I shall find a better resort than this.* [18:36] referring to his garden which he admired so much, forgetting God's favor when He gave it to him. He felt so proud for owning it that he bragged about it to humble another servant of God who was a better man than he. You can look this up in the story of this man and of the virtuous servant beginning with His saying, *And give them the example of two men to one of whom we gave two vineyards, surrounded them with palms, and between them made sown fields.* [18:32] Another of His deluded enemies said, *I shall surely be given wealth and children!* [19:77] Meaning in the hereafter. God gave him the lie and threatened him with His torment. About yet another God—Exalted is He—says, *Were I to be returned to my Lord, I shall have near Him a most excellent reward.* [41:50]

Now consider—may God have mercy on you—how God describes His loved ones, His friends, and those He loathes, His enemies. Of the two groups the one you emulate and imitate is that which you will join, for as has been transmitted, he who imitates certain people is one of them. It must have become clear to you that God's angels, Prophets, and virtuous servants hasten to acts of goodness, persevere in them, avoid sins and bad deeds, and are in fear and awe of God; and that His enemies are at the opposite of that, they disobey, abandon excellence, harbor illusions, feel safe from God's lures, and harbor false hopes in Him. Choose for yourself which of the two groups' company is preferable, then emulate them in deeds and attributes, you shall thus join them—God willing.

Know that hopes of forgiveness accompanied by laziness and wasting time are of the most noxious things to Man. They are widely to be heard from the confused people of these times. This is why we have discoursed on them at length in the hope that God may benefit those of them who read it, that they may abandon their distraction and awaken from their slumber, when they learn that Prophets and virtuous people experience great fear from God, to the extent that our Prophet Muḥammad—may God's blessings and peace be upon him—used to say, *Were God to bring us to reckoning, I and the*

64. Ibn Māja, *Sunan*, (4188); Aḥmad, *Musnad*, (24102, 24523).

Son of Mary, for what these two have done [meaning the thumb and index finger] *He would chastise us without us being wronged in the least.*[65] Since Prophets and virtuous people are more aware than others of God, His immense generosity, and His vast mercy, then it behooves the confused and the neglectful to be much more fearful, in every possible manner and in all situations.

And know that the arguments of he who harbors false hopes and deceives himself can be refuted with the greatest ease. For should he say, "God—Exalted is He—is neither harmed by my sins, nor does He profit from my acts of obedience, He is in no need of me or my deeds." Say to him, "True, but sins harm you and acts of obedience profit you. It is you who need the good works." Then say to him, "Abandon your efforts to earn a living, do nothing, strive not for your sustenance, for God—Exalted is He—has guaranteed your provision for you, and in His grip are the treasuries of the heavens and earth". When he says to you, "True, but one must strive and act. We have never seen something being obtained without effort." Say to him, "This world that God commands you to renounce, forbids you to desire, and guarantees you your needs from it, is still only to be obtained with effort and action. The hereafter which, on the contrary, God encourages you to desire and commands you to pursue, He informs you in His Book and through the words of His Prophet that you will only escape His torment and gain His reward only by striving for it and expending effort to obtain it. Yet we observe you neglecting it, not paying it any attention. You either are one who doubts or a self deceived fool. You have turned things upside down and placed things where they do not belong by using that argument. How will you dare meet God and His Messenger—may God's blessings and peace be upon him—whom He sent to you to invite you to prefer the hereafter to this world?" At this his argument will be destroyed and he will be at a loss, knowing not what to say.

Be certain—may God have mercy on you—that the stronger one's faith and the better one's works, the greater one's fear will be; and the weaker one's faith and the worse one's works, the less one's fear will be and the more likely one is to feel secure and deceive oneself. Observe this in yourself and in others, you will see how evident it is.

---

65. Ibn Ḥibbān, *Ṣaḥīḥ*, (659); Abū Nuʿaym, *Ḥilyat al-Awliyā'*, vol. 3, p. 414.

On the whole, the true believer is he whose works are good and sincere, and he hopes they will be accepted and rewarded by God's favor. He will also avoid sins, steer away from them, lest he may be afflicted with them, fear to be chastised for those he has already committed, and hope to be forgiven by God once he has repented and turned to Him. A believer who does not fulfill these conditions is one who is confused and is in great danger. Understand this and impose upon yourself its fulfillment so that—God willing—you will be saved and will have won.

Know that the sign of good fortune is that in his lifetime the servant is granted success in performing good works and that they be rendered easy for him. On the other hand, the sign of wretchedness is that they not be rendered easy for him and that, furthermore, he is afflicted with evil works. The Messenger of God—may God's blessings and peace be upon him—said, *Work, for to each will be rendered easy that for which he was created. He who was created for happiness, to him the works of the people of happiness will be rendered easy, while he who was created for wretchedness, to him the works of the wretched will be rendered easy.*[66] And when God grasped the two fistfuls, He said to the fistful of fortunate ones, "These are for the Garden and the works of the people of the Garden they shall do." And He said to the fistful of wretched ones, "And these are for the Fire and the works of the people of the Fire they shall do."

Also know that the believer possessed of discernment in religion, well steeped in knowledge and certainty, is he who excels in his works for the sake of God, exerts his utmost, then depends on God and His grace, not on his own works and brilliancy. Thus were the Prophets, the scholars, and the virtuous among the old and the recent generations—may peace, mercy, and satisfaction be upon them. To this refers his saying—may God's blessings and peace be upon him, *None shall enter the Garden by his works.* They said, "Not even you, O Messenger of God?" He said, *Not even I, save that God envelopes me in His mercy.*[67] And he strove to his utmost in good works—may God's blessings and peace be upon him—till his feet swelled up because he stood up for so long during his night prayers.

66. Bukhārī, *Ṣaḥīḥ*, (4568).

67. Bukhārī, *Ṣaḥīḥ*, (5241, 5982); Muslim, *Ṣaḥīḥ*, (5036, 5037); Aḥmad, *Musnad*, (9455, 9629).

He who strives in earnest in good works, then depends on them, is guilty of self-admiration and impudence toward his Lord. He may very well be tried so that he may come to realize his powerlessness and inability to do anything good without God's favor and mercy. As He says—Exalted is He, *Had it not been for God's favor upon you and His mercy, none of you would ever have been purified. But God purifies whom He will; and God is Hearing, Knowing.* [24:21] It has reached us that: *a certain devotee worshipped God for five hundred years. On Judgment Day, when God will say to him, "O my servant, enter the Garden by My mercy!" He will answer, "O Lord, by my works." God will then order him to be brought to reckoning. He will be shown the worth of the grace of eyesight and will find that it outweighs all his devotions put together, so that nothing will be left to balance the numerous other divine graces he had enjoyed. He will then be ordered to the Fire. At which point he will say, "O Lord, admit me to the Garden by Your mercy!" God will then order him to be taken to the Garden,* at which he will praise and laud Him—Majestic and High is He.[68]

It is now clear that two things are necessary: The first is to make one's works good, while the second is to depend on God, not on one's works. How excellent are the words of Shaykh Muḥyīddīn 'Abdal-Qādir al-Jīlānī—may God be pleased with him, "By you we do not arrive, yet you are indispensable." Meaning that effort without God's favor is ineffective, yet effort is indispensable in submission to God's orders. Shaykh Abū Sa'īd al-Kharrāz—may God have mercy on him—said, "He who thinks he will arrive [to God] by works, he is overburdening himself. But he who thinks that without works he will arrive he is deceiving himself." The self- deceiver is he who does nothing, yet claims he is depending on God's favor. This attitude is nothing but illusion and foolishness, for he is permitted to depend on God and His favor only after having expended the necessary effort. Al-Ḥasan al-Baṣrī—may God's mercy be upon him—has said, "Hopes of forgiveness have deceived some people so much that they left this world bankrupt." Bankrupt of good works that is. And he also said, "The believer joins excellence in works with fear, while the hypocrite joins evil works with security." I say: This is strange indeed, for he whose deeds are evil is more worthy of fear, since he thus exposes himself to God's chastisement. But he

68. Al-Ḥākim, *Mustadrak*, (7745); Bayhaqī, *Shu'ab al-Īmān*, (4442).

feels secure, although his works are evil, because his heart is upside down and his inner eye is blind, so that he is devoid of insight, but *He whom God guides, he is the rightly guided one, and he whom He leads astray, to him you will find no guiding ally*. [18:17]

O God! Guide us and be our guiding ally! Lead us to what pleases and satisfies You! We have entrusted our fate to You. Make us die as Muslims and join the virtuous.

As for using predestination as an argument, as many common Muslims do who are misled by the Devil, it is extremely perilous. When one of them neglects some duties or commits forbidden things and he is asked, "Why did you do this? Why did you contravene God's injunctions and His Messenger's?" He says, 'I was predestined to do so, it had already been written and decided." Thinking thereby that he has justified himself, escaped all blame, and argued successfully against God, to whom belongs the most conclusive arguments against all His creatures in all situations. *He is not questioned concerning what He does, rather they are questioned.* [21:23] I say: The argument of this sinner is a greater crime than his sin and more harmful to him in both this world and the next. For the implications of this argument indicate that it's holder harbors beliefs that shake the very foundations of his religion. Why should this sinner repent, why should he regret his loathsome behavior, when he perceives himself as coerced and forced to behave thus, without any choice on his part, nor ability? This is precisely the belief of the Jabriyya, who are a heterodox sect who teach that no free choice exists. The Mu'tazilites, on the other hand, another heterodox sect, teach the opposite. The belief of the people of truth, the people of *Sunna* and *Jamā'a* is a middle position between these two. As a certain scholar once said, "It comes out between filth and blood, milk that is pure, sweet to the drinkers".

The belief of *Ahl al-Sunna*- may God make us of them by His favor-is that no creature, small or large, exists save by God's decree, decision, will, and power. Human beings and their acts, whether good or evil, are created by God—Exalted is He. They should demand of themselves complete obedience to God's injunctions and seek no excuse for neglecting any of them. They should also demand of themselves that they refrain from all that is forbidden and avoid it altogether. Should they fall into any of it, they hasten to repent and ask God's forgiveness—Exalted is He. When they neglect any of their duties they hasten to requite it and repent to God—

Exalted is He—for neglecting it. They never use the argument of predestination against God, nor do they use it to attempt to justify their misdeeds, nor do they permit anyone else to do so. For God—Exalted is He—describes some of His foes in His Book as using the argument of predestination. He follows this by disparaging and reprimanding them, rejecting their argument, then accusing them of uttering falsehoods. *The idolaters will say: 'Had God so willed we would not have been idolaters, neither would our fathers, nor would we have forbidden anything'. Thus did those who were before them deny until they tasted Our might. Say: 'Have you any knowledge to bring forth to us? You follow only surmise, merely conjecturing'. Say: 'To God belongs the conclusive argument.'* [6:148-149] And in the other verse, *And the idolaters said, 'Had God so wished we would not have worshipped anything apart from Him, nor would our fathers, nor would we have forbidden anything apart from Him. Thus have those before them done, but what are the Messengers to do save deliver a clear message?* [16:35] So beware of imitating the idolaters in arguing against God, the Lord of the Worlds.

It is sufficient for you, as concerns the question of destiny, to believe in it, for good or evil. Having done so, impose upon yourself to obey God's orders and avoid His prohibitions. Be constantly repentant for not having fulfilled His rights, seek His Help, and depend on Him—Exalted is He. He has said,—may blessings and peace be upon him, *When destiny is mentioned keep silent.*[69] He thus forbade delving into it because of the perils and excessive harm that may come from this. A man once asked 'Alī—may God be pleased with him—about destiny. He replied, "It is a deep sea, so do not enter it; and a dark road, so do not travel it. It is the secret of God—Exalted is He—which is hidden from you, so do not seek to unravel it." And a man of eminence once asked Muḥammad ibn Wāsi'—may God have mercy on him—about destiny. He replied, "Your neighbors who are in their graves, to reflect upon them is sufficient to keep you so occupied as not to think about destiny."

The predecessors and their successors among the people of truth have all believed in destiny, good and evil, and have agreed on this by consensus—may God have mercy on them—and on refraining from using it as an argument when they neglect a duty or commit something forbidden. They saw this as one of the worst evils. If you belong to the people of truth, emulate them and take their way.

69. Ṭabarānī, *Kabīr,* (1411, 10296).

Should you not do this, you have already heard how God—Exalted is He—addressed those who took a path other than that of the believers. Hear it again now. God—Exalted is He—says, *He who disputes with the Messenger after guidance was made clear to him, and takes a way other than that of the believers, We entrust him to that he trusted, and We shall roast him in Hell, an evil end it is.* [4:115]

Know—may God have mercy on you—that it is not permissible for a believer to believe within himself that he will not be blamed, nor will he be held responsible if he neglects a duty or commits a forbidden thing, since he is vanquished by predestination. Then when such behavior actually issues from him that displeases God, should he use destiny as an argument to exculpate himself, when he still retains his faculties of discrimination and decision, he would be burdening himself with calumny and manifest sin.

I am afraid this affliction has spread among people to the extent of reaching some who are supposedly knowledgeable and virtuous. The sign that they are thus afflicted is that no great pain or regret appear on them when they commit something that is legally blameworthy.

Let every believer who notices some of this in himself fear God, make an effort to rid himself of it, and know that God will accept destiny neither as an excuse, nor as an argument, so long as he enjoys and retains his ability to choose. Should you ever hear this worthless argument used by a Muslim, rebuke him and inform him that his sin in using such an argument is greater than his sin in neglecting a duty or committing a forbidden thing. He should therefore fear God and avoid burdening himself with two calamities rather than one, thereby exposing himself to God's wrath in two ways rather than one.

As for speaking of destiny and reminding others of it when hardships, afflictions, and misfortunes strike, it is permissible, since it is an argument against the ego, not for it. For the afflicted servant who is suffering hardship, when he remembers that it is his Lord who has afflicted him, that He has compassion for him, that this hardship was decreed by God—Exalted is He—he becomes certain that there will be much good and benefit in it. The knowledge of this will allow him to accept it and surrender the matter to God, the Wise, the Omniscient.

It is now clear that using destiny as an argument when legal injunctions are in question is forbidden and blameworthy, so beware of this! But when hardship strikes it is beneficial, if only to those who understand what God—Exalted is He—wishes them to. He says—Exalted is He, *No misfortune befalls in the earth or in yourselves but it was in a book before We brought it to pass. That is easy for God. That you may not grieve for what you have missed, nor rejoice for what has come to you. And God loves not any who is proud and boastful. [57:22,23]*

For the servant afflicted by misfortune, to remember God's promises of high degrees and good things and of forgiveness of sins is a good thing that is of benefit for most Muslims and easy for them to understand. For to reflect on eternal knowledge and pre-existent destiny and decrees needs sagacity and insight such as most people lack. On the other hand, promises and threats concerning the hereafter are easy for everyone to understand. For this reason is reminding of promises and threats of widespread benefit, both when one is engaged in acts of obedience, when one is committing a sin, or when one is afflicted with hardship. This is why you see the Book of God—Exalted is He—and the *Sunna* of His Messenger—may God's blessings and peace be upon him—full of promises and threats, and exhortations containing reminders of both. Understand this and reflect on it, you will thus be wisely guided. Rely on God, for He likes those who rely on Him. There is neither power nor ability save by God, the High, the Formidable.

Chapter Two: On Knowledge

Know O brothers—may God bestow upon us and you wellbeing and certainty, and make us tread the paths of the God-fearing—that it is incumbent upon every Muslim man and woman to seek knowledge. No Muslim is to be excused from this. The knowledge in question is that without which faith and religion cannot be sound. In sum it is the knowledge of God, His Messenger, the Last Day, what is obligatory, and what is forbidden. The Messenger of God—may God's blessings and peace be upon him—said, *Seeking knowledge is an obligation upon every Muslim.*[1] He also said—may blessings and peace be upon him, *Seek knowledge, even if in China.*[2] China being an extremely distant region to which very few people go because it is so remote. If a Muslim is required to seek knowledge even in such a remote place, how will it not be required when he lives among scholars and will not incur much expense nor suffer much hardship seeking it?

As for the sciences of *Islām*, they are included in the Messenger of God's answer to Gabriel when he asked him in the famous *ḥadīth*, "Tell me about *Islām*." And he replied, Islām *is to testify that there is no God other than God and that Muhammad is God's Messenger, to perform the ritual prayer, pay out the Zakāt, fast Ramaḍān, and go to the House on pilgrimage when you are able to.* He then said, "Now tell me about *Īmān*." He said, Īmān *is to believe in God, His angels, His books, His Messengers, the Last Day, and destiny, whether good or evil.*[3]

That which it is incumbent on every Muslim to know regarding the science of *Īmān* is to be found in the concise expositions of beliefs produced by leading scholars for the common Muslim. An example is the Creed of Īmām al-Ghazālī—may God have mercy on him—which is comprehensive, beneficial, and includes many additions to the minimum required for every believer. These additions, however, confirm, strengthen, and complete one's faith. We shall adduce at the end of this book—God willing—a Creed that is brief

1. Ibn Māja, *Sunan*, (220); Ṭabarānī, *Kabīr,* (10286), *Awsaṭ,*(9, 2082, 2105); Bayhaqī, *Shu'ab al-Īmān*, (1613,1614, 1615, 1616). .

2. Bayhaqī, *Shu'ab al-Īmān*, (1612).

3. Bukhārī, *Ṣaḥīḥ*, (48, 4404); Muslim, *Ṣaḥīḥ*, (9, 10,11); Abū Dāwūd, *Sunan*, (4075); Tirmidhī, *Sunan*, (2535); Nasā'ī, *Sunan*, (4904, 4905); Ibn Māja, *Sunan*, (62); Aḥmad, *Musnad,* (346).

but inclusive of everything it is necessary to know of the sciences of *Īmān*.

As for the sciences of *Islām*, they are to be found in the works of the leading experts on jurisprudence (*fiqh*)—may God be satisfied with them. The obligatory amount is that which no Muslim should be ignorant of, such as knowledge of the obligation to perform the five ritual prayers, how to perform them, their conditions and times, how to purify oneself for them, and so on. It will also include knowledge of the obligation of *zakāt*, the amount required and the time at which it becomes obligatory; knowledge of the obligation to fast the month of Ramaḍān, the conditions of fasting and those things which invalidate it; and knowledge of the obligation of *Ḥajj* for those who are able to perform it and the conditions necessary for one to be considered able to do so.

In sum, it is obligatory upon the Muslim to know every obligation he must comply with and every forbidden thing he may ever fall into, such as adultery, homosexuality, intoxicating beverages, wronging others, stealing, treachery, lying, tale bearing, backbiting, and so on.

However, to know the details of the rulings on *zakāt* is not obligatory for those who are not in possession of enough money to make *zakāt* obligatory upon them. Similarly, those who are unable to go to *Ḥajj*, or those who have the ability but have yet to decide to go, for those it is not obligatory to know the integrals (*arkān*) of *Ḥajj* and the conditions necessary for its validity. However, knowledge that both *zakāt* and *Ḥajj* are incumbent upon all Muslims is in itself obligatory.

As for knowledge of the conditions of commercial transactions such as buying or selling and of marriage, it becomes obligatory on those intending to engage in such activities to learn about God's rulings concerning them, what makes them valid or invalid, both upon initiating such activities and during pursuing them. This is indispensable, for otherwise a person may do something that will bring God's wrath upon him, whether he intended it or not. The ignorant person exposes himself, because of his ignorance, to God's wrath and to falling into perilous situations. How can he avoid this when he may believe that some duties are forbidden, or not necessary, and believe that certain forbidden things are obligatory, or that they are acts of obedience, or that they are not forbidden? This is perilous and harmful to the extreme, for due to ignorance they may even fall into something which resembles disbelief, or is in actual fact disbelief, as anyone who observes them and their words and deeds will see. God will not excuse any of this, for He—Transcendent is He—has imposed seeking knowledge upon them, has given them the means to do so with ease, and has imposed upon scholars to teach them. Their negligence, following all this, because they are too occupied with worldly things and are following their whims, can only move them farther away from God and render them deserving to be loathed and expelled by Him.

All this pertains to obligatory knowledge that no Muslim should be ignorant of.

It is strange how you can observe the ignorant and deluded person tirelessly pursuing the world, night and day, avidly desiring it, most careful in amassing, guarding, and enjoying it, then coming up with numerous excuses for doing this, while remaining ignorant of his religion, never having sought knowledge and never having sat with a scholar to learn from him. When someone remonstrates with him about it, he justifies himself with such arguments as lack of free time and excessive occupation, all of which leads to his falling from the sight of God. For God—may He be praised—has made it easy for him to seek knowledge, for scholars abound and the effort required to learn the obligatory amount is insignificant, contrary to the affairs of this world where even small gains require strenuous efforts and enduring hardships. The cause of this is but death of the heart, the little consideration accorded to religion, and the carelessness with which things of the hereafter are taken. Such a person sees his need for the things of this world ever present before his eyes, while his need for knowledge is absent and remote from his mind, for he will only need it and recognize its benefits after he dies. But he has forgotten death and what comes after it, overcome as he is by his ignorance and lack of knowledge. Such a person is one about whom God—Exalted is He—says, *But most people do not know. They know some appearance of the life of this world, but of the hereafter they are forgetful.* [30:6,7]

Al-Ḥasan al-Baṣrī—may God have mercy on him—once said, "One of those will place the *Dirham* on his nail and tell you how much it weighs (so expert is he at things of this world) but were you to ask him about the conditions necessary for ritual purification and prayer, he will know nothing about them."

In summation, ignorance is the origin of all evils and afflictions in both this world and the next. Were all the enemies of an ignorant man to join hands to harm him, they would be unable to cause him as much harm as he causes himself.

A poet has said:

His foes never harm the ignorant
As much as the ignorant harms himself.

And another has said,

Ignorance is a death before death
For their bodies are tombs before their tombs.

The kind of ignorance that is unconditionally blameworthy is ignorance of that which God has made obligatory to know. So beware—O brother—from this. Leave the shadows of your ignorance for the lights of knowledge. It is not obligatory upon you to acquire much knowledge, but only the amount that you cannot do without.

You must also teach your wife, children, and anyone else you are responsible for. If you are incapable of teaching them, you should enjoin upon them to go to the scholars from whom they can learn the obligatory amount of knowledge. Otherwise both you and they will have burdened yourselves with wrongdoing. This applies to those of them who have reached the age of legal responsibility.

The amount of knowledge that is obligatory upon all Muslims is not much. The seeker of knowledge does not have to endure hardship—God willing—because it is so easy, and because God—Exalted is He—will help him and render things even easier for him should his intention be upright. An immense reward will be his.

The Prophet—may God's blessings and peace be upon him—said, *He who takes a path leading to acquiring knowledge, God will ease his path to the Garden.*[4] And he said—may blessings and peace be upon him—*The angels lay down their wings for the seeker of knowledge, so pleased are they with what he is doing.*[5] And he said—may blessings and peace be upon him, that to attend a teaching session is better than to pray a thousand *rak'as,*[6] and so on.

4. Abū Dāwūd, *Sunan*, (3157); Tirmidhī, *Sunan*, (2570, 2606); Ibn Māja, *Sunan*, (219); Aḥmad, *Musnad*, (7965, 20723).
5. Abū Dāwūd, *Sunan*, (3157); Tirmidhī, *Sunan*, (2606, 3458, 3459); Ibn Māja, *Sunan*, (222); Aḥmad, *Musnad*, (17394, 17398, 17401).
6. Ibn Māja, *Sunan*, (215).

And he said—may blessings and peace be upon him, *He who seeks knowledge, God guarantees his provision.*[7] I say: This is a special guarantee in addition to the universal guarantee God has given every moving creature on earth when he said, *There is no moving creature on earth but that its provision falls upon God.* [11:16] It means an increase in ease and decrease in the effort and hardship incurred in seeking provision. And God knows best.

In the long *ḥadīth* where he mentions the merits of knowledge, the Prophet—may blessings and peace be upon him—says near the end of the *ḥadīth, the fortunate are inspired it, while the wretched are deprived of it.*[8] Now all kinds of good are included in being fortunate and all kinds of evil are included in being wretched.

You now know, from the above, that there is no excuse before God—Exalted is He—for an ignorant person to neglect acquiring knowledge. Similarly, there is no excuse for a scholar to neglect practicing what he knows.

The likeness of the ignorant person who neglects seeking obligatory knowledge is that of a slave to whom his master sends a letter, commanding him to do certain things and refrain from other things. The slave, while able to read the letter, neglects to even look at it, let alone learn what it contains. And the likeness of the scholar who neglects to put into practice what he knows is that of another slave who reads his master's letter, learns what it contains, then obeys none of the commands nor refrains from any of the prohibitions he finds in the letter. Now consider—may God have mercy on you—is there any worse neglect than that of these two slaves with their master? Can they ever find justification before him? Is anyone more deserving of severe punishment for his impudence and disrespect for his master than they? So beware of being one of those two inauspicious men, the ignorant who does not learn, or the learned who does not act upon his knowledge. Otherwise you will perish along with those who shall perish, losing both this world and the next, which is the most manifest of all losses.

On the other hand, increasing one's knowledge of beneficial religious sciences, widening one's scope, and acquiring more than what is strictly necessary, is one of the best means to God and most meritorious things in His sight, provided that the acquisition of

7. Al-Shihāb al-Quḍā'ī, *Musnad al-Shihāb*, (373); Abū Ḥanīfa, *Musnad Abū Ḥanīfa*, (2); Abū Nu'aym al-Aṣbahānī, *Ma'rifat al-Saḥāba,* (2676).
8. Ibn 'Abd al-Barr, *Jāmi' Bayān al-'Ilm wa Faḍlih*, (219, 226)

knowledge be purely for God and that one imposes upon oneself to practice what one knows and teach it to God's servants, again for God and the Last Abode.

This is a rank that comes next to the rank of Prophethood. Every other rank belonging to the believers is beneath it, for the scholars who practice what they know are the mediators between the Messenger of God—may God's blessings and peace be upon him—and the Muslims. God—Exalted is he—says concerning the merit of scholars, *God bears witness that there is no god but He, and [so do] the angels and those who have knowledge,* [and that He is] *upholding justice.* [3:11] See how He mentions them along with the angels in bearing witness that He is One and that He upholds justice. And He says—Exalted is He, *Say: are they equal, those who know and those who do not know?* [39:9] which means that they will be equal neither in this world nor in the next, for God prefers those who know and grants them many more degrees. He says—Exalted is He, *God raises those of you who believe and those who are given knowledge many degrees.* [58:11] And the Prophet said—may blessings and peace be upon him, *Scholars are heirs to the Prophets. Prophets bequeath neither* Dīnār *nor* Dirham, *but they bequeath knowledge…*[9] And he said—may blessings and peace be upon him, *Envy is* [justifiable] *only in two cases: a man to whom God has given wisdom, he judges by it and teaches it; and a man to whom God has given wealth and the capacity to spend it all in a rightful manner.*[10] By envy is meant the [benign] non resentful kind that it is praiseworthy to feel in matters pertaining to the hereafter. And he said—may blessings and peace be upon him, *The superiority of the scholar over the worshipper is as my superiority over the least of my Companions.*[11] Another version runs, *as the superiority of the full moon over the rest of the planets.*[12] Now if the superiority of the scholar over the worshipper is that great, knowing that the worshipper must of necessity have knowledge, otherwise he would not have been called a worshipper, how greater will be the superiority of the scholar over the ignorant?

---

9. Abū Dāwūd, *Sunan*, (3157); Tirmidhī, *Sunan*, (2606).

10. Bukhārī, *Ṣaḥīḥ*, (71, 1320, 4637); Muslim, *Ṣaḥīḥ*, (1352); Tirmidhī, *Sunan*, (1859).

11. Tirmidhī, *Sunan*, (2606).

12. Abū Dāwūd, *Sunan*, (3157); Ibn Māja, *Sunan*, (219).

The merits of knowledge and scholars are innumerable. The Book of God, the *Sunna* of His Messenger—may God's blessings and peace be upon him—and the utterances of our virtuous ancestors concerning this matter are very well known and books are brimming with them. 'Alī—may God be pleased with him—said, "Knowledge is better than wealth, for knowledge protects you, while you must protect wealth. Also, knowledge increases when you spend of it, while wealth diminishes. Knowledge is a ruler, while wealth must be ruled."

Know that the scholar who does not behave according to what he knows has no merit whatsoever. He should not deceive himself with what God and His Messenger say about the merits of knowledge and imagine that this shall apply to him even when he does not act upon his knowledge. The Prophet has said—may blessings and peace be upon him, *Learn as you please, but by God, only when you act upon what you know will you be rewarded for it by God.*[13] And he has said—may blessings and peace be upon him, that he who increases in knowledge, but not in right-guidance, only increases in remoteness from God.

Knowledge enjoys such a high rank in the sight of God only because of the benefit it brings to every servant of His—Exalted is He. Thus when a scholar is incapable of drawing benefit form his own knowledge, how will others benefit from him? Know, therefore, that this is why he who knows but does not act on his knowledge is devoid of merit. He has said—may blessings and peace be upon him, *He who is to suffer the severest torment on Judgment Day is a scholar to whom God has not given to benefit from his own knowledge.*[14] And he used to ask for God's protection from knowledge that is of no benefit and a heart that feels no humility.

The scholar who does not practice what he knows possesses only the image of knowledge, its outward form, but not its essence and reality. One of our virtuous ancestors—may God have mercy on them—said, "Knowledge summons its practice, if it is not answered it departs." Meaning that its spirit, its light, and its *baraka* depart; as for its form, it does not depart, but subsists to constitute proof against the evil scholar.

---

13. Dārimī, *Sunan*, (266).

14. Ṭabarānī, *Kabīr*, (151); *Ṣaghīr*, (508); Bayhaqī, *Shu'ab al-Īmān,* (1732); Al-Shihāb al-Quḍā'ī, *Musnad al-Shihāb*, (1042).

However, if this scholar teaches others what he knows, thereby benefiting them with it, he will be like the candle which gives light to the people while itself being consumed, or like the needle which clothes people while remaining naked. He says—Exalted is He, *Will you enjoin good works upon others yet forget yourselves, and you recite the Book? Will you not understand?* [2:44] and a *ḥadīth* says, *A man will be ordered to the Fire, his entrails will spill out and he will drag them around in the Fire as the donkey goes round turning the mill. The people of the Fire will pass by him and say, 'What is with you?' He will answer, 'I used to enjoin good but not do it, and forbid evil, but do it…'*[15] I say: This scholar who teaches others but himself does nothing is a loser who is in extreme danger, yet he is better off than he who neither teaches others nor himself works, for this latter is a loser in every way and will perish no matter what, for no good at all remains in him and no benefit at all can come from him. I fear he might be one of those about whom the Prophet—may blessings and peace be upon him—said that the corrupt among those who have memorized the Qur'ān will be ordered to the Fire even before the idol worshippers, and when they will ask, 'Are we to precede the idol worshippers?' it will be said to them, 'He who knows is not as he who does not.'[16]

Now a scholar who, not only does not act on his knowledge, nor teaches it, but also enjoins evil, opens for the common people the doors to [false] interpretations and dispensation, and teaches them how to deceive others and trick them so as to avoid fulfilling their obligations to them and to enable them to appropriate what belongs to others, he is a rebellious demon, a corrupt man who is opposing God and His Messenger. The Devil has set him up as his deputy, making him do his work of temptation, misguidance, and seduction. In the sight of God he is one of those He likened to donkeys and dogs, so vile and base they are. Donkeys and dogs, however, are better than him, for they will end up back to dust, while he will end up in the Fire, He says—Exalted is He, *The likeness of those who were given the Torah to carry, but did not carry it, is that of a donkey carrying books. Evil is the likeness of those who denied the signs of God; and God guides not people who are unjust.* [62:5] And He says—Exalted is He, *And recite to them the story of him to whom We gave Our signs, but he cast them off, and the Devil followed*

15. Aḥmad, *Musnad,* (20801).
16. Bayhaqī, *Shu'ab al-Īmān,* (109).

him, so he became one of the beguiled. Had We wished We would have raised him up by them, but he was drawn to the earth and he followed his passion. His likeness is thus that of the dog, when you attack him he pants and when you leave him he pants. [7:175-176]

'Umar—may God be pleased with him—said, "That which I fear most for you is a hypocrite who speaks like a learned man." Such a corrupt hypocrite may make a thorough study of the Qur'ān and *Sunna*, and so become a source of sedition and affliction for the Muslims. About such people the Prophet said—may blessings and peace be upon him, *Other than the* Dajjāl *do I fear for you more than the* Dajjāl. They asked, "And what is that?" He said, *Misleading leaders.*[17] He described—may blessings and peace be upon him—people who will recite the Qur'ān as it was sent down, but it will not go beyond their clavicles, and they will shoot out of Islam as the arrow shoots out of its target.[18] A *ḥadīth* says, *The likeness of the hypocrite who recites the Qur'ān is that of sweet basil, its scent is fragrant, but its taste bitter.*[19]

It is not unlikely then, after the above, to consider he who acquires the likeness of knowledge to be a corrupt hypocrite. His sign is that neither he himself benefits from his knowledge, nor do others, but on the contrary, he harms himself and others.

On the whole the scholar who acts on his knowledge and teaches God's servants is the one who deserves to be considered an heir to the Prophets. The scholar who does not act on his knowledge but teaches others is in a perilous situation, but nevertheless is much better than he who neither behaves according to his knowledge, nor teaches others, and in addition invites to evil by opening the doors to it and rendering it easier for the people.

So distinguish between scholars and choose the best among them to emulate and follow his way, thus will you be rightly-guided. God guides whom He will to a straight path.

Now know—may God have mercy on you—that the scholar who acts on his knowledge, who is counted by God and His Messenger amongst the learned in this world and the next, has marks and signs by which he can be distinguished from the confused scholar who is counted by God and His Messenger amongst those whose

17. Aḥmad, *Musnad,* (20334, 20335); Abū Ya'lā, *Musnad,* (445).

18. Bukhārī, *Ṣaḥīḥ*, (6422, 7007); Muslim, *Ṣaḥīḥ*, (1358, 1765).

19. Nasā'ī. *Al-Sunan al-Kubrā*, (8081, 8082, 8084); 'Abdal-Razzāq, *Muṣannaf*, (20932).

learning is only verbose, who follow their whims and prefer this world to the next.

Among the signs of he who is counted amongst those who are learned in the sciences of the hereafter are that he be humble, modest, fearful, anxious, in awe of God, detached from the world, content with a little of it, spending in charity whatever exceeds his needs, of good counsel to the servants of God—Exalted is He, solicitous for their welfare, compassionate, enjoining good and forbidding evil, swift to good works, constant in his devotions, guiding to good, inviting to right-guidance, possessed of gravity and commanding respect, dignified, sedate, of good character, forbearing, gentle, affable with believers, neither arrogant nor overbearing, harboring no [worldly] hopes in people, not avid for worldly things, nor preferring this world to the hereafter, not given to amassing money, nor withholding it when it should rightfully be spent. He is neither coarse, nor rude, neither argumentative, nor quarrelsome, neither harsh, intolerant, nor of bad character, neither hypocritical, nor deceitful, nor cheating. He does not prefer rich to poor people, is not a frequent visitor to rulers, and does not refrain from rebuking them when capable of it. He is not avid for power, wealth, or position, on the contrary he dislikes them all, does not engage in any of them, nor accept any of them except when for a dire need or necessity.

In sum, he should be everything that his knowledge enjoins him to be in the way of virtuous character and good works and should avoid every bad character or deed that his knowledge enjoins him to avoid.

These attributes of those whose knowledge is for the hereafter are attributes which should adorn every believer. However, though every believer should strive to acquire them, a scholar is more worthy of them and should be the first to acquire them. It is more of a duty to him, since he is an example that people are guided by, a leader whom they emulate. Should he err, fall prey to temptation, or give precedence to this world over the next, he will carry his burden of sin and that of everyone who follows him. But if he is upright and God-fearing, he will receive his own reward as well as additional rewards equal to those of everyone who followed him.

The scholar well versed in the outward matters of religion should add to this the knowledge of inward attributes such as the attributes of the heart, knowledge of the secrets of works and of the things that blemish them, of the promises and threats in the Book and *Sunna* concerning the rewards of those who do good and the punishment of evildoers. In this way will a scholar complete himself and become fully beneficial both to himself and others. For these sciences cannot become complete without each completing the other, and they were the sciences of our virtuous ancestors, as will be recognized by anyone who peruses their biographies.

Knowledge of the inward cannot stand independently from knowledge of the outward. Similarly, outward knowledge cannot be complete without that of the inward.

As for knowledge of promises and threats, it is because they arouse the desire to live according to the injunctions of the Law and to virtue, and the fear of falling into prohibited things and vices.

It is unbecoming of a scholar to speak of the rulings concerning certain obligations, other virtuous works, or certain prohibited things, then when requested to produce some of what God and His Messenger have to say on this, prove incapable of quoting any relevant text. It is but by the words of God—Exalted is He—and His Messenger—may God's blessings and peace be upon him—that dilatation of the breasts of believers occurs, that their hearts find peace, and their resolution increases.

Reflect on this passage and study it well. Acquire a sufficient amount of each of these three sciences: the science of the outward rulings concerning acts of worship and transactions; the science of inward things such as good character and the attributes of the heart; and the science of promises and threats, which is what has been received from God and His Messenger concerning the merits of acts of obedience, which are the promises, and the punishment of evil deeds, which are the threats.

It is a most emphatic duty upon scholars to do their best to disseminate this knowledge, which no Muslim would fail to benefit from, and to spread it and teach it to every single Muslim.

When sitting with the common people, a scholar should talk only of duties and forbidden things, supererogatory devotions, and rewards and punishments for good and bad behavior. His words should be easy to understand and clear, so that his listeners recognize and understand them. He should expend more effort in clarifying those things which he knows they actually do. He should not remain silent until asked about something which he knows they need and which is necessary for them. For his knowledge of their need is tantamount to their asking him.

Most common people have become neglectful in matters of religion, as concerns both knowledge and works. Scholars should not help them in this by failing to teach and guide them, for then everyone will perish and hardship will increase. You seldom question a common man—and most people are common people—without finding him ignorant of duties, forbidden things, and matters of religion which it is neither permissible nor acceptable not to know. Even in the event of his not being ignorant of all of them, he will be found ignorant of some. And in the event when you find him aware of some of these things, he will have learned them from other common people, so that should you wish to turn what he knows into ignorance, you can do so with little effort, for it has no basis and is unsound.

When the seeker of knowledge comes to the scholar, the latter should decide whether he is qualified to understand and able to devote his time fully to studying, then he may counsel him to read books. But if he is a common Muslim wishing only to learn the obligatory minimum, he should teach him verbally, explain, make him understand, be brief, and not ask him to read books that he may not understand, nor have the time for, nor need most of what they contain. For the needs of common people in the way of knowledge are little.

Scholars, especially those who are judges, must counsel the common Muslims who come before them with their litigations. They must put fear into them with the words of God—Exalted is He—and His Messenger, speak harshly to them and threaten those who make false claims, are guilty of perjury, testify falsely, are guilty of corrupt transactions such as usury, and so on. They should tell them what the Sacred Law says concerning how forbidden such things are and how severe their punishment is. This is because ignorance is so widespread, and also greed and lack of concern for religion. How many a common Muslim, having heard how lying about claims, testimonies, and oaths is forbidden, has backed up from things that, owing to his ignorance, he had decided to do.

In sum, it is important for scholars to sit with the people to talk to them about religious sciences and explain them to them. They should discourse upon the matter which they came to them for. For instance, if they have come for a marriage contract, then they should speak to them about the rights of women in terms of dowry, current expenses, gentle treatment, and so on. But if they have come to them to record in writing a commercial transaction, they should speak to them of valid and invalid transactions, the duties of witnesses, and so on.

This—by God—is better and more appropriate in such situations than to talk of that which is of no use and is connected neither with the matter at hand, nor with religion.

A scholar should not chat with those who chat, nor spend any of his time in other than strengthening religion.

This that we have been stating, that the scholar is emphatically enjoined to make his times with common Muslims fully occupied with teaching, warning, and reminding them, has become in those days one of the most important duties of the learned. Heedlessness, ignorance and turning away from knowledge and its practice have become rampant among common people. Should the learned encourage them in this by failing to teach and remind them, corruption will dominate and everyone will come to harm. The neglect of religion by common Muslims is easily observable, while scholars maintain silence, neither teaching, nor explaining. There is neither power nor ability save by God.

It is one of the most imperative functions and courtesies of scholars to be for the people a good example, before they address them with their words, not to enjoin anything good upon them before being most careful to practice it, nor forbid anything evil to them without being most careful to avoid it and be most remote from it. They should also intend nothing with their knowledge, actions, and teaching but God and the Last Abode, and not desire any other thing such as eminence, wealth, power, or other worldly things. The Messenger of God—may God's blessings and peace be upon him—said, *Whoever seeks knowledge* [of the kind that is sought for God's sake] *to boast before scholars, or argue with fools, or attract important people to himself, he will go to the Fire.*[20]

O God, make us profit from what You have taught us, teach us what profits us and increase us in knowledge. Praise is God's in all situations. We seek God's protection from the states of the people of the Fire.

---

20. Ibn Māja, *Sunan*, (249, 256); Dārimī, *Sunan*, (381, 382); Al-Ḥākim, *Mustadrak*, (268); Ṭabarānī, *Kabīr*, (19113); *Awsaṭ*, (5869); Bayhaqī, *Shu'ab al-Īmān,* (1726).

Chapter Three: On Ritual Prayer

Know brothers—may God grant us and you the understanding of religion, inspire us with our guidance, and protect us from the evil in ourselves—that the ritual prayer is the basis of religion and, of the five bases of Islam, second in importance only to the two testimonies. It is to religion what the head is to the body. Just as there can be no life for a headless person, so there can be no religion for he who does not pray. Thus state many *ḥadīths*.

May God make us and you of those who carefully keep their prayers, perform them as they should, and persevere therein. For in His Book God orders His believing servants to do so, making this one of their [distinctive] attributes, when He says, *Carefully keep your prayers, and the middle prayer, and stand humble before God.* [2:238] The prayers meant here are the five obligatory ones which take place at midday, early afternoon, sunset, night, and before dawn. These are the prayers that a Muslim is allowed to neglect under no circumstance, even if extremely old or ill, so long as his mind is intact. As for the *middle prayer*, it is the afternoon prayer, as stated in a sound *ḥadīth*. God makes special mention of it to give it additional merit and honor. This is well known in Islam.

It has reached us that the reason for the dispensation in the Prayer of Fear is that the Muslims were with the Messenger of God—may God's blessings and peace be upon him—in one of their expeditions. As usual he led them in prayer—may peace be upon him—for the noon prayer, while the idolaters, who were not far off, watched. Once they were finished, one of the idolaters said, "Had you attacked them while they were in their prayer you would have defeated them." Others said, "They have, after this prayer, another which is dearer to them than their fathers and sons", meaning the afternoon prayer. Gabriel—may peace be upon him—came down to the Messenger of God—may God's blessings and peace be upon him—with the Prayer of Fear.[1] So observe how the merit of this prayer [*'aṣr*] was known even to the idolaters.

God—Exalted is He—says, *Humbly returning to Him, fear Him and establish the prayer, and do not be of those who associate [others with God].* [30:31] To establish the prayer is to perform it in the manner that God has prescribed. And He says—Exalted is He,

1. Muslim, *Ṣaḥīḥ*, (1388); Tirmidhī, *Sunan*, (2961).

Successful indeed are the believers who are humble in their prayers, who shun idle prattle, who pay the zakāt, *who guard their private parts, except from their wives and what their right hands own, for then they are not to blame. But those who seek other than that, they are the transgressors. And those who keep their trusts and their pledges, and those who are careful to keep their prayers…* [23:1 to 9] And He says—Exalted is He, *Except those who pray, who persevere with their prayers.* [70:22,23] Here he excludes those who pray from the generality of mankind who by nature become panicky and aggrieved when afflicted with hardship, but avaricious when blessed with affluence. As if God—Transcendent is He—is saying to them that those who pray and whose prayer is real neither panic, grieve, nor act avariciously. I say: This is because their attributes are reprehensible and He says—Exalted is He, *And establish the prayer, for prayer prevents from lewdness and reprehensible things; and the remembrance of God is even greater.* [29:45]

He who establishes the prayer in the manner prescribed by God and His Messenger, his prayer rebukes him from doing anything that may displease God, whether one of the above mentioned or other such reprehensible things.

The Prophet said—may God's blessings and peace be upon him, *Pray as you have seen me pray.*[2] He only will be considered by God to have established the prayer and preserved it who follows and emulates the Messenger of God—may God's blessings and peace be upon him—in his prayer, in the manner that the scholars of this community, both early ones and latecomers—may God be pleased with them all—have recorded and transmitted it.

Now the ritual prayer has an outward form and an inward reality. No prayer can be perfect or complete without both being performed properly.

As for the outward form, it is its standing up, recitation, bowing down, prostrating, and other such components of outward prayer. As for the inward reality, it is humility, presence of the heart, perfect sincerity, reflection, and understanding of the meanings of what is being recited, *tasbīḥ*, and all other components of inward prayer. The outward form of the prayer thus belongs to the body and the senses, while its inward belongs to the heart and the secret. The heart and secret are the location upon which falls the gaze of the Real.

2. Bukhārī, *Ṣaḥīḥ*, (595, 5549).

Imām al-Ghazālī—may God have mercy on him—says, "The likeness of he who performs the outward form of the prayer but neglects its inward reality is that of he who, wishing to offer a great king a gift, gives him a dead maid. As for he who performs the outward form of the prayer incorrectly, he is like one who offers the king a maid whose limbs have been cut off and whose eyes have been plucked out. Both are exposing themselves to punishment and perhaps torture because of their disrespect and contempt for the king." Says Ghazālī, "You offer your prayer but to your Lord. Beware of offering one like that, thereby deserving punishment."

It is part of keeping the prayer with care and propriety to perform ritual ablutions to perfection and carefully keep one's body, clothes, and place of prayer pure. The Prophet—may peace be upon him—said, *Ritual purity is the key to the Prayer*[3]. And in another *ḥadīth*, *Ritual purity is half of faith.*[4]

Complete ritual ablution is to repeat each of its motions three times, being neither too obsessive, nor too neglectful. Obsessions in either ritual purification or prayer are from the Devil, who confuses thereby those whose knowledge is deficient and reason weak. One of our predecessors said, "Obsessions are due either to ignorance of the *Sunna* or mental illness." The way of our predecessors in ritual purification is the praiseworthy manner of doing things, and so it is in all other things, for they are our exemplars, and we should emulate them. To renew one's *wuḍū'* for each prayer is of the *Sunna.* Maintaining oneself in a constant state of ritual purity is something to be encouraged and has many benefits. It has reached us that God said to Moses—may peace be upon him, "Should a calamity afflict you when you are not in ritual purity, blame only yourself."

Many authentic *ḥadīths* exist to the effect that he who performs his ritual ablution with care, all his sins are cast off the various parts of his body and he enters the prayer pure from sins.

It is part of keeping the prayer with care and propriety to hasten to perform it as soon as its time comes. There is great merit in this and it is a sign that one loves God—Exalted is He—and is swift to what pleases Him. The Prophet—may blessings and peace be upon him—said, *The beginning of the time is God's good pleasure, its end is God's pardon.*[5] And, *A man may perform a prayer [still within its*

3. Abū Dāwūd, *Sunan*, (56, 523); Tirmidhī, *Sunan*, (3, 221).
4. Muslim, *Ṣaḥīḥ*, (328); Tirmidhī, *Sunan*, (3439).
5. Dāraqutnī, *Sunan*, (998); Bayhaqī, *Al-Sunan al-Kubrā*, vol. 1, p. 436.

prescribed time], but would have missed, because of not performing it at the beginning of its time, what would have been worth to him more than his wife and children.[6]

It is ugly of a believer, engaged in a worldly pursuit when the time for the prayer comes, not to abandon it and hasten to perform the duty that God has prescribed for him. This can be caused only by excessive heedlessness, lack of knowledge of God, or weakness in one's desire for the hereafter.

As for delaying the prayer until its time runs out, or part of it is performed after its time, this is not permissible and is sinful.

The *adhān* and *iqāma* are parts of the rites of prayer and should be preserved. They drive devils away. He said—may blessings and peace be upon him, *When the prayer is called for the devil departs.*[7]

It is also part of keeping the prayer with care and propriety to be humble therein, present of heart, reflect on what one is reciting, understand its meanings, feel submission and powerlessness before God when bowing down or prostrating, have a heart full of the magnitude and holiness of God when uttering the *takbīr* and *tasbīḥ*, as well as throughout every other part of the prayer, avoid incidental thoughts and worldly preoccupations, and turn away from the ego's ruminations. One should concentrate solely on the proper performance of the prayer, in the exact manner that God has prescribed, for prayer accompanied by distraction and lack of humility or presence is useless. Al-Ḥasan al-Baṣrī—may God have mercy on him—said, "Every prayer where the heart is not present is more likely to bring about punishment." It has been transmitted that, "A servant owns only that part of the prayer during which he was attentive." And, *A man may pray and have only a tenth or a ninth, or an eighth or a seventh of it added to his record.*[8] This means that only that part will be recorded to his credit during which he was present with God and humble before Him. It may vary from little to much according to the proportion of distraction to attentiveness. He who is present and humble during the whole prayer, it will be recorded whole to his

6. 'Abdal-Razzāq, *Muṣannaf*, (2225); Ibn Ḥajar al-'Asqalānī, *Al-Maṭālib al-'Āliya*, (291).

7. Bukhārī, *Ṣaḥīḥ*, (573, 1146); Muslim, *Ṣaḥīḥ*,(585, 884).

8. Aḥmad, *Musnad*, (18122); Nasā'ī, *Al-Sunan al-Kubrā*, (612); Abū Ya'lā, *Musnad*, (1614).

credit; while he who is distracted and inattentive during the whole of his prayer, nothing of it will be recorded to his credit.

So strive—may God have mercy on you—to be humble and present in your prayer. Reflect on what you recite of the words of your Lord. Do not be hasty in your recitation, for reflection cannot co-exist with haste.

Bow down and prostrate yourself with composure, do not peck as chicken do, then your prayer will not be valid, for composure during bowing down, standing up afterwards, during the two prostrations and kneeling down in between, is necessary. It cannot be dispensed with, whether in obligatory or supererogatory prayers, and without it the prayer is invalid. He who neither performs his bowing down and prostrations to completion, nor is sufficiently humble, is the one who steals from his prayer, as mentioned in *ḥadīth*. It is also mentioned in *ḥadīth* that he who is careful with his prayer and completes it properly, his prayer comes out white and radiant, saying, "May God preserve you as you have preserved me." But when it is not performed properly, it comes out black and dark, and says, "May God neglect you as you have neglected me!" Then it is wrapped up just as a worn out garment is wrapped up, then his face is struck with it.[9] A *ḥadīth* says that the Prayer is but poverty, submission, and humility. Once when he noticed a man playing with his beard as he prayed, the Prophet said, *Had this one's heart been humble, his limbs would also have been humble*.[10]

Stillness of the body is part of the heart's humility, no prayer is complete without it. Our ancestors—may God be pleased with them—used to say, "He who is aware of who is standing on his right and on his left during prayer is not humble." Some of our ancestors were so humble during their prayers that birds alighted on them, for they stood or prostrated themselves for so long that the birds took them for a wall or some other inanimate object.

A pillar once fell in the great mosque at Basra. Out in the marketplace the people were terrified, except for one man praying in the mosque, who was so absorbed in his prayer that he felt nothing at all.

Another used to tell his family, "Once I commence praying, do what you will." Meaning: raise your voices and make noises as you

9. Ṭabarānī, *Awsaṭ*, (3213); Bayhaqī, *Shu'ab al-Īmān*, (2993).

10. Abū 'Abdal-Raḥmān al-Sulamī, *Adāb al-Ṣuḥba*, vol.,1, p. 186.

will for I shall not hear you. They sometimes beat the drums next to him without him hearing them.

Once as he was in prostration, the house of 'Alī ibn al-Husayn—may God be pleased with them both—started to burn. People shouted, "[Beware of] the fire, [beware of] the fire, O son of the Messenger of God!" But he did not raise his head. When his prayer was over and they asked him why he did so, he replied, "I was distracted from it by the fire of the hereafter."

A man was once asked, "Do you experience in your prayer the same worldly thoughts that we do?" He said, "I would rather be run through by spears than experience that." Another was asked, "Do you talk to yourself during prayer?" He said, "Is there anything more beloved to me than the prayer that I may talk to myself about it?"

A thief once stole al-Rabī' ibn al-Khaytham's mare while he was praying. Those who saw this began to invoke God against him. Al-Rabī' said, "I saw him when he untied it." They asked him, "Why then did you not pursue him and retrieve it?" He replied, "My prayer was dearer to me than the mare, and I now declare that I am relinquishing the mare to him."

A Companion of the Messenger of God—may God's blessings and peace be upon him—was once praying in his garden when he was distracted by birds flying from one tree to another. When he realized he had been distracted he was so aggrieved that he gave the whole garden away for the sake of God.

I say: This is all because our virtuous ancestors, may God be pleased with them—knew how great the importance of the prayer is and how essential it is to religion.

It has reached us that God—Exalted is He—has divided the various parts of the prayer among forty thousand ranks of angels, each rank made of seventy thousand angels. Ten ranks are ever standing up, never bowing down, ten bowing down, never prostrating, ten in prostration, never rising up, and ten sitting down, never standing up. All this He joined into two *rak'as* that His believing servant is given to pray, so see how immense His grace and favor are upon His believing servants. The Prophet may blessings and peace be upon him—said, *Imagine that a river flows near a man's doorstep and he bathes in it five times a day; do you think any dirt will remain on him*? They answered, "No dirt will remain on him." He said, *This is the likeness of the five Prayers with which God erases sins.* [11]

And he said- may blessings and peace be upon him—*One Prayer after another are expiations for what takes place between them, so long as major sins are avoided.*[12]

Whenever it was time to pray, Abū Bakr al-Ṣiddīq—may God be pleased with him—used to say, "Arise and put out this fire of yours which you have kindled!" By fire he meant their sins, while by putting it out he meant with prayer, for it expiates and erases bad deeds. God—Exalted is He—says, *Establish the prayer at both ends of the days, and in part of the night, for good works do away with sins. This is a reminder for those who remember.* [11:114] This verse was revealed after a man who was guilty of one of those things that may take place with a woman short of intercourse came to the Prophet requesting to submit to the statutory punishment (*ḥadd*). The Prophet gave him no answer, till after the ritual prayer was called for and they had prayed, he called him and recited this verse to him. The man asked, "Is this for me in particular or for the people in general?" He said, "For the people in general."[13] I say: This is evidence that minor sins are expiated by Prayer as well as by other good works. However, to refrain from them is better and safer. Also, no statutory punishment is prescribed for anything short of intercourse, such as kissing or touching, but the man thought there was [and wished to be thus purified]. And God and His Messenger know best.

It is part of keeping the Prayer with care and propriety to persevere in performing it in congregation, for congregational prayer is twenty seven times better than solitary prayer, as in the authentic *ḥadīth.* He who takes such religious profit lightly, even though this next-worldly profit is obtainable without undue effort or hardship, his forgetfulness of religious gains is great and his desire for the hereafter feeble, especially when he knows full well how much effort he expends and how many hardships he endures in his pursuit of puny insignificant worldly gains. Whenever he does achieve any of the latter, even something trivial at the cost of much toiling, he forgets his toil and considers what he has gained of this evanescent world an immense profit. He who is aware that he is thus, does he

11. Bukhārī, *Ṣaḥīḥ*, (497); Muslim, *Ṣaḥīḥ*, (1071, 1072); Tirmidhī, *Sunan*, (2794); Nasā'ī, *Sunan*, (458).
12. Muslim, *Ṣaḥīḥ*, (344); Aḥmad, *Musnad*, (10171).
13. Tirmidhī, *Sunan*, (3040).

not fear to be counted by God among the hypocrites or among those who doubt God's promises?

In all that was recorded and transmitted about the Messenger of God—may God's blessings and peace be upon him—there is no indication that he ever prayed on his own, not even once. Ibn Mas'ūd—may God be pleased with him—said, "I witnessed a time when none stayed behind [from the congregational prayer] except a known hypocrite. A man was brought, in the days of the Messenger of God—may God's blessings and peace be upon him—supported by two men, so old was he, till he was stood in the rank."

The blind ibn Umm Maktūm complained to the Messenger of God—may God's blessings and peace be upon him—that he had no one to lead him [to the mosque], that Madina in those days abounded in wells and reptiles, and that his house was far from the mosque. He hoped to receive from him a dispensation from attending the congregational prayer. Having heard him, the Prophet replied that he is to be dispensed, but when he rose to depart, he called him back to ask him, "Do you hear *Ḥayya 'ala'ṣ-ṣalā, Ḥayya 'ala'l-falāḥ*?" He answered, "Yes" He said, "Come then."[14] Meaning you must come to the Prayer for there is no excuse for you.

He said—may blessings and peace be upon him—*He who hears the Call, is unoccupied and healthy, but does not respond, for him there is no prayer.*[15] He once threatened to burn the houses of certain people who neglected the congregational prayer. There is a *ḥadīth* to this effect, threatening those who abandon the congregational prayer without a valid excuse with utmost severity.

A valid excuse is that which makes one entirely incapable of attending, or if capable then only at the cost of extreme hardship that most people would find difficult to bear. Nevertheless, attending is better and its reward greater, except in certain rare instances. An example would be continuous diarrhea, which would threaten to soil the mosque, and other similar instances.

To be excused means that there is to be no blame. If one is truly incapable, wishes sincerely that he could attend, feels in his heart sadness and grief for missing acts of obedience and not giving due reverence to his Lord's prescription, then he will receive his reward. As he once said—may blessings and peace be upon him, *We have left behind in Madina people who are with us even as we march*

14. Nasā'ī, *Sunan*, (842); Ibn Khuzayma, *Ṣaḥīḥ*, (1399).

15. Al-Ḥākim, *Mustadrak,* (860).

and as we cross each valley, for they were impeded by valid excuses.[16] It seems that they were those about whom God said, *Neither are they to blame who came to you requesting to be provided with mounts, but when you said to them, 'I am unable to provide you with mounts,' they turned back with tears overflowing from their eyes, aggrieved.* [9:92] This applies to all those who are true and sincere like them, have a powerful desire for what is with God, and are willing to sacrifice their lives and all else to obtain His good pleasure. So beware of leaving the congregational prayer for no impervious excuse such as you can present to God, the knower of the unseen. Should you decide to stay home for reasons to do with the soundness of either your religious or worldly affairs, then go out to the mosque at each prayer time to pray in congregation, or else arrange for someone to join you at home, even if one person, that you may avoid the blame and obtain the reward. The merit of congregation is obtained by one man leading the prayer and another following him; however, the greater the number the better.

The prayer is purer and of more reward when the leader is a man of goodness and virtue. It then becomes superior to that performed behind someone not of such qualities. Therefore, you should strive to pray behind those who are known for *taqwā*. This is only to achieve what is better and of more merit, for otherwise, the Prophet—blessings and peace be upon him—said, *Pray behind* [every man, whether he is] *good or corrupt.*[17]

Walking to the mosque to pray brings on a great reward, as in *ḥadīth*, for it is said that each single step a servant takes to the mosque is counted to his credit and recorded in his good deeds.

Also, waiting for one prayer after another is an act of worship. For example: to pray *Maghrib* then sit in the mosque waiting for *'Ishā'*. He who is waiting for a prayer is considered by God to be praying and the reward of those who are in actual prayer is recorded for him, whether he has already performed one prayer and is waiting for the next, or has come early to the mosque and is sitting waiting. He who remains where he has prayed will have the angels praying for him and asking forgiveness until either he breaks his ritual purity or talks. The Messenger of God—may God's blessings and peace be upon him—said, *Shall I inform you of that with which God erases sins and raises degrees? To perform ritual ablutions thoroughly,*

16. Bukhārī, *Ṣaḥīḥ*, (2627, 4071); Abū Dāwūd, *Sunan*, (2147).

17. Bayhaqī, *Al-Sunan al-Kubrā,* vol. 4, p. 19.; Dāraquṭnī, *Sunan*, (1788).

even in unpleasant circumstances, to walk many steps to the mosque, to wait for one prayer after another. This is standing guard![18] And he said—may blessings and peace be upon him, *You are in prayer as long as you are waiting for the prayer.*[19] And, *Give good news to those who constantly walk to the mosque in the dark that they shall have complete light on Resurrection Day.*[20] It has also been transmitted that when a man walks to the mosque it is recorded for him and his reward from God is that one step expiates one sin, the next step is recorded for him as a good deed, and the next raises him one degree. Then, just as his walking to the mosque was recorded to his credit, so will his walking back home.

The Prophet—may blessings and peace be upon him—said, *The angels will continue to pray for each of you as long as he remains where he has prayed, so long as he has not broken his ritual purity or spoken. They will say, 'O God, forgive him! O God, have mercy on him*!'[21]

It is of the utmost importance to strive persistently to pray in the first row, for he has said—may blessings and peace be upon him, *God and His angels bless those who pray in the front ranks.*[22] And he has also said, *Were people to know what* [merit] *lies in the Call and the first row, then found no way other than to draw lots, they would have drawn lots.*[23]

He who wishes to obtain the merit of praying in the first row should be there early, before people crowd [the mosque]. He should outstrip them to the first row, for if he comes late and still wishes to reach the first row he may need to cross over their shoulders, which is forbidden. In such cases it is better not to insist on praying in the first row, after which one must reprimand oneself for being so late as to have allowed other people to precede him there. A *ḥadīth* says, *Some people will persist in being late until it will be God that will hold them back.*[24]

18. Muslim, *Ṣaḥīḥ*, (369); Tirmidhī, *Sunan*, (47); Nasā'ī, *Sunan*, (143).
19. Bukhārī, *Ṣaḥīḥ*, (565, 802); Muslim, *Ṣaḥīḥ*, (1012).
20. Abū Dāwūd, *Sunan*, (474); Tirmidhī, *Sunan*, (207); Ibn Māja, *Sunan*, (773).
21. Aḥmad, *Musnad,* (10116); Dārimī, *Sunan*, (1458).
22. Nasā'ī, *Al-Sunan al-Kubrā,* (886); Ibn Ḥibbān, *Ṣaḥīḥ*, (2195).
23. Bukhārī, *Ṣaḥīḥ*, (580, 615, 2492); Muslim, *Ṣaḥīḥ*, (661).
24. Muslim, *Ṣaḥīḥ*, (662); Abū Dāwūd, *Sunan*, (581, 582); Nasā'ī, *Sunan*, (787).

An important *Sunna* that people seem to have forgotten is to straighten the ranks and line up in an orderly fashion. The Prophet—may blessings and peace be upon him—used to do this himself, commanded others to do it and encouraged them, saying, *By God, you will straighten your ranks or God will cause discord between your hearts*![25] And, *I see the devil penetrating the gaps in the ranks.*[26] It is therefore recommended to press elbows against each others as the ranks are straightened, so that none should stand ahead or behind another; this is the *Sunna*. Imāms should take special care of this and enjoin upon those who pray to conform to it. It behooves them more than other Muslims to do this, for they are those who help in benevolence and *taqwā*, for this is how God commanded them. He said—Exalted is He, *And assist each other in benevolence and* taqwā, *but assist not each other in sin and aggression.* [5:2]

Hasten to the first row—may God have mercy on you—help straightening the rows as much as you can, for it is one of the *Sunnas* that have died out, so that he who brings it back to life will be with the Messenger of God—may God's blessings and peace be upon him—in the Garden; as has been handed down.

Known that, as mentioned before, it is of the utmost importance to persevere in praying in congregation. However, it is even more important in *'Ishā'* and *Ṣubḥ* prayers, and there is more merit in it. For he has said—may blessings and peace be upon him, *He who prays the* 'Ishā' *prayer in congregation is as if he has stood in prayer half the night, and he who prays* Ṣubḥ *in congregation is as if he has stood in prayer all night long.*[27] And, *The difference between us and the hypocrites is that they cannot attend* 'Ishā' *and* Ṣubḥ *in congregation.*[28] And, *He who prays* Ṣubḥ *in congregation remains under God's protection till evening.* And he added, *Let not God ask you to account for those under His protection.*[29] Meaning: Never harm anyone who is under God's protection.

We have been told that al-Ḥajjāj, as iniquitous, tyrannical, and oblivious of God's limits as he was, always asked those who were

25. Abū Dāwūd, *Sunan*, (566); Aḥmad, *Musnad,* (17703); Ibn Ḥibbān, *Ṣaḥīḥ*, (2210).
26. Ibn Ḥibbān, *Ṣaḥīḥ*, (6445).
27. Muslim, *Ṣaḥīḥ*, (1049).
28. Imām Mālik, *Muwaṭṭa'*, (268).
29. Muslim, *Ṣaḥīḥ*, (1050, 1051); Tirmidhī, *Sunan*, (206, 2090); Ibn Māja, *Sunan*, (3935, 3936).

brought to him during the daytime, "Did you pray *Ṣubḥ* in congregation?" Whenever anyone answered yes he set him free, anxious that God should not ask him to account for a man under His protection.

Now that you are aware of what has been received from the Messenger—may blessings and peace be upon him—in the way of insistence upon never leaving praying in congregation without a valid excuse, know and be sure that he who abandons the *Jumu'a* prayer is much more deserving of those threats and insistence, for it is by consensus an obligation upon every individual. He said—may God's blessings and peace be upon him, *He who leaves three* Jumu'as *out of indifference, without excuse, God will stamp upon his heart.*[30] Ibn 'Abbās was once asked about a man who prayed all night and fasted every day, but attended neither *Jumu'a*, nor the other congregational prayers. He answered, "He is in the Fire."

No believer can leave *Jumu'a* without excuse, having heard His saying—Exalted is He, *O Believers, when the prayer is called for on Friday hasten to God's remembrance and leave commerce aside. That is better for you, did you but know.* [62:9] But you see people who pretend to be Muslims and believers, who hear God's words and those of His Messenger, then neglect *Jumu'a* without excuse, or with invalid excuses, acceptable neither to God, nor to the Messenger of God—may God's blessings and peace be upon him—excuses such as cannot relieve them of obligatory duties. We have already said that the valid excuse is that which renders one either entirely incapable of attending, or if capable, he must endure such hardship as is too difficult to bear, so that in practice he is not capable. This is much more applicable to *Jumu'a.* Only he would leave it without a valid excuse who is a doubting hypocrite who has missed the truth, and whose heart has lost the lights of reverence for God the Tremendous and for the rights of His Lordship. There is for the servant neither honor, nor degree, nor happiness, nor success in this world or the next, without regularly fulfilling these rights and persevering in doing so. So see how this evil servant disdains his own happiness and success, and cares little how he will fail and perish for neglecting God's rights and the obligatory rites He has imposed upon him.

We ask God for well-being and safety and seek His protection from being overtaken by wretchedness and evil destiny.

Know also that when, even though in possession of a valid excuse, one still attends *Jumu'a*, this is better, for it indicates that one

30. Aḥmad, *Musnad,* (14951); Abū Dāwūd, *Sunan*, (888).

is complete in one's reverence for God and respect for His rights, that one desires to the full what God has and fears to the full His wrath and punishment.

And know—may God make you happy—that Friday is the master of all days and that it is greatly honorable in the sight of God. In it Adam—may peace be upon him—was created. In it God will bring about the Hour. In it He permits the people of the Garden to visit Him. The Angels call Friday the Day of Increase because God opens the gates of mercy with such abundance, grants so much favor, and distributes so much good.

In the course of this day is a noble hour when all prayers are answered. It is not known which hour of the day it is, as have stated Imām al-Ghazālī and others.

Keep to good works and acts of worship on that day. Do not occupy yourself with other than that, unless it is absolutely necessary, for this day should be dedicated to the hereafter. It is sufficient that one occupies all other days with worldly pursuits. What a waste! What a loss! A believer should devote all his days and nights to his life to come. If he cannot because of worldly preoccupations, then the least he can do is to devote that one day to the hereafter.

It is a *Sunna* to recite *Sūrat'al-Kahf* and to invoke blessings on the Prophet in abundance on Friday and Friday eve, so keep to this, as well as to being early in going to the *Jumu'a* prayer. At the very least be there before or when the sun reaches its zenith. It is contrary to the *Sunna* to delay praying the *Jumu'a* prayer until half its time or so is gone. On the contrary, the *Sunna* is to pray as soon as the time for *Ẓuhr* comes, as the Prophet- may blessings and peace be upon him—used to do.

Listen attentively—may God have mercy on you—to the *khuṭba* and the counsels given, heed them, and feel that they are addressed to you personally.

Some of the craftsmen and others in the marketplace, upon whom *Jumu'a* is obligatory, are late coming to it. This is one of the most reprehensible *bid'as*. Governors should impose upon them to attend and punish those who do not, once they have explained the situation to them and warned them. Governors are not permitted to neglect this and other similar matters. God only gave them power over His servants so that they may establish among them the rites of religion, get them to perform its obligatory duties and avoid prohibited things. Worldly affairs must come second for those in charge. And God knows best.

It is part of the proper observance of the ritual prayer to persevere in performing the supererogatory prayers attached to them, both those that are strongly recommended and those that are less strongly recommended. This is because supererogatory devotions compensate for shortcomings in obligatory ones, as has been transmitted. Whenever the obligatory act is flawed or incomplete because of lack of humility or of presence of the heart, or for any other reason, supererogatory devotions compensate for these flaws and complete the rite. Therefore, he who has no supererogatory devotions, his obligatory acts remain incomplete, and he misses the immense reward he has been promised for these devotions. It has been handed down that the first thing a servant is asked to account for is the ritual prayer. Should it be found wanting, it is said, "See if he has any supererogatory prayers that his ritual prayer can be completed with." These firmly recommended prayers are too well known to deserve [detailed] mention.

The *Witr* prayer is one of the things that we are strongly recommended to perform and persevere in. The Messenger of God—may God's blessings and peace be upon him—said, *God is* Witr *and He loves what is* Witr*, so perform your* Witr*, O people of the Qur'ān.*[31] Every Muslim should be counted among the people of the Qur'ān, since he believes in it and is required to act by what it contains. He said—may blessings and peace be upon him, *The* Witr *is a truth, so he who does not perform the* Witr *is not one of us.*[32]

The maximum in *Witr* is eleven *rak'as*, while the minimum is one *rak'a*, but one should never confine oneself to one, rather the acceptable minimum is three. He who prays three *rak'as* should recite in the first, after the *Fātiḥa*, *Sabbiḥ'ismi rabbika'l-A'lā*, in the second, *Qul yā ayyuha'l-kāfirūn,* and in the third, *Qul Huwa'llāhu Aḥad.* He who prays more than three *rak'as* in his *Witr* may recite whatever he can of the Qur'ān before the last three *rak'as*. The longer the recitations the better. In the last three he should recite what we have just mentioned.

To perform one's *Witr* at the end of the night is better for he who is so accustomed to getting up that he rarely misses it. But he who

31. Abū Dāwūd, *Sunan*, (1207); Tirmidhī, *Sunan*, (415); Nasā'ī, *Sunan*, (1657).

32. Abū Dāwūd, *Sunan*, (1209); Aḥmad, *Musnad*, (21941).

is not so accustomed should perform his *Witr* before going to sleep, for this is better and more cautious. Once he has done so, should he awaken and wish to pray, let him pray to his heart's desire; his first *Witr* will suffice him.

It is a *Sunna* to persevere in praying the *Ḍuḥā* prayer. Its minimum is two *rak'as* and its maximum eight. According to some it is twelve. Its merit is great. The best time for it is when about a quarter of the day has elapsed. He said- may blessings and peace be upon him, *Morning comes and upon each of your joints a charity is due. Every* tasbīḥ *is a charity, every* taḥmīd *is a charity, every* tahlīl *is a charity, every* takbīr *is a charity, to enjoin good is a charity, to forbid evil is a charity, and two rak'as prayed during Ḍuḥā suffice for all this.*[33] And, *He who perseveres in the pair of* Ḍuḥā, *his sins are forgiven even if they are as* [profuse as] *the foam of the sea.*[34] The *pair* is two *rak'as*. In each human being there are three hundred and sixty joints, as the number of the days of the year. The *Ḍuḥā* prayer is called *Ṣalāt' al-Awwabīn*, which is the same appellation of the supererogatory prayer between *Maghrib* and *'Ishā'*. The *awwāb* is he who is ever turning back to God in times of distraction. These two times, that of *Ḍuḥā* and that between the two night prayers, are times of distraction, the first because people are engaged in earning their living, and the second because people are busy returning to their homes and eating their meals. Thus, he who returns to God and attends to His service in those times will have a [high] degree with Him.

It is recommended to pray *Ṣalāt' al-Tasbīḥ*, which consists of four *rak'as*. *Ḥadīths* have been handed down on its merits and that he who prays it all his sins, past and future, will be forgiven. The Prophet said to his uncle al-'Abbās—may God be pleased with him—as he taught it to him, *Pray it every day, every week, every month, every year, or even once in your lifetime.*[35] Some scholars have said—may God have mercy on them, "This prayer has been tried and found effective for obtaining important needs." And, "If it is prayed at night, it should be prayed with two *takbīrat' al-iḥrām*, two *tashahhuds*, and two *taslīms*. Two *rak'as* at a time. But if it is prayed by day time it will be four *rak'as* at one go, with one *takbīr* and one *tashahhud*. There are two manners of performing it: The

33. Muslim, *Ṣaḥīḥ*, (1181); Abū Dāwūd, *Sunan*, (1094).
34. Tirmidhī, *Sunan*, (438); Ibn Māja, *Sunan*, (1372).
35. Abū Dāwūd, *Sunan*, (1105); Ibn Māja, *Sunan*, (1376).

first is to say *takbirat' al-iḥrām*, recite the opening supplications, then say: *Subḥān'allāhi, wal-ḥamdu lil'llāhi, wa lā ilāha illa'llāhu, wa'l-llāhu akbar,* fifteen times. Then recite the *Fātiḥa* and a *sūra*; then repeat the invocations ten times, then bow down and repeat them ten times, then straighten up and repeat them ten times, then prostrate and repeat them ten times, then rise from prostration and repeat them ten times, then prostrate again and repeat them ten times, then rise up for the second *rak'a* and repeat them fifteen times before beginning recitation, and so on. The second manner is different from the first in that one does not recite the invocations before but after Qur'ān recitation, and this will be fifteen times, then one proceeds as mentioned above, except that they are repeated ten times after the second prostration, either before standing up, or after doing so but before reciting the *Fātiḥa*. So understand! Thus there will be seventy five invocations in each *rak'a*, to complete a total of three hundred in the four *rak'as*.

The scholars have also said, "The usual invocations recited during bowing down, rising up, prostrating, and sitting down, are still to be recited before the special invocations of *Ṣalāt' al-Tasbīḥ*. Also if the latter are forgotten during any of the phases of the prayer, they are recited in the next phase."

I say: no worshipper should neglect to perform this prayer every week, or at the very least every month. And God knows best.

It is firmly recommended to bring to life the period between the two night prayers, either with supererogatory prayers, which is best, or with recitations of the Qur'ān, or the remembrance of God- exalted is He—[in its various forms] such as *tasbīḥ*, *tahlīl,* and so on. The Prophet—may blessings and peace be upon him—said, *He who prays six* rak'a*s after* Maghrib*, without speaking evil in between, they will be equivalent for him to twelve years of worshipping.*[36] And, *He who prays twenty* rak'as *between* Maghrib *and* 'Ishā' *shall have a mansion built for him in the Gar*den.[37]

On the whole, this time is among the most noble and superior of times, so that it is most important to occupy it with devotions and avoid distractions and indolence.

36. Tirmidhī, *Sunan*, (399); Ibn Māja, *Sunan*, (1157, 1364).

37. Tirmidhī, *Sunan*, (399); Ibn Māja, *Sunan*, (1363).

It has been handed down that it is recommended not to sleep before *'Ishā'*,[38] so beware of this, for it is a Jewish custom. And also that he who sleeps before the *'Ishā'* prayer, may God forbid his eyes to sleep.

Persevere in praying four *rak'as* after *'Ishā'*. There is much merit in them, for he has said—may blessings and peace be upon him, *Four after* 'Ishā' *equal their like on* Laylat'ul-Qadr.[39] Each *rak'a* during *Laylat'ul-Qadr* equals thirty thousand on any other night. This can be calculated from His saying—Exalted is He, *The Night of Worth is better than a thousand months.* [97:3] So do reflect on this.

It is categorically discouraged to speak or chat after the *'Ishā'* prayer, unless what is said is appropriate and correct, such as studying or discussing religious knowledge, or any other such act of goodness.

As for night vigils, their merit is formidable, their reward profuse. So much has been said about them in the Book and *Sunna* that it would be too lengthy to enumerate their merits, nor would it be possible to exhaust them.

God- Exalted is He—said to His Messenger, *O enwrapped one! Keep vigil the night, save a little; half of it, or a little less, or a little more, and chant the Qur'ān distinctly.* [73:1 to 4] Then He said- Exalted is He, *Your Lord is well aware that you keep vigil nearly two thirds of the night, or half of it, or a third of it, and a group of those with you.* [73:20] And He said- Exalted is He, *Rise in prayer at night, a supererogation for you, that your Lord may resurrect you to a praiseworthy station.*[17: 79] And He said- Exalted is He—to describe the believers, *Their sides shun their beds, they call upon their Lord in fear and in hope, and of what We give them they spend.* [32: 16] And He said- Exalted is He, *They used to sleep but little of the night, then pray at dawn for God's forgiveness.* [51:17, 18]

The Prophet—may blessings and peace be upon him—said, *The best ritual prayers after the obligatory ones are those that are prayed at night.*[40] And, *Pray at night, for it was the custom of the virtuous before you. Night vigils are a devotion to your Lord, a re-*

38. Bukhārī, *Ṣaḥīḥ*, (535); Tirmidhī, *Sunan*, (153); Ibn Māja, *Sunan*, (694).

39. Ṭabarānī, *Awsaṭ*, (2840).

40. Muslim, *Ṣaḥīḥ*, (1982); Tirmidhī, *Sunan*, (402); Nasā'ī, *Sunan*, (1595).

pellent from evil deeds, a requital of sins, and a protection for the body from illness.[41] And, *O people! Always greet each other with* salām, *feed the people, preserve your kinship bonds, pray at night when people are asleep, and you shall enter the Garden in peace.*[42] And, *Pray at night, even for as little as milking an ewe.* And Gabriel once said to the Prophet that the honor of a believer is to keep vigil at night and his pride is to stand in no need of another human being.[43] And the Prophet said, may blessings and peace be upon him, *He who keeps vigil with ten verses shall not be written among the heedless. He who keeps vigil with a hundred verses shall be written among the humble. He who keeps vigil with a thousand verses shall be written among those possessing many* quintārs.[44] Another *ḥadīth* states that a *quintār* equals twelve thousand ounces, each ounce worth more than everything between heaven and earth.[45] Scholars have pointed out that from the beginning of [*sūra*] *Tabārak al-Mulk* till the end of the Qur'ān the verses number one thousand.

An authentic *ḥadīth* states that, *There is in the night an hour when no Muslim servant asks God for anything good, whether of this world or the next, without being granted it, and this occurs every night.*[46] Were this the sole *ḥadīth* on the merits of nighttime and of keeping vigil, it would have sufficed. But he has also said- may blessings and peace be upon him, *Our Lord descends to the Terrestrial Heaven when only the last third of the night remains and says, 'Is there anyone praying for something, that I may respond to him? Is there anyone making a request, that I may grant it to him? Is there anyone asking for forgiveness, that I may forgive him*?'"[47] Reflect on this *ḥadīth*- may God have mercy on you—and the one before it. Read them repeatedly, that your breast may expand to accept night vigils and that your resolution may increase. May your desire for them become sincere, and may laziness and heedlessness abandon

---

41. Tirmidhī, *Sunan*, (3472); Bayhaqī, *Shu'ab al-Īmān*, (2950, 2951).
42. Ibn Māja, *Sunan*, (3242); Aḥmad, *Musnad*, (22668); Al-Ḥākim, *Mustadrak,* (4250, 7386), Bayhaqī, *Shu'ab al-Īmān*, (3211, 8490).
43. Al-Ḥākim, *Mustadrak,* (8038), Bayhaqī, *Shu'ab al-Īmān*, (10145); Ṭabarānī, *Awsaṭ*, (4429).
44. Abū Dāwūd, *Sunan*, (1190); Bayhaqī, *Shu'ab al-Īmān*, (2124), Ibn Ḥibbān, *Ṣaḥīḥ*, (2624).
45. Ibn Māja, *Sunan*, (3650); Aḥmad, *Musnad*, (8403).
46. Muslim, *Ṣaḥīḥ*, (1259); Aḥmad, *Musnad*, (13835, 14017).
47. Bukhārī, *Ṣaḥīḥ*, (1077, 5846); Muslim, *Ṣaḥīḥ*,(1261, 1265).

you, and also too much sleep, which thing reduces the *baraka* in a lifetime and wastes time. It has been said that he who sleeps too much arrives a poor man on Judgment Day. It has also been said that two *rak'as* in the deep of the night constitute a treasure of goodness. And he has said- may blessings and peace be upon him, *The nearest the Lord comes to His servant is in the deep of the night. If you are able to pray at such times, then do so.*[48] And, *People will be gathered on even ground, then as herald will call, 'Where are those whose sides shunned their beds?' They will stand up at that and a few they will be. They will enter the Garden without judgment.*[49]

Know that night vigils are among the most difficult things for the soul, especially for one to rise after having slept a little. However, they become lighter to bear when one becomes accustomed to them and performs them regularly, when one has patience in enduring hardship and strives hard at the beginning. Then the door is opened to intimate comfort with God—Exalted is He, the sweetness of communing with Him, and the pleasure of being alone with Him—August and Majestic is He. At this point one not only no longer finds night vigils too difficult, nor is inclined to surrender to indolence, but on the contrary remains ever eager for more. This happens to the virtuous among God's servants. So much so that one of them said, "If the people of the Garden are in a state similar to ours during the night, they are living pleasantly indeed." Another said, "The people of the night in their nights have more pleasure than the people of frivolity in their play." Yet another said, "Were it not for night vigils and the company of brothers in God, I would not have wished to remain in this world." There are innumerable well known anecdotes to this effect. Many of them used to pray the dawn prayer having maintained their ritual purity since *'Ishā'*. May God be pleased with them. *Those are they whom God has guided, so emulate their guidance.* [6:90]

Therefore you must keep night vigils—may God have mercy on you—persevere in them, and repeat them often. Be one of *the servants of the All-Merciful who walk gently on the earth and when addressed by the ignorant say: Peace; who spend their night prostrate and standing before their Lord.* [25: 63, 64] Acquire the rest

48. Muslim, *Ṣaḥīḥ*, (744); Abū Dāwūd, *Sunan*, (741); Tirmidhī, *Sunan*, (3503).

49. Bayhaqī, *Shu'ab al-Īmān*, (3097).

of their attributes, those described by God in the verses following the above.

Should you find yourself unable to keep frequent night vigils, keep a few. He says—Exalted is He, *Recite what you can of the Qur'ān*. [73:20] The reference here being to recitation during night prayers. And he has said—may blessings and peace be upon him, *Pray at night, even if as little as one* rak'a.[50]

How beautiful and excellent would it be for he who knows the Qur'ān by heart to recite some of it every night in his prayers, so that he may recite it from beginning to end, completing its recitation during his night vigils. This he can accomplish in a month, forty days, or less, or more, according to how much energy and resolution he has.

Know that a little that is constant is better than more that is interrupted. He said—may blessings and peace be upon him, *The works that God likes best are those that are constant, even if few*.[51] So let those who would recite the Qur'ān in the manner just mentioned make a set amount of recitation their regular *wird* and persevere in it, requiting it at a later time whenever any of it is missed. In this manner will the soul become accustomed to it and trained to persevere. It should be missed only for a valid excuse. A *ḥadīth* states that he who is overcome by sleep and misses his regular *wird* of the Qur'ān or part thereof, then recites it between the Morning and Midday prayers, it will be recorded for him as if he had recited it by night. The Prophet—may God's blessings and peace be upon him—when prevented from keeping night vigil for any reason, whether this be sickness or any other excuse, prayed during the day what he had missed at night.

Now know that it is extremely reprehensible, sinful to the utmost, and the worst among forbidden things, for Muslims to neglect some of their obligatory prayers. Many authentic *ḥadīths* have been handed down to the effect that he who abandons ritual prayer is a disbeliever. He has said—may blessings and peace be upon him, *The pact that is between us and them is the ritual prayer; he who abandons it has disbelieved*.[52] And, *He who abandons the ritual*

50. Ṭabarānī, *Awsaṭ*, (7013).

51. Bukhārī, *Ṣaḥīḥ*, (5983, 5984); Muslim, *Ṣaḥīḥ*,(1303, 1305).

52. Tirmidhī, *Sunan*, (2545); Nasā'ī, *Sunan*, (459); Ibn Māja, *Sunan*, (1069).

prayer on purpose has disbelieved openly.[53] And, *He who abandons the ritual prayer on purpose, God and His Messenger will disown him.*[54] And, *He who preserves his ritual prayer, it will be for him a light, a proof, and a salvation on Resurrection Day. But he who does not preserve it, it will be for him neither a light, nor a proof, nor a salvation, and on Resurrection Day he will be in the company of Pharaoh, Korah (Qārūn), Hāmān, and Ubayy ibn Khalaf.*[55]

The Prophet—may God's blessings and peace be upon him—has explicitly declared he who abandons the prayer a disbeliever. So have many Companions and virtuous predecessors. One of the latter said, "I have heard the Companions of the Messenger of God—may God's blessings and peace be upon him—declare the abandonment of no works tantamount to disbelief except the ritual prayer." So beware! Beware of abandoning the prayer, wholly or partly. If you do this you are sure to perish along with those who are to perish, and you will have lost both this world and the next, and that would be the most evident loss.

Just as it is incumbent upon you to preserve your prayer and forbidden upon you to neglect it, so you should firmly enjoin upon your spouse, children, and everyone else you are responsible for, to perform it. You should allow them no room for abandoning it. You should threaten and punish those of them who do not comply. You should show them more anger than you would show had your property been damaged. Failing to act thus would only mean that you are one who belittles the rights of God the Exalted and His religion. Those whom you show anger to and punish but who nevertheless remain heedless and disobedient you must move them away from you and keep them thus, for such people are devils devoid of goodness and *baraka*. You are forbidden to befriend them or keep their company, and commanded to oppose and boycott them. They are those who oppose God and His Messenger. He says—Exalted is He, *You will not find any people who believe in God and the Last Day showing affection to those who oppose God and His Messenger, even though they may be their fathers, or their sons, or their brothers, or their clansmen. Those are they in whose hearts He has inscribed faith and has confirmed with a spirit from Him. He shall admit them*

53. Ṭabarānī, *Awsaṭ*, (3479); Bayhaqī, *Shu'ab al-Īmān*, (296).

54. Aḥmad, *Musnad*, (26098); Ṭabarānī, *Kabīr*, (12848).

55. Aḥmad, *Musnad*, (6288); Bayhaqī, *Shu'ab al-Īmān*, (2697); Dārimī, *Sunan*, (2777); Ibn Ḥibbān, *Ṣaḥīḥ*, (1489).

into gardens beneath which rivers flow, perpetually to dwell therein. God is well pleased with them and they are well pleased with Him. Those are God's party. Indeed God's party, they are the successful. [58: 22] Here He denies faith to those who show affection to those who oppose Him and His Messenger, even though they may be their nearest kin.

The utmost that can be allowed the common Muslim, distracted as he is and immersed [in worldly pursuits] is that when he misses a prayer, he should requite it at the earliest time, repent for having missed it, and resolve never to do so again. As for abandoning it altogether, never! Just to delay it from its appointed time is a great sin, even were it to be requited later on. Being too occupied with worldly affairs is no excuse, only sleep and forgetting are excuses.

Rulers should ensure that the common Muslims perform their obligatory prayers. Those who abandon it due to indolence should be asked to repent. If they refuse, they should be executed. It is greatly sinful and reprehensible for those in charge to be aware of this yet do nothing about it. There is no excuse for them to leave this or other similarly important matters of religion.

Praise belongs to God, Lord of the worlds.

Chapter Four: On *Zakāt*

Know O brothers—may God make us and you of those who purify themselves, mention the Name of their Lord, and pray, and do not prefer the life of this world over the next, for the next is better and more enduring- that *zakāt* is one of the five pillars of Islam and that God has bound it to the ritual prayer in His august Book. He says, *Establish the ritual prayer and give out the* zakāt. *Whatever good you send ahead for yourselves, you shall find with God. Truly God sees what you do.* [2:110] And He says, describing His faithful servants, *Those who establish the ritual prayer and expend of what We have given them, those are the believers in truth.* [8:3,4] And He says—Exalted is He, *And the believers, men and women, are allies to each other. They enjoin good, forbid evil, establish the ritual prayer, pay the* zakāt, *and obey God and His Messenger. To those shall God show compassion. God is August, Wise.* [9:71] There are many more such verses.

The Messenger of God—may God's blessings and peace be upon him—said, *He who believes in God and His Messenger, let him pay the* zakāt *due on his possessions.*[1] These words imply that he who does not is not a believer.

Know that he who prays, fasts, goes on pilgrimage, but does not pay the *zakāt* due on his possessions; God shall accept from him neither his prayers, nor his fasts, nor his pilgrimage, until he does. This is because these are all connected together. God does not accept part of them unless the rest is performed, as the Messenger of God—may God's blessings and peace be upon him—is reported to have stated.

And know that *zakāt* is obligatory on certain specified things, which are a *niṣāb* (minimum amount required for the tax to be due) in gold or silver, mercantile goods, grains and fruits, and certain domestic animals. It becomes due at a specified time, which is once a year for monies, mercantile goods, and animals, and at the time they are reaped for crops and fruits. The obligatory amount is specified at a quarter of a tenth (2.5%) for monies and commerce, a tenth for grains and fruits that are watered without appliances, and half the tenth for those watered with the help of appliances. As for animals, these are specified to be camels, cattle, sheep, and goats. There are

1. Ṭabarānī, *Kabīr*, (13385).

many details of relevance here and the place to look for them is in the books of *fiqh*. He who owns any of the above mentioned things is obliged to acquire sufficient knowledge to be able to pay out his *zakāt*. He must know the *niṣāb*, the amount to be given away, the deserving recipients, and so on.

He who pays his *zakāt* receives a great reward, a generous recompense. By so doing he will enjoy many benefits, both religious and worldly. There are in wealth afflictions, temptations, and problems. He who pays his *zakāt* will be safe from these, God willing. The Prophet—may God's blessings and peace be upon him—said, *When graciously you pay the* zakāt *due on your possessions, you shall have diverted away from you the evil in them.*[2] The possessions of he who pays his *zakāt* remains safe from damage or ruin, for he has said—may God's blessings and peace be upon him, *No wealth perishes at sea or on land except because of withholding the* zakāt; *so protect your possessions with* zakāt *and remedy your sick with charity…*[3]

Possessions for which *zakāt* has been paid is protected, guarded by God, for it is good and full of *baraka*, but possessions for which *zakāt* has not been paid will suffer damage, for it is evil and devoid of *baraka*. He has said—may God's blessings and peace be upon him, Zakāt *never mixes with wealth without destroying it.*[4]

What good, what benefit can there be in wealth the *baraka* of which has been removed, leaving the evil and temptations?

The destruction in question may be visible or invisible. The first kind is for the wealth to depart, leaving the wealthy poor, panicky, fearful, and full of resentment against God's decree. This has indeed happened to numerous people who had been neglectful as concerns their *zakāt*. As for the second or invisible kind, it is for the wealth to be there in abundance, but without its owner being able to enjoy any of its benefits, either in a religious way, by spending of it in charitable ways and doing good, or to his own profit, to preserve his honor and reputation. On the contrary, it may bring him great harm when he withholds it when it should be spent, or spends it where it should not be, on sins for instance—may God protect us- or on bestial appetites that are wasteful and of no benefit.

2. Ibn Khuzayma, *Ṣaḥīḥ*, (2071, 2273); Al-Ḥākim, *Mustadrak*, (1390).
3. Ṭabarānī, *Musnad al-Shāmiyyīn*, (16) *Al-Du'ā'*, (30).
4. Bayhaqī, *Shu'ab al-Īmān*, (3367); Al-Shihāb al-Quḍā'ī, *Musnad al-Shihāb*, (729).

To withhold *zakāt* is one of the greatest of major sins. Against such behavior great threats and severe warnings have been proffered by God and His Messenger. It is to be feared for the withholder of *zakāt* that he will suffer an evil end and leave this world other than as a Muslim. He may also be punished before his death, as has happened to Korah (Qārūn) the Israelite when he withheld *zakāt*. God—Exalted is He—says, *We made the earth to swallow him and his house*. [28:81]

It has been transmitted that every wealth the *zakāt* of which had been withheld shall take the form of a great serpent on the Day of Resurrection and shall be wrapped around the culprit's neck. God—Exalted is He—says, *They shall have that which they had avariciously withheld wrapped around their necks on the Day of Arising*. [3:180] The Prophet—may God's blessings and peace be upon him—said, *Each possessor of gold or silver who does not pay out its due shall have them on Judgment Day made into leaves, which shall be heated in the fire of Hell, then his forehead, flank, and back shall be burned with them. Whenever the leaves grow cold, it shall all be repeated, on a day the length of which is fifty thousand years…*[5] It is also stated in *ḥadīth* that he who owns cattle but does not pay the *zakāt* due on it, they will come on Resurrection Day, more numerous than they had ever been, to trample him underneath their hooves, bite him with their teeth, and stab him with their horns.

It is part of the good manners of paying *zakāt* to do it willingly, with pleasure, feeling good about it, grateful to those who deserve to receive it, never acting as if they were indebted to you. To give away one's *zakāt* while seeming to reproach the recipient for taking it annuls its reward. As He says—Exalted is He, *O believers! Render not your charity null by reproach and injury.* [2:264]

He who pays *zakāt* should never be averse to doing so. Let him beware of this, for it is the attribute of hypocrites. God—Exalted is He—says, *They never come to the ritual prayer but indolently and they never spend* [in charity] *but reluctantly*. [9:54]. In this verse *spending* means *zakāt*. He indicates—Transcendent is He—that the hypocrite may indeed pray, but only lazily, and may pay his *zakāt*, but reluctantly. He whose behavior resembles that of certain people is one of them.

It is part of the good manners of paying *zakāt* to do so from the best of one's possessions. This is the most praiseworthy manner of

5. Muslim, *Ṣaḥīḥ*, (1647).

doing it. The obligatory manner is to make what is to be given away of average quality as compared with one's possessions. To make it of the lowest quality is forbidden, unless all possessions are of the same quality. God—Exalted is He—says, *Seek not the worst amongst it to spend.* [2:267]

It is a duty upon he who pays *zakāt* not to give it away according to his whims, but according to the dictates of the Book and *Sunna*. To distribute it according to one's whims means to give all or part of it to those who, although deserving, are engaged in rendering one worldly services in one way or another. Should a person give another because he serves, visits, or shows respect to him, he would be acting improperly and his *zakāt* may even be rejected [by God] even though he who receives it is deserving. There is no harm if the deserving person is given the *zakāt* strictly for being deserving, without any real concern for whether he is known to the giver, likely to be of any use to him, or even happens to render some service. We are drawing attention to this because some wealthy people are unconcerned with proper conduct in this matter and incapable of behaving with discernment.

Problems arise when a wealthy man gives a poor one some of his *zakāt*, but makes it seem like an ordinary donation, a gift, or something similar. The same applies should he give it to some of his needy relatives, such as parents or children, whose expenses already are his obligatory responsibility. As for giving it to relatives for whom he is not legally responsible, it is not only permissible, but preferable, because they are his kin and may be harboring expectations to receive something from him.

As for *Zakāt'al-fiṭr*, it is due every Ramaḍān and is obligatory upon every Muslim who is able to afford it, whether he is an adult or a child, a free man or a slave. He who is responsible for others is obliged to pay their *Zakāt'al-fiṭr*, which is four measures (*mudd*) of the Prophet 's measures—may God's blessings and peace be upon him—of dates, wheat, corn, barley, or any other kind constituting the staple diet used by the people. It is better for a person to give of the same kind of food that he himself consumes or of one of better quality.

Zakāt'al-fiṭr is subject to strict injunctions that ordinary Muslims are frequently unaware of, so that they end up not paying it, in the mistaken assumption that they belong to the category of those unable to. Scholars—may God have mercy on them—have stated that if needs be one should sell of his possessions everything that exceeds the provisions required for the eve and day of ʿĪd and the necessary as regards clothes, shelter, and so on, to be able to pay one's *zakāt*. There can be no stricter instructions than those. This is what *Sharīʿa* requires, so let every Muslim beware of not paying out his *zakāt* when able to.

Know that when a just ruler demands that *zakāt* be paid to him, then this becomes a duty. By obeying one would have fulfilled one's obligation. It then becomes the ruler's responsibility to distribute it.

If the ruler is unjust and demands that *zakāt* be paid to him, then one should comply to avoid sedition and strife. Should the ruler then distribute it to those designated by God as deserving, who are those he can locate that belong to the eight kinds, then God shall reward him with an immense reward, as He will reward those who paid him their *zakāt*. But if he distributes it to other than those designated in His saying—Exalted is He, *Charity is only for the poor and the needy, for those who collect it, for those whose hearts need to be reconciled, for the ransom of slaves, for debtors, for the way of God, and for the travelers. This is an obligation ordained by God, and God is Knowing, Wise.* [9:60] he would be committing a grave sin and a monstrous injustice. He would be wronging the wealthy by placing their *zakāt* where it does not belong, and the poor by not giving them that which God has decreed is their rightful share of the possessions of the wealthy. God made *zakāt* obligatory that it might be a purification for the wealthy and a help for the poor. He who uses it in other than that commits a great falsehood and sin.

When the unjust ruler gives the *zakāt* to the undeserving, it is better and more cautious for those who have paid it and find in themselves the willingness to do so to pay it again directly to deserving people. But this is by no means obligatory.

If those who must pay the *zakāt* are able to withhold it in whole or in part from the unjust ruler, they are permitted to do so, on condition that no sedition ensues and no act of disobedience to God, such as manifest lying, a false oath, or anything similar. Also, they should make it their intention to save the ruler from the sin of misplacing the *zakāt*, as well as to assist the poor in upholding their religious duties by giving them that which God has made rightfully theirs. Success comes from God.

As for charity of freewill, spending in ways of goodness and benevolence, intending the good-pleasure of God and wishing for His reward, so numerous are the verses and *ḥadīth*s detailing the merits of this that they would be too lengthy to exhaust. God—Exalted is He—says, *Whatever good you expend it is for yourselves, for you expend only for the sake of God. Whatever good you expend, it shall be repaid to you in full and you will not be wronged.* [2:272] *Those who expend of their wealth night and day, secretly and in public, their wage is with their Lord. No fear shall be on them and they shall not grieve.* [2:274] *Believe in God and His Messenger and expend of what He has entrusted you with. For those of you who have believed and expended there shall be a great wage.* [57:7] *Who is he who will lend God a good loan, and He will multiply it for him, and his shall be a generous wage.* [57:11] Imagine in your mind this wage that God calls great and generous, what a wage shall this be! Also, multiplication was not restricted by God to a specific number of times, for He says, *He shall multiply it for him.* [57:11] And in another verse, *many times over.* [2:245] He says *many times* and does not specify their number. What encouragement can exceed this, coming from the Liberal, the Generous? How unfortunate is he who is incapable of grasping God's intention or understanding His verses, so much so that avarice overcomes him and he withholds in a miserly fashion what God has favored him with. This may even reach the point where he withholds not only charity of freewill, but obligatory expenditure. Had such a person been poor, it would have been better and more gracious for him.

The Prophet—may God's blessings and peace be upon him—said of the merits of charitable expenditure, *God—Exalted is He—says, 'O Son of Adam! Expend and I shall expend upon you.'*[6] And he said—may God's blessings and peace be upon him, *Morning never comes upon the people without two angels coming down, one of whom says, 'O God! Compensate him who expends.' while the other says, 'O God! Cause damage to him who withholds.'*[7] I say, the prayers of angels are always accepted [by God].

But when the wealth of him who withholds is not seen to suffer, it is nevertheless damaged in reality, for he will benefit little from it, either in the hereafter or in this world. This is even worse than visible damage.

He has said—may God's blessings and peace be upon him, *He who gives in charity something he has earned in a goodly manner—*

6. Muslim, *Ṣaḥīḥ*, (1658); Aḥmad, *Musnad,* (6997).
7. Bukhārī, *Ṣaḥīḥ*, (1351); Muslim, *Ṣaḥīḥ*, (1678).

and God accepts only that which is good—the All-Merciful shall take it in His palm and increase it for him, just as one of you looks after his foal, till it becomes like a mountain.[8] The same was said for a piece of *ḥalāl* bread, [*ḥalāl* being] the only kind that God accepts. And he said—may God's blessings and peace be upon him, *O Son of Adam! To give away the superfluous is better for you, while to withhold it is worse for you. You shall not incur any blame if all you possess is the strict necessary. Start with those for whom you are the provider. The upper hand is better than the lower hand.*[9] I say: By "*superfluous*" the Prophet means that portion of your wealth which is in excess of the strict necessary. By "*necessary*" he means the minimum needed. By "*those for whom you are the provider*" he means those whose expenses are your responsibility and whom you are permitted neither to neglect, nor fail to provide them with their expenses, leaving them in need, while at the same time giving to others. By "*upper hand*" he means the hand that gives. He states that it is better than the hand that accepts to encourage people to guard their independence, avoid as much as possible having to ask or need others. However, if really in need, he who accepts receives as much reward as he who gives. He said—may God's blessings and peace be upon him, *He who accepts due to necessity receives no less a reward than he who gives out of affluence.*[10] And he said, *Protect yourselves against the Fire, with even as little as half a date. If you possess not even that, then with a good word.*[11] And, *Charity extinguishes sin, just as water extinguishes fire.*[12] It has been said that people shall be gathered on Resurrection Day more naked, hungrier, thirstier, and wearier than they had ever been. He who had clothed others for the sake of God, God shall clothe him. He who had fed others for the sake of God, God shall feed him. He who had given to drink to others for the sake of God, God shall give him to drink.[13] "For the sake of God" means that it was done truly for this, with no trace of ostentation, pretence, or desire for praise from others. He

8. Imām Mālik, *Muwaṭṭa'*, (1581); Aḥmad, *Musnad,* (9055); Nasā'ī, *Al-Sunan al-Kubrā*, (7759, 11227); Ṭabarānī, *Kabīr*, (132, 640).

9. Muslim, *Ṣaḥīḥ*, (1718); Tirmidhī, *Sunan,* (2265).

10. Ṭabarānī, *Kabīr*, (13384); *Awsaṭ*, (8471).

11. Bukhārī, *Ṣaḥīḥ*, (1324, 5564, 6058); Muslim, *Ṣaḥīḥ*, (1688, 1689, 1690).

12. Tirmidhī, *Sunan,* (558, 2541); Ibn Maja, *Sunan*, (4200).

13. Aḥmad ibn Ḥanbal, *Kitāb al-Zuhd*, (1101).

said—may God's blessings and peace be upon him, *He who feeds his brother bread until he is satiated and gives him water to drink until his thirst is quenched, God removes him away from the Fire the width of seven trenches; the distance between each of these two trenches being five hundred years.*[14]

Many other *ḥadīth*s exist as to the merits of feeding people and giving them water to drink, so strive to do this with diligence and do not go feebly about it. And know that what is little becomes much with God. Every act of goodness is a charity. Never disdain any act of goodness to the extent of failing to do it. He said—may God's blessings and peace be upon him, *Disdain not any act of goodness, even as simple as to meet your brother amiably.*[15] Give a charity every day, however small and start early in the day with your charity, for hardship does not bypass charity.[16] The meaning here is that the charity you give becomes a barrier that prevents the hardships that threaten you from reaching you.

Should a beggar come to you, never send him away disappointed, but give him something however small. Should you choose not to or are unable to, beware of rebuking or insulting him, but send him away gently and amiably. It is possible for a person to rebuke a beggar in such a manner that were he to give him half his wealth, it would still outweigh it; neither will the reward for giving it ever equal the sin of that rebuke.

Never refuse the first person who comes soliciting from you; beware of this!

When you give charity, begin with your poor relatives and kinsmen, and your needy neighbors, for they are more deserving than others, and the reward for giving them is greater and more abundant. The Prophet—may God's blessings and peace be upon him—said, *Charity to the indigent is charity, but charity to kin is both charity and nurturing of* [kinship] *bonds.*[17] And, *He who bypasses with*

---

14. Al-Ḥākim, *Mustadrak*, (7276); Bayhaqī, *Shu'ab al-Īmān*, (3218).

15. Muslim, *Ṣaḥīḥ*, (4760); Aḥmad, *Musnad,* (19717); Bayhaqī, *Shu'ab al-Īmān*, (3225, 3306).

16. He said—may God's blessings and peace be upon him, *Start early in the day with your charity, for hardship does not bypass charity*. Bayhaqī, *Shu'ab al-Īmān*, (3204, 3306); Ṭabarānī, *Awsaṭ*, (5801).

17. Tirmidhī, *Sunan*, (594); Nasā'ī, *Sunan*, (2535); Ibn Māja, *Sunan*, (1834).

his charity is as he who has withheld it.[18] Bypassing means giving strangers and far away people, while aware that relatives and neighbors are more in need.

Make your charity secret, for it is stated in *ḥadīth* that its reward is seventy times that of publicly donated charity. He said—may God's blessings and peace be upon him, *Secret charity extinguishes the Lord's wrath.*[19] What can be more threatening than His wrath—Transcendent and Exalted is He? Secret charity extinguishes it only because it is so great in His sight—Transcendent and Exalted is He. He says—Exalted is He, *If you show your charities, they are still excellent, but if you hide them and give them to the poor, it shall be better for you and it shall requite your sins for you. And God is aware of what you do.* [2:271]

Secret charity is better because it is more likely to be sincere, and sincerity is the spirit of works. It is less likely to be subject to ostentation which ruins works. So beware of ostentation in your charity and in all your other works. Beware of showing the poor how obliged you expect them to be, for there are severe threats against such behavior.

Never request those to whom you give to do something for you, or serve, or respect you, for if you do, this will be all the reward that you will receive. Our virtuous ancestors used to reward the poor who prayed for them, having received their charity, by giving them an equal amount of prayers, to avoid their own rewards being diminished. This is being thoroughly cautious.

Never request the poor to thank or praise you, nor to mention to others what you have given, for this will either diminish or altogether cancel your reward.

Never refrain from giving charity for fear of poverty or diminution in your wealth, for the Prophet has said—may God's blessings and peace be upon him, *No money has ever diminished because of charity.*[20] On the contrary, charity is that which attracts wealth and affluence, and protects from poverty and need. Refraining from charity brings about the opposite, it attracts poverty and drives away

18. Abū Dāwūd, *Sunan*, (1352).
19. Al-Ḥākim, *Mustadrak*, (6491); Ṭabarānī, *Kabīr,* (7939, 16362); *Awsaṭ*, (956, 3584).
20. Tirmidhī, *Sunan*, (2247); Aḥmad, *Musnad,* (17339); Ṭabarānī, *Awsaṭ*, (2361); *Ṣaghīr* (142).

affluence. God—Exalted is He—says, *Whatever you expend, He will compensate for it; and he is the best of providers.* [34:39]

Know that for the poor to give a small amount is better in the sight of God from the wealthy giving much. He has said—may God's blessing and peace be upon him, *One* Dirham *has outstripped a hundred thousand* Dirhams. They asked him, "How so?" He replied, A *man who possessed only two* Dirhams *gave one away, and another took a hundred thousand* Dirhams *from his wealth and gave them away. This one* Dirham *has outstripped a hundred thousand.*[21] This is how one *Dirham* from the poor becomes better than a hundred thousand from the affluent.

It is blameworthy and forbidden to reproach or shame the poor for their poverty, or despise them, for poverty is the garment of Prophets and the attribute of the elect. The same applies to acting toward them with arrogance, belittling them, making light of their rights, or giving precedence to the rich over them for worldly reasons. All these are forbidden crimes, so beware of them.

Be they rich or poor, people should be shown esteem according to their esteem for God and His Messenger, their upholding His religion, and their knowledge of His rights. Should they happen to be equal as concerns religious matters, the poor should be treated better because they are poor, broken hearted, and likely to be ignored by most people, for the latter are heedless and tend to esteem the rich as a result of their esteem for the worldly things in their possession.

You must give charity and expend of those things that you love best in order to attain goodness. God—Exalted is He—says, *You shall never attain goodness till you expend of what you love.* [3:92] Commentators have said that the goodness referred to here is no other than the Garden.

You must prefer others to yourself, which means that when you possess something which you need, you must nevertheless give it to a needy brother believer. You shall thus be one of the successful, who are those who will ultimately triumph. God—Exalted is He—says, *They prefer others to themselves even though they are in need. Those who are protected from the avarice in themselves, they are the successful.* [59:9]

Rejoice when someone solicits at your door, for he is God the Exalted's gift to you. He has a right due to him, even were he to

21. Nasā'ī, *Sunan*, (2480, 2481); Ibn Ḥibbān, *Ṣaḥīḥ*, (3416); Ibn Khuzayma, *Ṣaḥīḥ*, (2247); Al-Ḥākim, *Mustadrak*, (1466).

come on horseback, as has been transmitted. The least you can do is send him away in a gracious manner.

Give the beggar with your own hand, if not every time then sometimes, for the Prophet—may God's blessings and peace be upon him—used to give them with his own noble hand. This is because God receives the donation with His Holy Hand from the hand of the giver. The *ḥadīth* states that it falls into God's Hand before reaching the recipient's. As He says—Exalted is He, *Do they not know that God is He who accepts repentance from His servants and takes the donations; and that God it is who is the Relenter, the Compassionate*. [9:104]

As for the poor, they should endure their poverty with patience, be satisfied with what God has chosen to allot them and contented with His decree to make them poor. They must beware of being anxious, panicky, or resentful. The Prophet—may God's blessings and peace be upon him—is said to have addressed the poor saying, *O poor people! Offer God contentment from your hearts and you will receive the reward for your poverty*. Otherwise you will not. He also said that poor people who are patient shall be God's companions on Resurrection Day. And he said, *Poverty is not far from being disbelief.*[22] This is when the poor person is angry with God's decree and discontented with what He has given him. He may even fall into the calamity of objecting to God the Exalted's decision to prefer some of His servants over others in provision. When a poor person is devoid of patience as well as of knowledge of God, he may be in danger of falling into this.

The poor person should be thankful to God and to those servants of God who help him. The Prophet—may God's blessings and peace be upon him—has said, *He has not thanked God who has not thanked people*.[23] Thus should the poor person praise benevolent people and pray for them. He has said—may God's blessings and peace be upon him, *He who says to him who has rendered him a service, 'May God reward you well', he has thanked him abundantly*.[24]

The poor person should neither disparage nor defame he who gives him nothing, for this would be blameworthy to the extreme. In

22. Bayhaqī, *Shu'ab al-Īmān*, (6336).

23. Abū Dāwūd, *Sunan*, (4177); Tirmidhī, *Sunan*, (1877, 1878); Aḥmad, *Musnad,* (7191, 7598,7676, 8673, 9565).

24. Tirmidhī, *Sunan*, (1958); Bayhaqī, *Shu'ab al-Īmān*, (8838).

reality, none gives nor withholds but God the Exalted. Creatures are subjected to His will, He does with them as He pleases.

Let the poor person beware of being constantly watching other people, desiring their help, and coveting what they possess, for greed is in itself instant poverty. He who places his hopes in other than God, or attaches his heart to other than Him, he is a loser and a failure. So let him behave with decency and find his sufficiency in God. The Prophet—may God's blessings and peace be upon him—said, *He who is too decent to ask, God will suffice him; and he who does without, God renders him independent of others.*[25] He promises him sufficiency and freedom from need, should he behave with reserve and restraint. The promise of God and His Prophet is certain to be fulfilled.

Let the poor person beware of lying, saying, "So and so has given me," to deceive someone else to induce him to give him; or on the contrary say, "He has given me nothing," when in fact he has given him, for fear that the second should not give him. Let him beware of hiding whatever God has favored him with and constantly complaining to people, exhibiting his neediness for all to see. Some poor persons may do this, imagining that those who hear them will be induced to give them. Should what they say be also lies, they would have committed the sin of lying as well as that of acquiring things by deceit. Many poor persons may be afflicted with such things because of their ignorance and greed for what other people possess.

Soliciting is exceedingly reprehensible except in dire need. It is a villainous act, as has been transmitted, and it is the only villainy [deemed] permissible [by *Sharīʿa*]. The Messenger of God—may God's blessings and peace be upon him—said, *One of you would keep begging until he meets God with not one piece of flesh left on his face.*[26] And, *Soliciting is not licit for he who is not in need, nor he who is strong and healthy.*[27] He who is in no need is he who does possess some money or has a relative willing to help him, and is thus not obliged to solicit. He who is strong and able to work and earn, but instead begs, commits a sin and his begging is forbidden by *Sharīʿa*. As for he who gives him, he never sins, but on the contrary is rewarded for his donation. No donation is ever sinful, unless it

25. Bukhārī, *Ṣaḥīḥ*, (5989); Bayhaqī, *Shuʿab al-Īmān*, (9376, 9377).
26. Bukhārī, *Ṣaḥīḥ*, (1381); Muslim, *Ṣaḥīḥ*, (1724, 1725).
27. Tirmidhī, *Sunan*, (590).

is given to one whom you know will use it in sinning against God. Know this!

Beware—may God have mercy on you—and warn your brother Muslims to beware not to solicit from people when not in need. The Prophet—may God's blessings and peace be upon him—said, *Were you to know what soliciting really means, no man would ever go to another to ask him for something.*[28] And, *For a person not in need, soliciting is a fire, small if small, great if great.*[29] I say: "*Not in need*" does not mean one who has much money, but one who is able to earn, or has a little to suffice his immediate needs.

If ever you are forced to solicit, avoid being importune or insistent, let your heart concentrate on God, asking of Him. Once you are given what is sufficient for the immediate situation, refrain from further requests, thank he who has given you, and excuse he who has not, for nothing in the latter's possession had been allotted to you. Had that been the case, he would not have been able to withhold it from you. Do not solicit from someone standing in the midst of other people, with the intention of embarrassing him before them so that he would give you. Imām al-Ghazālī—may God have mercy on him—when speaking of a man being solicited in public and giving a donation out of embarrassment which he would not have given in private, says that for the recipient, "that which is taken in this manner, through embarrassment, although licit in outward appearance, is in reality illicit for the taker."

Were you to be given something without having asked nor desired it, take it and do not refuse it, especially if you need it. You may refuse it if you feel that doing so is better for your religion or your heart. However, if you refuse for the sake of acquiring a reputation, so that it be said that you refuse worldly things, then you have a problem. So beware of this.

Accept nothing illicit, nor strongly suspect, even if it comes to you without asking. Know this and be wise. Success comes from God; He is our sufficiency and the best of guardians.

---

28. Nasā'ī, *Sunan*, (2539).

29. Ṭabarānī, *Kabīr,* (14814); Bazzār, *Musnad,* (3018).

Chapter Five: On Fasting

Know O brothers—may God ease us and you into what is easy, protect us from what is hard, and forgive us in the hereafter and in this life- that the month of Ramaḍān is a month of immense importance and rank in the sight of God and His Messenger. It is the master of all months. God made it obligatory upon Muslims to fast it. He said—Exalted is He, *O Believers! Prescribed for you is the fast, even as it was prescribed for those that were before you, that you may be God-fearing*. [2:183]

In the month of Ramaḍān God revealed His Book and made one of its nights, the Night of Worth (*Laylat'ul-Qadr*), better than a thousand months, better therefore than more than eighty three years. Do give this due reflection. What may this night be that is better and more superior in the sight of God than this long period? He says—Exalted is He, *The month of Ramaḍān in which the Qur'ān was sent down, a guidance for the people and clear signs of guidance and discernment*. [2:185] And He says, *We did send it down on the Night of Worth; and how will you know what is the Night of Worth? The Night of Worth is better than a thousand months. In it the angels and the Spirit descend, by the leave of their Lord, with all His commands. Peace it is, until the break of dawn*. [97:1-5] Thus did He make it known to us—Transcendent is He—that He had sent the Qur'ān down in Ramaḍān, specifically in the Night of Worth. This sending down was from the Guarded Tablet to the House of Might in the Terrestrial Heaven. The entire Qur'ān was sent down to the House of Might [on that night], then revealed portion by portion by the trustworthy Gabriel, at God's command, to His Messenger—may God's blessings and peace be upon him and upon Gabriel- over a period of about twenty three years, which is the period of revelation to the Messenger of God- may God's blessings and peace be upon him—for the first revelation came from God when he was forty, and he died at the age of sixty three. This is what has been stated by scholars of authority, both the early ones and the latecomers.

Concerning the merits of Ramaḍān, the Messenger of God- may God's blessings and peace be upon him—said, *The five ritual prayers, Friday to Friday, and Ramaḍān to Ramaḍān, these re-*

quite sins, so long as major ones are avoided.[1] He also said about Ramaḍān, *It is the month of patience, and the reward for patience is the Garden.*[2] And he said in the same *ḥadīth*, *Its beginning is mercy, its middle is forgiveness, and its end is freedom from the Fire.*[3] He also said that God the Exalted sends His gaze upon the Muslims on the first night of it. He upon whom He gazes He never torments; then He forgives them on the last night.[4]

Gabriel once said to the Messenger of God- may God's blessings and peace be upon them both, "He upon whom Ramaḍān comes and he is not forgiven, may God banish him! Say *Āmīn*!" The Messenger of God- may God's blessings and peace be upon him—said, "*Āmīn*!"[5] I say: This is because in Ramaḍān everything that leads to forgiveness is made easier than in other months, so much so that only he is not forgiven whose turning away from God is excessive and whose impudence is great, for only thus will he deserve remoteness and banishment from before the gate of God. We ask God for safety from His wrath, torment, and every other hardship.

It has been transmitted that the gates of the sky and those of the Garden are kept open in Ramaḍān, while those of the Fire are locked. The demons among jinn are shackled and cast into the seas, so that they are unable to spoil the Muslims' fasting and night prayers; and every night in Ramaḍān a herald cries, "O seeker of goodness, make haste! O seeker of evil, retreat!"[6] It has also been transmitted that an obligatory act of worship offered to God the Exalted in Ramadān will equal seventy such acts at other times, while a supererogatory act will equal an obligatory act offered at other times.[7] It is with regard to the reward they attract that the supererogatory devotions of Ramaḍān are equal to obligatory ones at other times, while its obligatory devotions are multiplied seventy times.

The Prophet—may God's blessings and peace be upon him—said, *He who fasts Ramaḍān and keeps vigil out of faith and the wish*

1. Muslim, *Ṣaḥīḥ*, (344); Aḥmad, *Musnad,* (8830); Bayhaqī, *Shu'ab al-Īmān*, (3466).
2. Ibn Khuzayma, *Ṣaḥīḥ*, (1780); Bayhaqī, *Shu'ab al-Īmān*, (3455).
3. Ibn Khuzayma, *Ṣaḥīḥ*, (1780); Bayhaqī, *Shu'ab al-Īmān*, (3455).
4. Bayhaqī, *Shu'ab al-Īmān*, (3450).
5. Ibn Ḥibbān, *Ṣaḥīḥ*, (410, 909); Ṭabarānī, *Kabīr,* (1990, 10952, 16004); Bayhaqī, *Shu'ab al-Īmān*, (3469).
6. Tirmidhī, *Sunan*, (618); Ibn Māja, *Sunan*, (1632).
7. Ibn Khuzayma, *Ṣaḥīḥ*, (1780); Bayhaqī, *Shu'ab al-Īmān*, (3455).

for the recompense, he will be forgiven all his past sins.[8] I say: Faith here is to believe in God's promise, while sincerity is to have no other intention but God. And God knows best.

There are good manners for the fast, without which it cannot be complete. Among the most important are that one keeps one's tongue from lying and backbiting, as well as from what does not concern one, to keep one's eyes and ears from looking at or listening to that which is prohibited or that which is superfluous. One should also keep forbidden and suspect food from reaching one's stomach, especially at the time of breaking the fast, at which time one should do one's utmost to eat nothing but *ḥalāl* food. One of our virtuous ancestors said, "When you fast, observe what you break your fast with and in whose house you do it." Indicating that one should be circumspect and careful about what one breaks one's fast with. He who fasts should also guard all his members, first from sin, then from unnecessary things. This is how the fast becomes complete and pure. How many a person may fast, suffer the hardship of hunger and thirst, yet because he does not restrain his bodily members from sin spoils his fast. The Prophet—may God's blessings and peace be upon him—said, *How many a fasting person gains nothing from fasting but hunger and thirst.*[9]

To refrain from sin is always mandatory, for fasting and non-fasting persons alike. However, it is more emphatically incumbent upon the fasting person, more of a duty for him. So understand!

He has said—may God's blessings and peace be upon him, *Fasting is a protection* [from the Fire]. *When it is a day of fasting for one of you, let him refrain from lewd speech and quick tempered reactions. Should a man insult him or quarrel with him, let him say, 'I am fasting.'*[10]

It is good manners for the fasting person not to sleep too much by day, nor eat too much by night. Let him be moderate in both, that he may feel some hunger and thirst, that his soul may be disciplined, his appetites weakened, and his heart illuminated. This is the secret and purpose of fasting. Let him avoid luxuries and, as we have just said, excess in indulging his appetites and pleasures. The least he can do is not to exceed in Ramaḍān his habitual degree of comfort

8. Tirmidhī, *Sunan*, (619); Ibn Māja, *Sunan*, (1316).

9. Aḥmad, *Musnad*, (8501); Ibn Khuzayma, *Ṣaḥīḥ*, (1875); Bayhaqī, *Shu'ab al-Īmān*, (3487); Ṭabarānī, *Kabīr,* (13232).

10. Aḥmad, *Musnad*, (7714, 9568).

at other times. However, self-discipline and refraining from indulging the appetites of one's soul have a great effect in illuminating the heart and are more incumbent in Ramaḍān.

As for those who make Ramaḍān a time for self-indulgence and pleasures that go beyond their habitual practice at other times, they are being deceived by the Devil, for he is jealous of them and wishes to deprive them of the blessings of the fast and prevent its effects from appearing on them in the form of lights and unveilings, humility and brokenness before God the Exalted, and the pleasure of communing with Him, reciting His Book, and invoking Him.

Our virtuous ancestors—may God have mercy on them—used to reduce their habitual and their pleasurable activities in Ramaḍān, while increasing their good works. This was their normal pattern at all times, but they intensified it even further in Ramaḍān.

It is good manners not to be overly concerned with worldly affairs during the month of Ramaḍān. One should free oneself for the worship and constant remembrance of God, and not engage in any worldly endeavor unless it is strictly necessary, either for oneself or those for whom one is responsible, such as children and so on. This is because Ramaḍān among months is similar to Friday among days. A believer should devote both that day and that month to his life-to-come.

It is of the *Sunna* to hasten to break one's fast and that it be done with dates, or if dates are unavailable, with water. The Prophet—may God's blessings and peace be upon him—used to break his fast before praying *Maghrib*. He said, *The people shall remain in a good state so long as they hasten with breaking their fast and delay their* suḥūr.[11] Therefore, delaying *suḥūr* is also a *Sunna*.

The fasting person should eat in moderation, so that the effects of fasting may show on him and he may attain its secret and goal, which are disciplining the soul and weakening its appetites. Hunger and an empty stomach have a great effect in illuminating the heart and infusing the bodily members with energy for worship. On the contrary, satiety is at the origin of hardness, distraction, and laziness in obedience. The Prophet said—may God's blessings and peace be upon him, *The Son of Adam never fills a vessel worse than his stomach. It is sufficient for the Son of Adam to have a few morsels*

11. Aḥmad, *Musnad*, (20350).

to keep his back straight. If he must, then a third for his food, a third for his beverage, and a third for his breath.[12]

Someone once said, "When the stomach is satiated, all the members become hungry, but when the stomach is hungry, the members are satiated." I say: Hunger for the members is to demand and insist to satisfy their appetites. The tongue desires to talk, the eye to look, the ear to listen, and so on. They are only moved to demand what is in excess of their needs when the stomach is full. On the other hand, when it is empty, they become quiet and tranquil, which is expressed as the "satiety of the members". This is an observable fact. And God knows best.

It is strongly recommended to help those about to break their fast by offering them something, preferably dates if possible, if not then water. He said—may God's blessings and peace be upon him, *He at whose hands a fasting person breaks his fast shall receive an equal wage, without this diminishing his wage in any way.*[13] Meaning that the wage of the fasting person remains undiminished. This reward belongs to him at whose hands the fast is broken, even if only with water. As for he who feeds a fasting person who has already broken his fast, whether by inviting him to his house or elsewhere, he does not receive this particular reward, but that of feeding people, which is also immense, and that, equally great, of feeding the fasting person to satiety, should he offer him enough food to satiate him fully.

The *Tarāwīḥ* Prayers every night of Ramaḍān are a *Sunna*. The custom of the virtuous ancestors—may God have mercy on them—was to divide the Qur'ān in parts, one of which to be recited every night, so as to complete it during one of the last nights of the month. He who can emulate them in this, let him be diligent, for good comes in opportunities that must be seized. *Whatever good you send forward for yourselves, you shall find it with God.* [73:20] He who is unable to emulate them, let him beware of shortening his prayers excessively, as many ignorant people do with *Tarāwīḥ*, to the extent that they may miss some of the obligatory parts of the prayer, such as not pausing at all during bowing down or prostrating, or reciting the *Fātiḥa* so quickly that it comes out incorrectly. In the sight of God such people have neither prayed and won the reward, nor aban-

12. Tirmidhī, *Sunan*, (2302); Ibn Māja, *Sunan*, (3340); Aḥmad, *Musnad*, (16556).

13. Tirmidhī, *Sunan*, (735); Ibn Māja, *Sunan*, (1736); Aḥmad, *Musnad*, (16419, 16429, 20687).

doned the prayer altogether, thereby feeling neglectful, which feeling keeps them safe from self-admiration. This and similar things are for believers among the greatest deceptions of the Devil. He allows one of them to perform the act, but causes it to become nullified. So beware of this and be attentive, O brothers!

When you pray *Tarāwīḥ*, or any other prayer, complete your standing up, recitation, bowing, prostration, humility, presence, and all other duties and courtesies. Do not give the Devil sway over you, for he has no power over those who believe and rely on their Lord, so be of those. His authority is over those who take him for an ally and associate others with God; so do not be of those!

Strive to make your acts of goodness and benevolence as abundant as you can in Ramaḍān, for it is a blessed time when wages are multiplied, reward is abundant, and good works are made easy. As for the multiplication of wages, it has been transmitted that a supererogatory devotion in Ramaḍān attracts a reward equal to that of an obligatory one [of the same kind] at any other time, while an obligatory devotion equals seventy such devotions performed at other times. Why should one miss such profit and be too lazy to seize the opportunity of such a transaction, one that can never lose? As for good works being made easy, it is because the soul that incites to evil is imprisoned by hunger and thirst, and the devils that discourage people from good works and place obstacles before them are shackled, unable to spread corruption. Therefore, nothing stands between one and good works, no barriers exist, save for those who are overcome by their wretchedness and misfortune—may God protect us! For such people Ramaḍān is similar to any other time. They are ever forgetful of God. Some may even become more forgetful and distracted in Ramaḍān.

Just as the believer should intensify his good works in this month and show diligence, so should he be extremely careful to avoid transgressions and maintain himself at a distance from them, for sins committed during blessed times are much worse and deserving of much more severe punishment, as a counterpart for the multiplication of rewards for good works at those same times.

It has been transmitted that the Prophet—may God's blessings and peace be upon him—used to intensify his efforts in Ramaḍān, then intensify them even more in the last ten days and nights. I say: This is because of the superior merit of the last ten days and nights, and his instructions—may God's blessings and peace be upon him—

to seek *Laylat'ul-Qadr* in them. Scholars have stated further that it is more likely to be one of the odd nights.

In brief, the sagacious believer should be ready for *Laylat'ul-Qadr* every Ramaḍān night. He must remain watchful and constantly engaged in good works. The important thing is that when it does come it finds him absorbed in his good works, remembering God the Exalted, neither distracted, heedless, nor absorbed in frivolity. It is unimportant whether he actually witnesses *Laylat'ul-Qadr* or not, for the works of he who is absorbed in devotions during it will be equivalent to the works of a thousand months, whether he is aware or not which specific night it is. We say: He should watch for it and be prepared every night of the month, because much disagreement exists between scholars as to which night it is. Some have gone so far as to say that it is hidden and can be any night in the month; also that it shifts and is not the same night every year. I am inclined to accept this last opinion. I believe it can occur in other than the last ten nights, but more frequently does in them. This is also the opinion of the majority of scholars.

In this noble month one should increase one's charities, assistance and comfort to the poor, and inquire after the widows and the orphans. It has been transmitted that the Prophet—may God's blessings and peace be upon him—was always more openhanded with donations than a whirlwind, but was more so than ever in Ramaḍān.[14]

One should increase one's recitations and studying of the Qur'ān, secluding oneself in mosques (*I'tikāf*), especially during the last ten days, which is the time when the Prophet—may God's blessings and peace be upon him—used to seclude himself.

And know that the month of Ramaḍān is one that has always been charged with benedictions for the Muslims. On the seventeenth of it took place the Battle of Badr, the Day of Decision, the day the two factions met. Also in Ramaḍān did the conquest of Makka the Honorable take place, and people entered the religion of God in throngs. In it comes *Laylat'ul-Qadr*, which is better than a thousand months, so that he who is engaged in devotions during it for twelve years will be as if he has spent a thousand years worshipping God. Can there be anything more tremendous and of more worth than this? How many are the benedictions and graces of Ramaḍān! Blessed is he who recognizes its worth, seizes the chance to profit from its days

14. Bukhārī, *Ṣaḥīḥ*, (6021); Muslim, *Ṣaḥīḥ*, (4268).

and hours, and remains engaged throughout its nights and its days in that which draws him nearer to his Lord. This is God's favor which He grants to whom He will. God's favor is immense.

Know that the best of fasts is that of Ramaḍān, and the same applies to every other obligatory act of worship, for they are all more meritorious in Ramaḍān than at other times. He has said—may God's blessings and peace be upon him, *My servant draws nearer to Me with nothing better than what I have prescribed as obligatory for him; and My servant ceases not to draw nearer to Me with devotions of freewill until I love him…*[15]

Next in merit to Ramadan comes fasting during the four Sacred Months, Dhul-Qa'da, Dhul-Ḥajja, Muḥarram, and Rajab. God—Exalted is He—says, *The number of months with God is twelve months, in the Book of God, on the day when He created the heavens and the earth. Four of them are sacred.* [9:36]

It has been transmitted that fasting one day in the Sacred Months is equivalent to fasting thirty days at other times, and fasting one day in Ramaḍān is equivalent to fasting thirty days in the Sacred Months. It has also been transmitted he who fasts three consecutive days in any of the Sacred Months, Thursday, Friday, and Saturday, God shall pull him away from the Fire.

It is a *Sunna* to fast six days in Shawwāl, after Ramaḍān is over, to bid the latter farewell and compensate for any deficiency in one's fast, for supererogatory devotions compensate for deficiencies in obligatory ones.

The Prophet—may God's blessings and peace be upon him—has said, *He who fasts Ramaḍān, then follows it up with six from Shawwāl, he will be as if he had been fasting uninterruptedly.*[16]

It is meritorious to fast the Day of 'Arafāt, which is the Day of *Ḥajj*, the ninth of Dhul-Ḥajja. It has been transmitted that to fast it is equivalent to fasting two years. Scholars have said that it is the best day of the year in which one can fast, except for Ramaḍān, but that it is not recommended for pilgrims to fast it, so that they may retain their strength for *du'ā'* during the Gathering and the other rites.

Then comes the Day of 'Āshūrā', which is the tenth day of Muḥarram. It has been transmitted that to fast it expiates the sins of a full year.

15. Bukhārī, *Ṣaḥīḥ*, (5, 1769, 3290); Aḥmad, *Musnad*, (24997).
16. Muslim, *Ṣaḥīḥ*, (1984); Tirmidhī, *Sunan*, (690).

It is strongly recommended to fast three days every month. Many *ḥadīths* exist to the effect that they are the equivalent of a continuous fast. It is better and more meritorious for the person wishing to fast to make them the White Days, since it has been related that the Prophet—may God's blessings and peace be upon him—never omitted to fast the White Days[17], whether he was at home or traveling. These are the thirteenth, fourteenth, and fifteenth of every month, and should be given priority. However, to fast any other three days is also good, even if not consecutively.

Those intent on worshipping should never neglect fasting three days every month, since the fast will be light, but of immense merit. It should suffice you to know that they would be the equivalent of a continuous fast. The Prophet—may God's blessings and peace be upon him—recommended it to a number of his Companions—may God be pleased with them. He said that Noah used to fast continuously, while David fasted half continuously, he used to fast one day and eat the next, and Abraham fasted continuously and broke his fast continuously, for he used to fast three days of every month.[18] May God's blessings and peace be upon them all. I say: The most preferable manner of fasting is that of David—may peace be upon him—which is to fast one day and break one's fast the next. It is preferable than fasting continuously, as stated in many authentic *ḥadīths*. Imām al-Ghazālī—may God the Exalted have mercy on him—says, "It is more effective in disciplining the soul and more powerful in opposing it than a continuous fast."

To fast every Monday and Thursday is also extremely meritorious. The Prophet—may God's blessings and peace be upon him—used to fast them and say, *These are two days on which works are presented to the Lord of all Beings. It pleases me that my works are presented even as I am fasting.*[19]

To fast on Friday is recommended, due to the merits and rank of that day, but on condition that it be paired with either Thursday or Saturday, for it has been transmitted that the Prophet—may God's blessings and peace be upon him—discouraged the people from fasting it on its own.

---

17. So called because they are the three nights of the lunar months when the moon is at its fullest.

18. Bayhaqī, *Shu'ab al-Īmān*, (3688).

19. Nasā'ī, *Sunan,* (2318); Aḥmad, *Musnad,* (20758).

Generally speaking, one should fast with frequency, for it is a most effective manner of disciplining the soul and breaking its passion, in softening and illuminating the heart, and in refining the senses and imposing rectitude upon them. There is in it an immense wage and a generous reward that has neither limit nor end.

The recompense for every good work is known except for fasting, its recompense is neither determined, nor limited. The Prophet—may God's blessings and peace be upon him—said, *God the Exalted says, 'Every work of the Son of Adam is multiplied ten to seven hundred times, except fasting, for it is Mine and I Myself shall reward for it. A person will leave his food, beverage, and passion for My sake. The fasting person shall have two joys: one joy when he breaks his fast, the second when he meets his Lord. And the bad odor of the fasting person's mouth is more fragrant near God than the scent of musk.*[20] So reflect profoundly—may God have mercy on you—on His saying—Exalted is He, "*except fasting, for it is Mine and I Myself shall reward for it.*" Reflect on the promise of limitless reward from the Generous, Liberal, and Compassionate Master. Reflect also on the odor of the fasting person's mouth being more fragrant near God than the scent of musk. Imagine the meaning of being "near God" which is the attribute of the fasting person. I say: Because of this it is discouraged to brush one's teeth with *siwāk* after midday and until sunset when one is fasting, since it will diminish this odor or remove it altogether.

The Prophet—may God's blessings and peace be upon him—has said, *The Garden has a door called Al-Rayyān, it is for those who fast to enter from on Judgment Day, no one else enters from it, and, once they have entered, it is locked.*[21] And, *Fasting is half of all patience. To everything a* zakāt*: the* zakāt *of the body is to fast.*[22] And, *Fasting is a protection, a strong fortress protecting from the Fire.*[23]

Know that fasting has an outward form and an [inward] spirit. Its outward form is to refrain from eating, drinking, and intercourse from before dawn until sunset, having first formed a specific intention. He who deliberately and knowingly eats, drinks, or has intercourse during daytime annuls his fast. This is the outward form of

20. Muslim, *Ṣaḥīḥ*, (1945); Nasā'ī, *Sunan*, (2185).
21. Bukhārī, *Ṣaḥīḥ*, (1763); Muslim, *Ṣaḥīḥ*, (1947).
22. Ibn Māja, *Sunan,* (1735); Bayhaqī, *Shu'ab al-Īmān*, (3420, 3421).
23. Aḥmad, *Musnad,* (8857); Bayhaqī, *Shu'ab al-Īmān*, (3413).

the fast. As for its spirit, it is to refrain from sins and prohibited things, and neglect no obligation or duty. He who refrains from eating, drinking, and intercourse, but does not refrain from contraventions will have gained nothing from his fast but pains and discomfort.

When you fast or engage in any other good work, do it well. Strive to perform all good works with excellence, perfection, and sincerity, so that God may allow you to profit from them and grant you the immense reward on the day when you return to Him. To Him—Transcendent is He—belongs the whole matter, so worship Him and rely on Him. Your Lord is not unaware of what you do. There is no other god than He, to Him is the final end.

Chapter Six: On Pilgrimage

Know O brothers—may God make us and you of those predestined for good fortune and those who have said, "Our lord is God!" then were upright—that the pilgrimage to God's Sacred House (*Ḥajj*) is one of the cornerstones of Islam. It is an obligation that is mandatory once in a lifetime for every Muslim capable of it, and so is *'Umra.* God—Exalted is He—says, *It is a duty upon all people toward God to come to the House for pilgrimage, for those able to.* [3:97] And He said to His Intimate Friend, Abraham—may peace be upon him, *Proclaim among men the Pilgrimage and they shall come to you walking and on every lean beast. They shall come from every deep ravine to witness benefits for them and mention the Name of God during the designated days over such beasts of the flocks that He has provided them. 'So eat of them and feed the indigent poor'. Then let them complete their rites, fulfill their vows, and circumambulate the Ancient House. This* (is what is required) *and he who magnifies the sacred things of God, it shall be better for him with his Lord.* [22:27,28,29,30] And the Messenger of God—may God's blessings and peace be upon him—said, *Islam is built on five: The testimony that there is no god other than God and that Muḥammad is the Messenger of God, the ritual prayer,* zakāt, *going on pilgrimage to the House, and fasting Ramaḍān.*[1] And he said- may blessings and peace be upon him, *He who possesses provision and a mount that would allow him to reach the House of God the Exalted, then does not go on pilgrimage, it is equal to him if he dies a Jew if he so wishes, or a Christian if he so wishes.*[2] There can be no more severe threat than that for he who neglects to go on pilgrimage when able to.

A believer should not postpone, act lazily, or procrastinate, producing excuses year after year, when he is able to go. How can he be sure that death will not overtake him, or that he will lose the ability he now possesses. He will remain indebted with pilgrimage and when he meets God, will do so as a disobedient sinner. Ability is for the person to possess the provision and mount that he will need in his pilgrimage journey on the way there and back, as well as

---

1. Bukhārī, *Ṣaḥīḥ*, (7); Muslim, *Ṣaḥīḥ*, (21).
2. Tirmidhī, *Sunan,* (740); Bayhaqī, *Shu'ab al-Īmān*, (3818); Bazzār, *Musnad*, (776).

whatever else is necessary, in addition to the expenses of such of his dependents as his wife and children until he returns.

Ability varies with the variation in people and places, whether the latter are near or far.

He who yearns so much for the Sacred House of God and is so eager to perform that religious obligation that he strains himself to go to pilgrimage, although he is not able in every way, his faith is more complete and his reward greater and more liberal. On condition, however, that none of God the Exalted's rights are wasted, either in the course of his journey, or at home, otherwise he would be guilty of disobedience and deserving of blame. Examples of this is that he sets out leaving without provision those whom God the Exalted made him responsible for, or depends on begging during his journey, thus his heart will be preoccupied with watching the people he hopes to beg from, or that he neglects some of his obligatory ritual prayers because he is traveling, or falls into something prohibited. The person who goes to pilgrimage in such a manner, when God has granted him permission not to when unable, is like he who builds a mansion, but destroys a town. We have drawn attention to this because many common people travel in this manner, thinking they are drawing nearer to God the Exalted by going to His House on pilgrimage, when in fact they are most remote from their aim, since they have not entered the matter from the proper door. Because this is so for the obligatory pilgrimage, it is even more reprehensible for supererogatory ones.

Everything we have just said applies to the weak and powerless. As for the strong and able, we have already said that he must hasten to perform his obligatory pilgrimage, after which it is recommended for him not to neglect supererogatory pilgrimages. One of our ancestors—may God have mercy on him—said, "The least he can do is never to allow more than five years to pass without going to pilgrimage once. It has reached us that God—Exalted is He—has said, *'A servant to whom I grant good health in his body and ample provision, yet he lets five years elapse without visiting Me, he is indeed deprived.'*[3] I say: The Muslim who has the ability to perform the pilgrimage should do so repeatedly because of what it entails as a manner of magnifying the sacred things of God and His rites, since the magnification of these is the piety of the heart, and because of its immense merit, as has been stated in *ḥadīth*. The Messenger of

3. Ibn Ḥibbān, *Ṣaḥīḥ*, (3773); Bayhaqī, *Shu'ab al-Īmān*, (3975).

God—may God's blessings and peace be upon him—said, *The best* Jihād *is an acceptable* Ḥajj.[4] And, *The pilgrimage obliterates whatever has preceded it.*[5] Which means the sins that have been committed prior to it. And, *He who performs the pilgrimage, avoiding lewd speech and corrupt behavior, he will exit from his sins* [and revert to being] *like the day his mother gave birth to him.*[6] *Lewd speech and corrupt behavior* include every possible reprehensible behaviour. And, *One* 'Umra *after another expiate the sins committed in between and the accepted* Ḥajj *has no reward short of the Garden.*[7] And when asked what the acceptability of the pilgrimage depended upon, he answered, *feeding the people and speaking gently to them.*[8] And, *Those who perform* Ḥajj *and* 'Umra *are God's guests. When they ask, they are given, when they pray, they are answered, and when they expend, they are compensated.*[9]

It is most important for he who is about to set out for the pilgrimage to do his utmost to make his provision *ḥalāl* and his expenses from a licit source, for he who uses illicit money for the pilgrimage will not be accepted by God. When he will say, "*Labbayk*!" after entering the state of *iḥrām*, God—Transcendent is He—shall answer, "No *labbayk* and no *sa'dayk*! Your provision is illicit and your mount is illicit. Your pilgrimage has been rejected." But he who expends from a licit source, when he will say, "*Labbayk*!" God—Exalted is He—will say, "*Labbayk* and *sa'dayk*! Your provision is licit and your mount is licit. Your pilgrimage has been accepted." This is how it has been transmitted in *ḥadīth*.[10]

Let the pilgrim feel pleased when he spends his money in the course of his journey, for these are expenditures that he will be compensated for and the consequence of which will be goodness, benedictions, ease, and affluence. It has been transmitted that that which is spent on pilgrimage is similar to that spent on *Jihād,* the reward for every *Dirham* will be seven hundred.

---

4. Bukhārī, *Ṣaḥīḥ*, (1423, 2576); Abū Ya'lā, *Musnad*, (4595).
5. Muslim, *Ṣaḥīḥ*, (173); Ibn Khuzayma, *Ṣaḥīḥ*, (2315).
6. Bukhārī, *Ṣaḥīḥ*, (1424, 1690, 1691); Muslim, *Ṣaḥīḥ*, (2404).
7. Bukhārī, *Ṣaḥīḥ*, (1650); Muslim, *Ṣaḥīḥ*, (2403).
8. Al-Ḥākim, *Mustadrak*, (1733); Bayhaqī, *Shu'ab al-Īmān*, (3964, 3965).
9. Bayhaqī, *Shu'ab al-Īmān*, (3949, 3950); Ibn Māja, *Sunan*, (2883); Ṭabarānī, *Kabīr,* (1103).
10. Ṭabarānī, *Kabīr,* (1299); *Awsaṭ*, (5386).

If the pilgrim is wealthy, let him be liberal in giving to the poor and the destitute, in helping the weak and the needy, followed by all other Muslims. Let it be done sincerely for the Lord of the worlds.

During his journey, let him be humble, modest, and submissive. This is how he should approach the King, the Compeller and Proud. Behaving with arrogance or indulging in extreme forms of comfort will cause him to be rejected by God. The Prophet—may God's blessings and peace be upon him—said that it is proper for the pilgrim to be unkempt and covered with dust.[11] When he went on his pilgrimage—may God's blessings and peace be upon him—he used a worn out saddle and sat on a cheap cloth not worth four *Dirhams*. The more humble and modest the pilgrim, the poorer he looks for the sake of God, the better, purer, more honorable and complete will his pilgrimage be.

The Proof of Islam, al-Ghazālī—may God have mercy on him—says, "God made the pilgrimage journey in the likeness of the journey to the hereafter. Therefore, one should bring to mind, with every act during the journey, the corresponding or equivalent act pertaining to the hereafter. When you bid your family and friends farewell, remember how you will bid them farewell in your last moments before death. When you prepare your provisions for the road, remember the provisions that have to be prepared for the hereafter. The long distance that you travel together with the fear of predators and brigands should remind you of the road to the hereafter, the questioning by Munkar and Nakīr, and the torment of the grave. Wrapping the iḥrām clothes around your body should remind you of the shroud that will wrapped around you in due course. Going between Ṣafā and Marwa should remind you of which of the two sides of the Scales you should make heavier. The gathering on 'Arafāt should remind you of the gathering on Judgment Day." This is the summary of what he said. You can look up the full text in his book. The matter is indeed as he says—may God have mercy on him and reward him on behalf of all Muslims with the best reward.

Once the pilgrim arrives at God's sanctuary, His sacred Secure Town, Makka the honorable—may God increase it in honor-he should be full of veneration and reverence for God, as submissive and humble as he possibly can, full of reverence, awe, and powerlessness before God the Exalted. Let these attributes be his inner and outer garments wherever he goes in these noble places.

11. Bayhaqī, *Al-Sunan al-Kubrā*, vol. 5, p.58.

He should circumambulate the House and pray before it assiduously. It has been transmitted that, *He who does the round of this House seven times, it will be for him the equivalent of freeing a slave. And he who is circumambulating the House never lifts his foot, nor puts it down, without a bad deed being erased, a good one recorded, or his rank being raised by a degree.*[12] The reference here is to the reward for freeing a slave purely for the sake of God the Exalted. And, *Every day a hundred and twenty mercies alight on the House, sixty for those who are circumambulating it, forty for those praying before it, and twenty for those looking at it.*[13]

Let him recite the Qur'ān in abundance during his circumambulation, and also invocations and prayers, especially those specifically related to circumambulation.

Let him touch the blessed Black Stone with great frequency, for it is the right hand of God on earth with which He shakes the hands of His servants. The same applies to praying in the *Ḥijr,* for it had been part of the House, but was left out by the Quraysh when they ran short of licit funds as they were rebuilding it in the days of ignorance.

Let him also drink from Zamzam assiduously, for it is the best water on the face of the earth, as he said—may God's blessings and peace be upon him. He also said, "The water of Zamzam is good for what it is drunk for.[14] It is food for he who needs to be fed and a cure for the sick."[15] Many a great man has drunk of it, having formed noble intentions, and was granted them as a favor from God, through the *baraka* of the Messenger of God—may God's blessings and peace be upon him.

When he is standing at 'Arafāt, let the pilgrim ask forgiveness and make *du'ā'* in great abundance. Let him implore God and weep, and beseech Him with sincerity eagerness, concentration, and repentance. Let him ask for himself, his two parents, his loved ones, then all Muslims, that everything that concerns them, whether of this world or the next, be rendered good. He will be asking one who

12. Al-Ḥākim, *Mustadrak,* (1756); Aḥmad, *Musnad,* (5443); Ibn Khuzayma, *Ṣaḥīḥ,* (2545); Tirmidhī, *Sunan,* (882).
13. Ṭabarānī, *Kabīr,* (11085, 11313); *Awsaṭ,* (6496); Haythamī, *Bughyat al-Bāḥith an Zawā'id al-Ḥārith,* (389).
14. Ibn Māja, *Sunan,* (3053); Aḥmad, *Musnad,* (14320).
15. Bayhaqī, *Dalā' il al-Nubuwwa,* (513); Bazzār, *Musnad,* (3343, 3348); Ibn Ḥajar al-'Asqalānī, *Al-Maṭālib al-'Āliya,* (1357).

is Generous and Liberal, in whose hand is all good, who possesses the treasuries of the heavens and the earth.

This gathering is the greatest and most comprehensive of all Islamic gatherings. Innumerable angels and men of God attend it. It has been transmitted that God—Exalted is He—boasts of the people of the gathering before the denizens of heaven, then asks His angels to bear witness that He had accepted those of them that had done good, and given those who had done evil to those who had done good. It has also been transmitted that the greatest of sinners is he who stands on 'Arafāt then goes away thinking that he had not been forgiven. Another *ḥadīth* says that Iblīs—may God curse him—is never seen more humiliated, vanquished, or enraged than on the day of 'Arafa. This is because he witnesses the mercy that is descending and God's forgiveness for the sinners standing on 'Arafāt.[16]

It is important that the pilgrim's only intention should be to come to the House of God for pilgrimage and for honoring what He made sacred. If his intention is not so, then let him beware to the extreme from taking along worldly things that may distract him from performing the rites and honoring them as he should and is expected to. This occurs with many who are forgetful of God and enamored with the world. They are so occupied with commercial transactions that they fail to honor the sacred things or perform the rites properly. With some of them it may even reach the point where their main intention becomes commerce, while the pilgrimage becomes subsidiary. This is a major error and is greatly reprehensible. As for commerce as such during the course of the pilgrimage, there is no harm and no sin in it so long as it is not distracting or damaging to the correct performance of it. God has permitted it and revealed concerning it, *There is no fault in you should you seek bounty from your Lord. But when you press from 'Arafāt, then remember God at the Sacred Monument, and remember Him as He has guided you, for before this you were astray.* [2:198] However, it is preferable if one's sole intention is to perform the pilgrimage. In this case it will do no harm to carry along some merchandise, provided it is not likely to distract from the rites, nor disperse the heart's concentration. It is what distracts from the rites and disperses the heart's concentration that is reprehensible. So beware of it O pilgrim if you

16. Imām Mālik, *Muwaṭṭa'*, (840); 'Abdal-Razzāq, *Musannaf,* (8125, 8832); Bayhaqī, *Shu'ab al-Īmān*, (3910, 3911).

desire your pilgrimage to be complete and accepted, and your effort rewarded.

It is also reprehensible to go on pilgrimage, as certain common people do, with the intention of discharging one's duty to perform the obligatory pilgrimage, in order to be eligible to be hired by others to perform their pilgrimages on their behalf. The desire of such a man is but the fee he will receive. His is an ugly passion for this world. It is possible that God the Exalted does not accept the obligatory pilgrimage of he whose mind harbors such things. So let him fear God and beware of such intentions that are devoid of all goodness. We have mentioned this because some common people lacking wisdom have been observed doing it. They should be warned against it and this knowledge should be disseminated.

There is nothing wrong or blameworthy in hiring someone to perform the pilgrimage on one's behalf. The person hired should intend to visit the House, magnify the sacred things of God, and discharge his Muslim brother's obligation to perform the pilgrimage, out of compassion for him. In this manner will this person receive a great reward by the grace of God the Exalted. As for the hired person who desires nothing but his fees, he is not safe from peril. Imām al-Ghazālī—may God have mercy on him—says, "He who is hired to perform the pilgrimage should make going to the House his primary intention and the fee secondary to it, not reverse the priority, giving the fee primacy and making the pilgrimage secondary."

A pilgrim should perform the pilgrimage in the most complete manner as concerns both its obligatory and supererogatory aspects. He should conform to all the *sunnas* and courtesies, according to the manner in which the pilgrimage of the Messenger of God—may God's blessings and peace be upon him—was described. Knowledge of all this is to be found in the books of rites authored by the scholars—may God' s mercy be upon them. Among the best is that by Imām Nawawī—may God have mercy on him. No pilgrim should go without one of these works, so that he may know what he is doing and what his Lord wishes him to do.

He should visit all the places of special importance and the locations that are especially to be honored. These are very well known.

Let him be most careful to visit the Messenger of God—may God's blessings and peace be upon him—and beware to the utmost from neglecting this, if able to do it, especially following his obligatory pilgrimage. It has been transmitted that he has said—may God's blessings and peace be upon him, *He who performs the pilgrimage but does not visit me will have treated me coldly*. And, *He who visits me after my death will be as if he has visited me in my lifetime*.[17]

A believer should never neglect to visit his Prophet—may God's blessings and peace be upon him—unless he has a powerful excuse, for his rights upon his community are immense. Were someone to come from the place on earth that is farthest from his honorable grave walking on his face or eyesight to visit him—may God's blessings and peace be upon him—he would still have not fulfilled what he owes his Prophet. May God reward him on our behalf and that of all Muslims with the best reward He has ever granted a Prophet on behalf of his community, for he has conveyed the message, clarified the evidence, counseled the community, removed the gloom, and left us on a pure white path, a clear well-traveled road of truth, its night as [clear as] its day. May God's blessings, benedictions, and peace upon him and his family be better and more permanent than those He has granted any of His creation, and multiplied by the number, weight, and size of everything that He knows.

17. Bayhaqī, *Shu'ab al-Īmān*, (3993, 3996); Dāraquṭnī, *Sunan*, (2726); Ṭabarānī, *Kabīr*, (411); *Awsaṭ*, (3507).

Chapter Seven: On Reciting the Qur'ān and Remembrance

Reciting the Qur'ān

Know O brother—may God make us and you of those who recite His August Book as it should be, who believe in it, memorize and are preserved by it, uphold and summon to it- that reciting the formidable Qur'ān is one of the best acts of worship, greatest things to offer to God, and highest devotions. In it is an immense wage, a generous reward. God—Exalted is He—says, *Those who recite the Book of God, establish the prayer, and expend of what We have provided them secretly and in public, they hope that their commerce will never lose. He shall give them their wages in full and increase them of His favor. He is ever-forgiving, thankful.* [35:29,30] And the Prophet—may God's blessings and peace be upon him—has said, *The best of my community's acts of worship is the recitation of the Qur'ān.*[1] And, *He who recites a letter from the Book of God, a good deed is recorded to his credit, and a good deed is rewarded with ten times its equivalent. I do not say that* Alif-Lām-Mīm *is one letter, but* Alif *is one letter*, Lām *is one letter, and* Mīm *is one letter.*[2] And, *God the Exalted says, 'He who is too occupied with the remembrance of Me and the recitation of My Book to petition Me, I shall grant him better than what I grant those who ask.' And the superiority of the speech of God the Exalted over other speech is as the superiority of God over His creation.*[3] And, *Recite the Qur'ān, for it shall intercede on Resurrection Day for those who do.*[4] 'Alī—may God honor his countenance-said, "He who recites the Qur'ān as he stands in prayer shall receive for each letter [the reward for] a hundred good deeds. He who recites it as he prays sitting down shall receive for each letter fifty good deeds. He who recites it outside of prayer, but being ritually pure, shall receive for each letter twenty five good deeds. And he who recites it without ritual purification shall receive for each letter ten good deeds."

---

1. Bayhaqī, *Shu'ab al-Īmān*, (1964); Al-Shihāb al-Quḍā'ī, *Musnad al-Shihāb*, (1186).
2. Tirmidhī, *Sunan,* (2835); Bayhaqī, *Shu'ab al-Īmān*, (1928).
3. Tirmidhī, *Sunan,* (2850); Dārimī, *Sunan*, (3419).
4. Muslim, *Ṣaḥīḥ*, (1337); Bayhaqī, *Shu'ab al-Īmān*, (2281).

Know that recitation has both outward and inward courtesies to be observed. A servant is not truly a reciter whose recitation is pure, nor does he receive consideration from God, until he conforms to these good manners. The recitation of those who neglect or do not master them remains incomplete. However, they will not be deprived of reward altogether, but will be treated according to their performance.

One of the most important and mandatory good manners is for the recitation to be for no other purpose than for God the Exalted, seeking His noble countenance, intending to draw nearer to Him and win His reward. Ostentation, affectation, or seeking to look good in the sight of created beings should be avoided, and so also to obtain immediate and ephemeral profits. One's secret and heart should be full of the immensity of the Speaker—August and High is He—submissive to His majesty, of humble heart and bodily members, so full of reverence and humility as to be as if standing before God the Exalted, reciting His Book in which are His commands and prohibitions. He should be so by right, or even more perfect than that, he who has come to know the Qur'ān and the Speaker. How can he not be so when God—Exalted is He—says, *Were We to reveal this Qur'ān to a mountain, you would have seen it humble, split asunder from the fear of God. These examples We strike for mankind, that they may reflect.* [59:21] If this is what would happen to a mountain, solid and hard as they are, should the Qur'ān be sent down upon it, how much more should it be with a weak human being created from water and clay, were it not for the distraction and hardness of hearts, and their lack of knowledge of God's immensity, His inaccessible rank and majesty.

God—Exalted is He—says in describing those of His servants who are awed by the recitation of the Qur'ān, *Those who were given knowledge before it, when it is recited to them, fall down upon their chins in prostration and say, 'Transcendent is our Lord! Our Lord's promise will surely come true. And they fall down upon their chins weeping, and it increases them in humility.* [17:107-109] And He says—Exalted is He, *God has sent down the best of discourses as a Book the parts of which resemble each other, paired. It makes the skins shiver of those who fear their Lord, then their skins and their hearts soften to the remembrance of God.* [39:23]

Magnification, awe, humility, and submissiveness when reciting the Qur'ān are attributes of sincere believers, aware of the majesty of the Lord of the Worlds.

Distraction, hardness, inattention, and frivolity when reciting the Qur'ān are the attributes of those who have turned away and are mixing good with bad deeds, whose faith is weak and certainty scarce, whose hearts are devoid of the realities of the knowledge of God and His speech. We ask God for safety from all this, for us and you, and from all kinds of hardships and perils.

Also among the most important and incumbent good manners is to be present of heart when reciting, to reflect on the meanings and strive to understand. God—Exalted is He—says, *A Book We sent down to you, blessed, that they may reflect on its verses, that those may remember who are possessed of acute minds.* [38:29] And He says—Exalted is He—reprimanding and rebuking certain people, *Do they not reflect on the* Qur'ān*, or are there locks on their hearts?* [47:24]

'Alī—may God honor his countenance-said, "There is no good in a recitation without reflection." He has spoken the truth—may God be pleased with him—for the Qur'ān was sent down to reflected upon, for it is by reflection that the intended meaning is understood, one is able to acquire the knowledge in it, then put it into practice, which is the purpose of sending it down and conveying it to the people through the Messenger of God—may God's blessings and peace be upon him. Therefore, when you recite, strive to reflect and understand, for a little that you recite with reflection and understanding is better than much that is recited without. One of our virtuous ancestors—may God's mercy be upon them—said, "To recite *Idhā zulzilat* and *al-Qāri'a* with reflection and understanding is more satisfying to me than to read the whole Qur'ān." Another was asked about two persons, one of whom recited *al-Baqara*, while the other recited *al-Baqara* and *Āl-'imrān*, yet they started and finished together, which of the two was better? He answered, "The one who read *al-Baqara* only is better." I say: This is because, although the other had recited about twice as much, the first had recited with reflection and deliberation, as shown by his taking the same time as he who had recited more.

It should now have become clear to you that the goal is reflection and understanding, for these are what count when reciting the Qur'ān. So do this—may God have mercy on you.

Al-Ḥasan al-Baṣrī—may God have mercy on him—said, "Those who were before you perceived this Qur'ān as messages from their Lord to them, so they reflected on these by night, then put them into practice by day."

The more a person has knowledge of God, the more he will reflect on the Qur'ān and strive to understand its contents. This is why for those firmly established scholars and rightly-guided imams who possess the gnosis of God, the possibilities of reflecting on the Qur'ān and understanding it become vast. Abū Dharr—may God be pleased with him—said, "The Messenger of God—may God's blessings and peace be upon him—led us in prayer at night, reciting only His words—Exalted is He, *If you torment them, they are but Your servants, but if You forgive them, You are the August, the Wise*." [5:118]

'Umar—may God be pleased with him—used to repeat the same verse during his night vigils and reflect upon it till he became so over come with fear and awe that he fell down, sometimes becoming so ill that people visited him for his illness.

Tamīm al-Dārī once kept repeating the following verse in his night prayer, till dawn, *Or do those think, who commit evil deeds, that We shall make them as those who believe, equal in their life and their death? How ill they judge!* [45:21]

And Sa'īd ibn Jubayr—may God have mercy on him—repeated the following words a whole night, *Keep apart today, O criminals!* [36:59]

Such stories about our virtuous predecessors abound in record. Fear and weeping overcame them when reciting the Qur'ān, so well did they know God, reflect on His Book, and understand it. Many of them are known to have lost consciousness on occasions, when they recited the Qur'ān, or heard it being recited. Some have even died. This is well known from their anecdotal stories and biographies. May God have mercy on them and cause us to benefit from them.

Thus when you recite the Qur'ān, reflect, understand, and meditate. Halt at each verse containing one of the commands of God or His prohibitions, or a promise, or a threat, then consider, if you find yourself obeying His orders, refraining from what He prohibited, believing with certainty in these promises and threats, thank God, and know that it is through His assistance and His providentially granted success that you have achieved this. On the other hand, should you find yourself neither obeying His orders, nor refraining from His prohibitions, your certainty in His promises and threats weak, then ask your Lord for forgiveness, repent to Him from your neglectful attitude, and resolve to obey His commands and refrain from His prohibitions, and impose upon your heart complete certainty in His promises and threats.

Similarly, when you recite the verses relating to the oneness of God and His holiness—August and Majestic is He—and the verses mentioning His lofty attributes and most beautiful names, then halt and reflect on the meanings they contain concerning His majesty and His sublime glory and perfection. Then your heart will be full of His oneness and holiness, and with magnification and reverence.

When you recite the verses mentioning the attributes of believers and virtuous servants of God the Exalted, describing their praiseworthy character, reflect on these and study them, then impose it upon yourself to acquire these attributes.

But when you recite the verses mentioning the foes, be they disbelievers or hypocrites, their ugly attributes and character, reflect on them and search within yourself to see if any of them apply to you, in which case you should rid yourself of them and repent to God, lest some of the wrath and punishment that befell them should befall you.

This is the pattern according to which you should reflect upon the verses of God, each verse according to its meaning and context, for the verses of the Qur'ān are numerous, of many kinds and categories, containing vast abundant sciences that know of no limit or end. He says—Exalted is he, *We have neglected nothing in the Book.* [6:38] And, *We sent down the Book upon you, making clear all things.* [16:89] And the *ḥadīth* says, *Every verse has an outward and an inward, a limit and a place of ascent.*"[5]

To assist you in reflecting upon and understanding the meanings of the Qur'ān, recite correctly and with deliberation, without haste, without allowing it to become a jabber, for it has been transmitted that this is not permissible. God—Exalted is He—says to His Messenger—may God's blessings and peace be upon him, *Recite the Qur'ān distinctly.* [73:4]

When Umm Salama and other Companions—may God be pleased with them—described the recitation of the Messenger of God—may God's blessings and peace be upon him—they said it

5. Al-Qāsim ibn Salāma, *Faḍā'il al-Qur'ān,* (64, 65); Abū Ya'lā, *Musnad*, (5024).

had been deliberate, distinct, letter by letter. He said—may God's blessings and peace be upon him, *The reciter of the Qur'ān shall be told, 'Recite and climb, and chant it as you used to do in the world, your degree shall be with the last verse you recite.'*[6] A certain scholar—may God have mercy on them—said, "The number of degrees in the Garden is equal to that of the verses of the Qur'ān. Therefore, he who recites the complete Qur'ān shall be in the highest degree." I say: This applies to the reciter whose recitation is excellent and who puts into practice what he recites, not the distracted entangled reciter. This is understood from the authentic *ḥadīths* describing the punishment of he who recites the Qur'ān as it was revealed, but puts into practice none of it. The verses of the Qur'ān number over six thousands, therefore the degrees of the Garden according to the opinion of the quoted scholar are the same. And God knows best.

It is recommended to make one's voice melodious when reciting the Qur'ān. This helps the heart being attentive, awed, and sad, and stimulates one to listen carefully. He said—may God's blessings and peace be upon him, *Embellish the Qur'ān with your voices.*[7] And, *He is not of us who does not chant the Qur'ān melodiously.*[8] And he said in praise of Abū Mūsā al-Ash'arī—may God be pleased with him—having heard him recite the Qur'ān melodiously, *He has been given a flute like the flutes of David.*[9] However, this should be done in a manner that is consonant with the reverence and respect due to the Qur'ān. It should never resemble singing, or the rhythmic chanting of poetry, as is done by certain fools.

When you are reciting, you should be in the most complete state as concerns purity, facing the *Qibla*, motionlessness of bodily members, avoiding turning your head around, concentration, avoiding looking here and there, cleanliness of body, clothes, and place, and fragrance of smell. This is the best and most complete manner of doing it. Should one recite without ritual purity, not facing the *Qibla*, or while standing, walking, or lying down, it is still permissible and there is still merit and reward in it, but less than that for he who fulfills all the conditions of proper courtesy.

---

6. Abū Dāwūd, *Sunan*, (1252); Tirmidhī, *Sunan*, (2838).
7. Abū Dāwūd, *Sunan*, (1256); Nasā'ī, *Sunan*, (1005, 1006), Ibn Māja, *Sunan*, (1332).
8. Bukhārī, Ṣaḥīḥ, (6973); Abū Dāwūd, *Sunan*, (1257).
9. Bukhārī, *Ṣaḥīḥ*, (4660); Muslim, *Ṣaḥīḥ*, (1321).

Know—may God have mercy on you—that the reciter of the Qur'ān and he who has learned it by heart have a rank in the sight of God. The Prophet said—may God's blessings and peace be upon him, *He who recites the Qur'ān skillfully is with the scribes that are noble and loyal. As for he who recites it but stutters and finds it difficult, his shall be two rewards.*[10] And, *The people of the Qur'ān are God's own people, His elect.*[11]

Many other merits have been stated in detail in numerous well known *ḥadīth*s.

Nevertheless, he who recites the Qur'ān should know its rights upon him, the respect and reverence due to it, that it is incumbent upon him to learn what it contains, then put it into practice, be guided by what it enjoins in the way of excellent attributes, noble character, and good works. Although this is required of all Muslims, it is more incumbent upon he who recites the Qur'ān, for he is more worthy of it, because of his merit and the merit of that which he knows of the Book of God, its evidences and proofs.

'Umar—may God be pleased with him—said, "O reciters! Lift up your heads, your path has become clear, so compete for goodness."

'Abdallāh ibn Mas'ūd—may God be pleased with him—said, "The man of Qur'ān should be recognizable by his [behavior at] night, while people sleep, his [fasting by] day, while people eat, his sadness, while people are happy, his weeping, while people laugh, his silence, while people prattle, and his humility, while people boast." I say: The meaning of ibn Mas'ūd's words is that the men of Qur'ān should distinguish themselves from common people by their zeal in obeying God, their hastening to acts of goodness, the thoroughness with which they guard themselves against distraction and avoid frivolity, and their complete fear and awe of God the Exalted.

Ibn Mas'ūd—may God be pleased with him—also said, "The Qur'ān was sent down to be put into practice, but you have turned studying it into a job."

As for the distracted reciter whose works are mixed, who does not practice what is in the Qur'ān, does not obey its injunctions, is not held back by its rebukes, and does not stop at its limits, many

10. Muslim, *Ṣaḥīḥ*, (1321); Abū Dāwūd, *Sunan*, (1242); Tirmidhī, *Sunan*, (2829).

11. Ibn Māja, *Sunan*, (211); Aḥmad, *Musnad*, (11831, 11844).

ḥadīths have been transmitted as to how blameworthy he is, how severely he will be treated, and what he is threatened with. He has said—may God's blessings and peace be upon him, *Recite the Qur'ān so long as it restrains you* [from evil]. *If it is not restraining you, you are not reciting it.*[12] And, *He who places the Qur'ān before him, it will lead him to the Garden, but who places it behind him, it will drive him to the Fire.*[13]

It has been transmitted that the Fire will be swifter to reach corrupt reciters than to reach the idolaters; and that the Qur'ān remains a stranger inside the unjust. It has also been transmitted: How many a reciter recites the Qur'ān while it is cursing him? Meaning: because he is disobeying it and acting against its injunctions. It has reached us that some of those who know the Qur'ān by heart will be rushed to the Fire ahead of the idol worshippers. They will ask, "What, are we to be punished before the idol worshippers?" They will be answered, "He who knows is not as he who does not know." It has also been said that when the reciter of the Qur'ān commits sins, the Qur'ān calls him from inside him, "Where are my rebukes? Where are my threats? Where are my counsels?" and so on.

Maymūn ibn Mihrān—may God the Exalted have mercy on him—said, "Some of them when they recite the Qur'ān curse themselves." He was asked, "How so?" He replied, "They recite, *We shall cast the curse of God upon the liars*, [3:61] even as they are lying, and *May the curse of God be upon the unjust*, [11:18] even as they are being unjust.

A hadīth says, *The hypocrite who recites the Qur'ān is like myrtle, its smell is good, but its taste is bitter.*[14] And in the same hadīth, *Some people recite the Qur'ān, but it goes not beyond their clavicles. They exit from Islam even as the arrow passes through its target.*[15] We ask God the Exalted for ease and security, for success in holding fast to His Book, learning, understanding, and putting its guidance into practice, together with good endings and good consequences to all our affairs, for us, our loved ones, and all Muslims.

---

12. Ṭabarānī, *Musnad al-Shāmiyyin*, (1313); Al-Shihāb al-Qudā'ī, *Musnad al-Shihāb*, (374, 692).
13. Ibn Hibbān, *Ṣaḥīḥ*, (124); Ṭabarānī, *Kabīr*, (8573, 10298); Bayhaqī, *Shu'ab al-Īmān*,(1954).
14. Bukhārī, *Ṣaḥīḥ*, (5007); Muslim, *Ṣaḥīḥ*, (1328).
15. Bukhārī, *Ṣaḥīḥ*, (3341, 6422); Muslim, *Ṣaḥīḥ*, (1765, 1773).

It is one of the greatest devotions and most tremendous merits to learn the noble Qur'ān and teach it. It is one of the most mandatory *kifāya* obligations. The Messenger of God—may God's blessings and peace be upon him—said, *The best among you are those who learn the Qur'ān and teach it.*"[16] And when Sufyān al-Thawrī—may God's mercy be upon him—was asked, "Is a man who learns the Qur'ān more pleasing to you or one who fights in the way of God?" He answered, "He who learns the Qur'ān."

The person who has learned the Qur'ān by heart must recite it frequently by day and by night, with reflection, understanding, and extreme courtesy and respect. Let him beware to the utmost from neglecting to recite it and abandoning to look after it, for this might lead to forgetting it, which is one of the greatest sins. The Prophet—may God's blessings and peace be upon him—said, *The sins of my community were shown to me and I saw none greater than that of a man who was given a* sūra *or verse of the Qur'ān, then forgot it...*[17] And, *He who forgets the Qur'ān, having learned it by heart, will come to meet God on Resurrection Day as a leper.*[18]

The Prophet—may God's blessings and peace be upon him—has enjoined upon he who has learned the Qur'ān to preserve it, for as he said, it is swifter to escape from the breasts of men than hobbled camels are to escape from their tethers.

Our virtuous predecessors—may God have mercy on them—were very careful with the Qur'ān, they varied in their habits, some completing its recitation every month, some every ten nights, every eight, seven, or three nights. Some completed two full recitations every day and night, others two, others four. The maximum was eight complete recitations in a day and night. Imām al-Nawawī—may God have mercy on him—says, "This is the maximum that has come to our knowledge. However, certain scholars have stated that to make it a habit to complete it in less than three days was to be discouraged, since he has said—may God's blessings and peace be upon him, *He will not understand who recites the Qur'ān in less than three.*[19]

16. Bukhārī, *Ṣaḥīḥ*, (4639); Abū Dāwūd, *Sunan*, (1240); Tirmidhī, *Sunan*, (2832, 2833, 2834).

17. Abū Dāwūd, *Sunan*, (390); Tirmidhī, *Sunan*, (2840).

18. Abū Dāwūd, *Sunan*, (1260); Aḥmad, *Musnad*, (21419, 12426, 21696).

19. Abū Dāwūd, *Sunan*, (1186); Tirmidhī, *Sunan*, (2870, 2873).

The man of Qur'ān should have a daily *wird* of recitation during his night prayers, completing the Qur'ān in a month, forty days, or more or less, according to determination and circumstances. He should never abandon this, nor feel so lazy as to neglect it. The *ḥadīth* says, *The Qur'ān and the fast intercede with God on behalf of the servant. The Qur'ān will say, "I prevented him from sleeping at night, so permit me to intercede on his behalf." And the fast will say, "I prevented him from eating by day, so permit me to intercede on his behalf." They will then be permitted to intercede.*[20] God—Exalted is He—says, *They are not equal. Of the people of the Book are a community that stand reciting the verses of God during the night, prostrating themselves. They believe in God and the last day, enjoin good and forbid evil, and hasten to good works. Those are of the righteous.* [3:113,114] Thus the reciter of Qur'ān must pray at night, reciting what he can. As He says—Exalted is He, *Recite what you can of it.* [73:20] And he said—may God's blessings and peace be upon him, *He who keeps vigil with ten verses shall not be recorded among the forgetful. He who keeps vigil with a hundred verses shall be recorded among the humble. And he who keeps vigil with a thousand verses shall be recorded among those who will receive many* quintārs."[21]

Al-'Āmerī—may God have mercy on him—says in his *Bahjat*, "The reciter of the Qur'ān should complete it twice a month, once at night during his vigils, and once during the day." He adds, "And this is easy and to persevere in it is also easy." He has spoken the truth—may God have mercy on him. He who will succeed is he to whom God grants success.

The person who wishes to conclude the Qur'ān (*khatm*) should do so at the beginning of the night or the day, to give time to the angels to pray for him. There is a tradition to the effect that he who concludes the Qur'ān by night, the angels will pray for him until morning, or by day, they will pray for him until evening. There is every goodness and happiness in the prayers of the angels for the servant, which consist in asking God to forgive him and to grant him all good things.

---

20. Aḥmad, *Musnad*, (6337); Al-Hakim, *Mustadrak,* (1994); Bayhaqī, *Shu'ab al-Īmān*,(1938).

21. Abū Dāwūd, *Sunan*, (1190); Bayhaqī, *Shu'ab al-Īmān*, (2124); Ibn Ḥibbān, *Ṣaḥīḥ*, (2624).

He must make *du'ā'* in abundance at the time of completion, for it is a noble and blessed time when prayers are accepted and mercy descends. Imām al-Nawawī—may God have mercy on him—says, "He should devote much of his prayers at the time of completion to the wellbeing of all Muslims in every possible way." Then he quotes some of the prayers to be recited at the time of completing the Qur'ān. This is in his book *Al-Tibyān*, which is a most valuable and important book in which he has brought together an ample amount of the good manners necessary for both those who know the Qur'ān by heart and those who read it, such as they cannot do without.

One of the things that should be firmly held on to and persevered in, especially in these blessed times, is the blessed *ḥizb* that people have made a habit of reciting every day in many lands, after the morning prayer and between *Maghrib* and *'Ishā'*. It is known as the weekly *ḥizb,* is begun on Friday eve and completed on Thursday. It has been transmitted that 'Uthmān—may God be pleased with him—began reciting the Qur'ān on Friday eve and completed it on Thursday eve. The *ḥizb* we have mentioned conforms to this as regards its beginning and end, and is not far from what has been said concerning 'Uthmān—may God be pleased with him—and others of our predecessors, as for when and how much to recite. The jurist Abū 'Abdallāh ibn 'Abbād—may God have mercy on him—who wrote a commentary on the *Ḥikam*, mentioned this weekly *ḥizb* in one of his treatises, saying, "It is an excellent innovation (*bid'a*) onto which one must hold on firmly, especially in these times when care for the rites of religion has weakened." Things are as he said—may God have mercy on him.

However, he who perseveres in this blessed *ḥizb* should not forget two of its courtesies, as many have done. The first is not to confine his recitation of the Qur'ān to the *ḥizb*, for it is mostly recited in a group, the number of which may be large, so that the share of each of its individuals is small. He second is not to doze off while others are reading and only become aware of what is going on when they awaken him to take his turn. Others may talk to their neighbors and continue their conversation until their turn comes. This is not how it should be. On the contrary, this is blameworthy and repulsive, especially in a mosque, where speech other than the remembrance of God and recitation of His Book is extremely reprehensible. It has been transmitted that talking in a mosque consumes good deeds, just as fire burns dry wood. We have drawn attention to these two courtesies because we have seen many who read the *hizb*, yet seem unaware of them. He in whose presence the Book of God is being recited while he dozes off or engages in small talk is in a problematic state and perilous situation. He is as if turning away from the Book of God the Exalted, inattentive to it. So let him beware who fears God and respects His sacred things.

He who does not know the Book of God the Exalted by heart, let him listen to it frequently and be attentive. God—Exalted is He—says, *When the Qur'ān is recited, listen to it and be attentive, that you may find mercy.* [7:204] The Prophet—may God's blessings and peace be upon him—said, *To him who listens to a verse of the Book of God, a multiplied good deed is recorded. To him who recites it, it will be light on Resurrection Day.*[22] The injunction to listen is not confined to those who do not know the Qur'ān by heart, but to everyone. The Messenger of God—may God's blessings and peace be upon him—said to ibn Mas'ūd, *Recite to me.* He asked, "How can I recite to you, when it is upon you that it was sent down?" He said, *I desire to hear it from another.* So he recited to him, starting from the beginning of *sūrat'al-Nisā'*. When he reached, *How then shall it be, when We bring from every community a witness, and bring you to witness against those?* [4: 41] At this point the Prophet said, *Enough*, and they saw tears streaming from his eyes.[23] The Prophet—may God's blessings and peace be upon him—listened to the recitation of ibn Mas'ūd and that of Sālim, Abū Ḥudhayfa's servant, then praised God for raising in his community one like him. He also listened, accompanied by Abū Bakr and 'Umar, to the recitation of ibn Mas'ūd, then said, *He whom it would please to recite the Qur'ān as fresh as when it was sent down, let him recite it emulating the recitation of ibn Umm 'Abd.*[24] Ibn Umm 'Abd being ibn Mas'ūd—may God be pleased with them all.

It is important to persevere in reciting those *sūras* and verses of which the specific merits, abundant reward for reciting them, and encouragement to do so at specific times deserved mention in *ḥadīth*. An example is the recitation of *sūrat'al-Kahf* on Friday or Friday eve. The *ḥadīth* states that he who recites it thus is forgiven till the next Friday[25] and a light shines for him, extending from be-

22. Aḥmad, *Musnad,* (8138); Bayhaqī, *Shu'ab al-Īmān,*(1925).
23. Bukhārī, *Ṣaḥīḥ*, (4216, 4667); Muslim, *Ṣaḥīḥ*, (1332, 1333).
24. Ibn Māja, *Sunan*, (135); Aḥmad, *Musnad,* (35, 170, 256).
25. Al-Ḥākim, *Mustadrak,* (3349).

neath his feet to the sky, or in another version, *light shines for him between him and the Ancient House.*[26] It has also been transmitted that he who learns by heart the first ten verses of *sūrat'al-Kahf* shall be protected from the Impostor (*dajjāl*) whenever he appears.[27]

As for *sūrat'al-Baqara*, the Prophet—may God's blessings and peace be upon him—said, *Recite* sūrat'al-Baqara, *for to do so is a benediction, to neglect it brings remorse, and evil people are incapable of it.*[28] And, *The house in which* sūrat'al-Baqara *is recited is not approached by a devil for three days.*[29]

Another example is the blessed *Ya-sīn*. He said—may God's blessings and peace be upon him, Ya-sīn *is the heart of the Qur'ān. No man shall recite it, desiring God and the Last Abode, without his being forgiven.*[30] And, *He who recites it is as if he has recited the Qur'ān ten times.*[31]

Another is to recite *sūrat Tabārak (al-Mulk)* every night. He said—may God's blessings and peace be upon him, *It is beneficial and saves from the torment of the grave.*[32] *I wish it were in the heart of every believer.*[33] *It once interceded for a man and he was forgiven.*[34] He was accustomed—may God's blessings and peace be upon him—never to go to sleep at night before reciting *Alif-Lām-Mīm al-Sajda,* and *Tabārak'al-Mulk.*

Also, to recite *sūrat'al-Dukhān*. He said—may God's blessings and peace be upon him, *He who recites* Ḥā-Mīm al-Dukhān *at night is forgiven before morning.*[35]

And he said—may God's blessings and peace be upon him—of *sūrat'al-Waqi'a, He who recites it every night is never afflicted with poverty.*[36]

---

26. Bayhaqī, *Shu'ab al-Īmān*,(2345, 2903); Dārimī, *Sunan*, (3470).
27. Muslim, *Ṣaḥīḥ*, (1342, 5228); Abū Dāwūd, *Sunan*, (3764, 3765).
28. Muslim, *Ṣaḥīḥ*, (1337); Aḥmad, *Musnad,* (21126, 21136).
29. Bayhaqī, *Shu'ab al-Īmān*,(2285).
30. Aḥmad, *Musnad,* (19415); Ṭabarānī, *Kabīr*, (16905, 16931).
31. Dārimī, *Sunan*, (3479).
32. Tirmidhī, *Sunan*, (2815); Ṭabarānī, *Kabīr*, (12630).
33. Al-Ḥākim, *Mustadrak,* (2030); Bayhaqī, *Shu'ab al-Īmān*,(2404).
34. Aḥmad, *Musnad,* (7927).
35. Tirmidhī, *Sunan*, (2814).
36. Bayhaqī, *Shu'ab al-Īmān*,(2396, 2397, 2398); Haythamī, *Bughyat al-Bāḥith an Zawā'id al-Ḥārith*, (720).

And he said—may God's blessings and peace be upon him—of *sūrat Idhā zulzilat,* that it was the equivalent of half the Qur'ān.[37]

And he informed them of *sūrat Alhākum'ul-takāthur* that it was worth a thousand verses.[38]

And of *Qul huwa'llāhu aḥad, it is the equivalent of one third of the Qur'ān.*[39] And, *He who recites it ten times, a mansion is built for him in the Garden.*[40] It has been transmitted that one should recite it ten times after each ritual prayer, in addition to mornings, evenings, and before sleep. It has also been transmitted that it is to be recited together with the *Mu'awwidhāt* three times for protection from all kinds of harm or anxieties.

And he said—may God's blessings and peace be upon him—about the *Fātiḥa* that it is the greatest *sūra* in the Qur'ān, the seven paired ones and the immense Qur'ān,[41] that it had been revealed together with *Āyat'al-kursī* and the final two verses of *sūrat'al-Baqara* from a treasure under the Throne, that the *Fātiḥa* is good for whatever purpose it is recited for, and that it is a true curative invocation.

As for *Āyat'al-kursī,* it was transmitted that it is the supreme verse in the Qur'ān, that nothing stands between he who recites it after each obligatory prayer and the Garden but death, and that he who recites it before sleep cannot be approached by a devil until morning.

It has also been transmitted that he who recites the verses at the end of *sūrat'al-Baqara* at night, they will suffice him. He advised his companions—may God's blessings and peace be upon him, to teach them to their women and their children, saying that they constituted prayer, Qur'ān, and supplication all at once. And 'Alī—may God be pleased with him—said, "I know of no one who having accepted Islam, and being possessed of understanding, would sleep before reciting the last three verses of *sūrat'al-Baqara.*" The last three verses being the following, *To God belongs all that is in the heavens and earth. Whether you reveal what is in your souls or hide it, God shall ask you to account for it. He will forgive whom He*

37. Tirmidhī, *Sunan,* (2819); Al-Ḥākim, *Mustadrak,* (2033); Bayhaqī, *Shu'ab al-Īmān,* (2411).

38. Al-Ḥākim, *Mustadrak,* (2037); Bayhaqī, *Shu'ab al-Īmān,* (2414).

39. Bukhārī, *Ṣaḥīḥ,* (4627, 4628); Muslim, *Ṣaḥīḥ,* (1344, 1346).

40. Dārimī, *Sunan,* (3492); Ṭabarānī, *Kabīr,* (265), *Awsaṭ,* (286).

41. Bukhārī, *Ṣaḥīḥ,* (4114, 4622).

will, and torment whom He will. God has power over all things. The Messenger believes in what was sent down to him from his Lord, and the believers, each one believes in God and His angels, His Books, and His Messengers. 'We make no distinction between any of his Messengers and another', and they say, 'We hear and obey, your forgiveness O our Lord, to You is the final end.' God charges no soul save to its capacity, for it what it has earned and against it what it has deserved. 'Our Lord, take us not to task when we forget or err. Our Lord, charge us not with a burden such as You laid upon those before us. Our lord, impose not upon us that which we cannot bear. And pardon us, and forgive us, and have mercy on us, You are our protector, so give us victory over the disbelieving people.' [3:284-286]

The two verses meant by his saying—may God's blessings and peace be upon him, *he who recites them in any particular night, they shall suffice him.*[42] Are the last two of the above three verses. Scholars have said that the meaning of *they shall suffice him*, is that either they are enough to relieve his anxieties, or to constitute sufficient night vigil for him. Imām al-Nawawī—may God have mercy on him—says, "It is acceptable that it may mean both at the same time."

This subject, that of the merits of particular verses or *sūras*, is substantial and there is much textual evidence, well known to the learned, relating to it. The intention was to point out some of the more important things, that those who desire goodness may attain to the reward attached to it, as well as to protection and safety from affliction.

God it is who provides success and assistance. There is no lord and no divinity other than Him. God is our sufficiency and the best of guardians.

Remembrance

Know, O brothers—may God make us and you of those who remember Him in abundance, those whom neither possessions nor children distract from the remembrance of God-that remembering God the Exalted is one of the greatest injunctions, best devotions, and means most conducive to reunion. God says-and August is the Speaker, *Remember Me and I shall remember you. Thank Me and do not be ungrateful.* [2:152] And, *O believers! Remember God with*

42. Bukhārī, *Ṣaḥīḥ*, (3707, 4624); Muslim, *Ṣaḥīḥ*, (1340, 1341).

an abundant remembrance, and glorify Him mornings and evenings. [33:41,42] And, *Remember God within yourself, imploringly, fearfully, without raising your voice, mornings and evenings, and be not one of the forgetful.* [7:205] And, *Those who believe and whose hearts become tranquil with the remembrance of God; indeed it is by the remembrance of God that hearts find tranquility.* [13:28]

The Messenger of God—may God's blessings and peace be upon him—said, *God—Exalted is He—says, 'I am as My servant thinks of Me, and I am with him whenever he remembers Me. Whenever he mentions Me within himself, I mention him within Myself, and whenever he mentions Me in company, I mention him in a better company. Whenever he draws nearer to me by a hand-span, I draw nearer to him by an arm-span. Whenever he draws nearer to Me by an arm-span, I draw nearer to him by two arm-spans. And whenever he comes to Me walking, I come to him running.'*[43]

And he said—may God's blessings and peace be upon him, *Shall I inform you of which of your works is best, purest in the sight of your Sovereign, most elevating for your degrees, better for you than spending gold and silver, or encountering your enemy so that you cut off their necks and they cut off yours*? They said, "Yes!" He said, *The remembrance of God.*[44] And he said—may God's blessings and peace be upon him, *The Son of Adam never does anything more likely to save him from God's torment than the remembrance of God.*[45] And, *To remember God mornings and evenings is better than breaking your swords fighting in the way of God the Exalted and from spending money liberally.*[46] And, *The likeness of he who remembers God and he who does not is that of a man alive and another dead, or that of a green tree among dry ones. He who is remembering God amidst the forgetful is as he who stands his ground amidst those who flee.*[47]

The verses of the Qur'ān and the *ḥadīth*s enjoining the remembrance of God and detailing its merits are too numerous to exhaust.

Scholars—may God have mercy upon them—have said, "The best remembrance is that which involves both the heart and the

43. Bukhārī, *Ṣaḥīḥ*, (6856, 6982); Muslim, *Ṣaḥīḥ*, (4832, 4851).

44. Tirmidhī, *Sunan*, (3299); Ibn Māja, *Sunan*, (3780).

45. Aḥmad, *Musnad*, (21064); Bayhaqī, *Shu'ab al-Īmān*,(549, 551); Ṭabarānī, *Kabīr*, (16765).

46. Ibn Abī Shayba, *Muṣannaf*, vol.7, p.72; vol. 8, p. 235.

47. Bayhaqī, *Shu'ab al-Īmān*, (591, 592).

tongue. The remembrance of the heart alone is better than that of the tongue alone. I say: Remembrance of the heart means that it is present with either the form or the meaning of the invocation uttered by the tongue. In the first instance, when the invoker says with his tongue *Lā ilāha illa'llāh,* he should be repeating it within his heart simultaneously. In the second, the meaning of this noble utterance, which is that divinity is the exclusive prerogative of the Real, should be present in his heart.

The Proof of Islam—may God have mercy on him—says, "Remembrance is of four degrees: The first is that of the tongue only. The second is that of the tongue and heart together, but with the exertion of effort. The third is for the remembrance to become the attribute of the heart, so that it is effortlessly and constantly on the tongue. The fourth is for the Remembered to overpower the heart so that it becomes absorbed therein. The first degree, which is remembrance with the tongue while the heart is distracted, is of little benefit and feeble effect." This is undoubtedly so, but it is better than abandoning remembrance altogether. A certain Gnostic was once told, "We remember God, but achieve no presence." He replied, "Thank God for adorning one of your bodily organs [the tongue] with the remembrance of Him."

He who invokes God with his tongue should exert himself to achieve presence of the heart, so that he may be remembering with both, even if with difficulty at the beginning. Then let him persevere in this until such time as the heart tastes the pleasure of remembrance and the lights of it dawn upon it. When this happens, presence will be effortless and easy. He may even reach the stage when he can no longer bear to abandon remembrance or allow himself to be distracted from it.

Now know—may God have mercy on you—that there are courtesies to be observed during remembrance and that the most important and necessary is presence of the heart. So strive for it, for the invoker attains to almost none of the intended benefits and results of remembrance without presence.

Among the good manners of remembrance are also that the invoker maintain utmost courtesy, proper outward as well as inward demeanor, and complete cleanliness and ritual purity. He should be humble, full of awe before the majesty of God, facing the *Qibla*, his head ever bowed down and his body as still as during the ritual prayer.

The servant, being required to remember God at all times and in all situations, may be able to maintain the above mentioned good manners all the time, as for instance those in spiritual retreat or permanent service to God the Exalted. But more often than not this is not possible, so he must assign a time for remembrance when he may sit with all the required good manners, those we mentioned as well as others in the same vein. At all other times he should still remember God without limits or conditions, whether he is standing up, sitting, or lying down. As God—Exalted is He—says, *So remember God, standing, sitting, and on your sides.* [4:103] Let him beware of being distracted from remembrance at any time, for this is immensely harmful. The Prophet—may God's blessings and peace be upon him—said, *He who sits for a while without remembering God the Exalted, it will bring him remorse; and he who lies down for a while without remembering God the Exalted, it will bring him remorse.*[48] Remorse means regrets coupled with grief, or regrets on the day when one is asked to account. The Devil may influence the distracted and be able to control him, because he is forgetful of his Lord. As He says—Exalted is He, *He who blinds himself to the remembrance of the All-Merciful, we shall assign a devil for him, who shall be his companion.* [43:36] And, *The Devil has gained mastery over them and made them forget the remembrance of God.* [58:19]

It is natural to the believer to remember God in abundance, just as it is the attribute of the hypocrite to remember Him but a little. God—Exalted is He—says concerning the hypocrites, *They show off to the people, but remember God but a little.* [4:142]

Persevering in remembrance and being constant drives the Devil away and stops its whisperings. It has been transmitted that, *The Devil has his trunk over the heart of the son of Adam so that whenever he remembers God he retreats, but whenever he is distracted he gobbles up his heart.*[49]

It is most important to keep to the remembrance of God and persevere throughout the day and in most circumstances. When a man said to the Prophet—may God's blessings and peace be upon him, "O Messenger of God, the injunctions of Islam are too numerous for me, so enjoin upon me a single thing that I can hold on to firmly."

48. Abū Dāwūd, *Sunan*, (4215, 4400); Bayhaqī, *Shu'ab al-Īmān*, (571, 572).

49. Bayhaqī, *Shu'ab al-Īmān*, (567).

He answered, *Keep your tongue ever moist with the remembrance of God.*[50]

Scholars—may God have mercy on them—have always considered that remembrance had more merit and priority over other kinds of good works, because one can practice it all the time and under any circumstance. It has no set times, but is required at all times. It can be practiced by the ritually impure, whether the impurity is minor (*ḥadath*) or major (*janāba*), as well as by those who are free and those who are occupied, which thing does not apply to other devotions such as ritual prayer, fasting, or reciting the Qur'ān, for these have prior conditions and there are times when they are not allowed. The best of all good works is the ritual prayer, yet is forbidden during about a third of the day, from after the dawn prayer until the sun rises high above the horizon, and from after the afternoon prayer until sunset. As for fasting, it is forbidden in other than the daytime, while reciting the Qur'ān is forbidden during major ritual impurity, and discouraged when one is occupied with worldly things so that he cannot collect his heart. This is because of the Qur'ān's sacredness and majesty. Remembrance on the other hand was left unrestricted by God the Exalted, as a mercy to His servants and a favor, together with making it lighter and less arduous compared with other devotions. Because of all that, remembrance is superior to other devotions, although some are superior to it in other respects. It is special to remembrance to be light despite its merits and to be capable of being practiced uninterruptedly, to the extent that when in a situation where to invoke God with the tongue is inappropriate, in the bathroom or during intercourse for example, one should nevertheless avoid being too distracted to remember God in one's heart. So have said the scholars who have knowledge of God—may God have mercy on them.

Therefore persevere in constant remembrance—may God have mercy on you—whether you are a craftsman, a manual worker, or otherwise engaged in worldly affairs. Keep to remembrance in your heart and with your tongue as much as you are able to.

When you remember God the Exalted in your heart, which means allowing none to hear but yourself, you have done well and hit the mark. The Prophet—may God's blessings and peace be upon him—said, *The best remembrance is that which is hidden and the*

50. Tirmidhī, *Sunan*, (3297); Ibn Māja, *Sunan*, (3783).

best provision is that which suffices.[51] The noble verse states, *Remember your Lord in yourself, imploringly and fearfully, without raising your voice, mornings and evenings.* [7:205]

Should you raise your voice with remembrance, being sincere with God, not distracting to others who might be praying or reciting the Qur'ān to the extent of causing them confusion, then there is no harm in raising your voice. It is not forbidden, on the contrary it is recommended. This may be done in a group that has gathered for the remembrance of God. If they conform with the conditions we mentioned earlier, namely sincerity and not distracting others who are praying, or engaged in something similar, then this recommended and encouraged. There are *ḥadīth*s to that effect. He said—may God's blessings and peace be upon him, *No group of people ever gather to remember God the Exalted, intending it to be solely for Him, without His forgiving them and turning their bad deeds into good ones.* [52] And, *No group of people ever sit together in a house of the houses of God, remembering God the Exalted, without the angels surrounding them, mercy enveloping them, peace descending upon them, and God mentioning them to those who are with Him.*[53] And, *Whenever you pass by the meadows of the Garden, revel in them.* They asked, "What are the meadows of the Garden?" He answered, *The circles of remembrance.* [54] Another version says, *Teaching sessions.*[55] Also, in the long *ḥadīth* which begins with, *God has angels roaming the earth, searching for sessions of remembrance…* He says at the end, *God says to the angels, "I ask you to bear witness that I have forgiven them, given them what they have requested, and protected them from what they have sought protection from.' The angels say, 'Among them is so and so, a sinful servant who happened to be passing by and joined them.' He will say—Exalted is*

51. Aḥmad, *Musnad*, (1397, 1477, 1537); Ibn Ḥibbān, *Ṣaḥīḥ*, (810); Bayhaqī, *Shu'ab al-Īmān*, (578, 579, 9982).
52. Aḥmad, *Musnad*, (12000); Bayhaqī, *Shu'ab al-Īmān*, (562, 714); Ṭabarānī, *Kabīr*, (5907); *Awsaṭ*, (1614).
53. Muslim, *Ṣaḥīḥ*, (4867, 4868); Abū Dāwūd, *Sunan*, (1243); Ibn Māja, *Sunan*, (221).
54. Aḥmad, *Musnad*, (12065); Bayhaqī, *Shu'ab al-Īmān*, (557); Tirmidhī, *Sunan*, (3432).
55. Ṭabarānī, *Kabīr*, (10995).

He, 'They are the people whose companions never suffer wretchedness.[56] This *ḥadīth* is very well-known.

Some Sufis have opted for remembrance aloud and in congregation, and their manners of doing this are well-known. Others have opted for silent remembrance. They have all been granted good patterns and straight paths from their Lord. May God have mercy on them and grant others to benefit from them.

Sufis acknowledge no equal to the remembrance of God. Upon it they depend and with it they are constantly occupied, once they have discharged their obligations satisfactorily and avoided forbidden things. They enjoin it upon their disciples and those who tread their path, and they take their oaths that they will persevere in it and make it their constant companion. Of the conditions and courtesies in the path, the most important and necessary is the remembrance of God.

There are many kinds of remembrance, each having its own immense merits and reward. There are numerous benefits there, as well as noble results and effects.

The most noble and superior of all invocations is *Lā ilāha illa'llāh*. The Prophet—may God's blessings and peace be upon him—said, *The best remembrance is* lā ilāha illa'llāh*, and the best* du'ā' *is* al-ḥamdu li'llāh.[57] And, *The best thing that I and the Prophets before me have said is* lā ilāha illa'llāhu waḥdahu la sharīka lah.[58] And, speaking for God the Exalted, he said, "Lā ilāha illa'llāh *is My fortress and he who enters My fortress shall be safe from My torment.*"[59] And he said—may God's blessings and peace be upon him, *Renew your faith.* They asked, "How shall we renew our faith?" He answered, *Frequently repeat* lā ilāha illa'llāh.[60] And he said—may God's blessings and peace be upon him, Subḥān'Allāh *fills half the scales*, al-ḥamdu li'llāh *fills them fully, and there is no veil between* lā ilāha illa'llāh *and God.*[61] A *ḥadīth* also says that a pillar of light stands before God the Exalted. When someone says *lā ilāha illa'llāh* this pillar trembles and when God the Exalted says,

56. Bukhārī, *Ṣaḥīḥ*, (5929); Tirmidhī, *Sunan*, (3524).
57. Tirmidhī, *Sunan*, (3305); Ibn Māja, *Sunan*, (3790); Bayhaqī, *Shu'ab al-Īmān*, (4201).
58. Imām Mālik, *Muwaṭṭa'*, (449, 841); Tirmidhī, *Sunan*, (3509).
59. Al-Shihāb al-Quḍā'ī, *Musnad al-Shihāb*, (1329).
60. Aḥmad, *Musnad,* (8353); Al-Ḥākim, *al-Mustadrak,* (7766).
61. Tirmidhī, *Sunan*, (3440).

"Be still!" it answers, "How can I be still when You are yet to forgive he who has uttered it." God the Exalted says, "I have forgiven him." Only then will it cease to move.[62] Another *ḥadīth* says that no servant says *lā ilāha illa'llāh*, day or night, but that it erases evil deeds from his record, until it finds a good deed and nestles against it.[63] And that, *Were the seven heavens and the seven earths and what they contain on one side of the scales and* lā ilāha illa'llāh *on the other,* lā ilāha illa'llāh *would outweigh them.*[64]

Much that is very well known has been handed down concerning the merits of this sentence. The intention here is to give examples, not to be exhaustive. It is sufficient to know that it is the word a human being enters Islam with and that whose life is concluded with it at the time of death wins perpetual bliss and will no longer be subject to unhappiness. O God! O Generous One! We ask You to make us live, die, and be resurrected saying *lā ilāha illa'llāh* with sincerity, as also our two parents, our loved ones, and all Muslims, *Āmīn*!

About *lā ilāha illa'llāhu waḥdahu lā sharīka lahu, lahu'l-mulku, wa lahu'l-ḥamdu, wa huwa 'alā kulli shay'in qadīr*, the Prophet—may God's blessings and peace be upon him—said that he who utters it ten times is as if he had freed from slavery four souls of the descendants of Ishmael—may peace be upon him.[65] And he who utters it a hundred times in one day it shall be equivalent for him to setting free ten slaves, a hundred good deeds are inscribed in his record, a hundred bad ones erased, it shall protect him from the Devil until evening, and none shall have done better save one who had repeated it more times.[66] And he said—may God's blessings and peace be upon him, "Saying *lā ilāha illa'llāhu waḥdahu lā sharīka lahu, lahu'l-mulku, wa lahu'l-ḥamdu, wa huwa 'alā kulli shay'in qadīr* cannot be outstripped by any other work, nor does it leave a sin remaining."[67]

Among the best and most comprehensive formulae of remembrance is saying *Subḥān'Allāhi, wa' l-ḥamdu lillahi, wa lā ilāha*

---

62. Haythamī, *Majma' al-Zawā'id*, vol. 4, p.366.
63. Abū Ya'lā, *Musnad*, (3514).
64. Aḥmad, *Musnad,* (6295, 6804); Al-Ḥākim, *al-Mustadrak,* (144, 1891); Ibn Ḥibbān, *Ṣaḥīḥ*, (6324); Nasā'ī, *Al-Sunan al-Kubrā*, (10670, 10980).
65. Muslim, *Ṣaḥīḥ*, (4859); Nasā'ī, *Al-Sunan al-Kubrā*, (9948).
66. Bukhārī, *Ṣaḥīḥ*, (3050, 5924); Muslim, *Ṣaḥīḥ*, (4857).
67. Ibn Māja, *Sunan*, (3787); Ṭabarānī, *Kabīr*, (7409); *Awsaṭ*, (7909).

illa'llāhu, wa'llāhu akbar. It has been handed down that he said—may God's blessings and peace be upon him—that it was the most superior of words and the best liked by God the exalted.[68] And he said—may God's blessings and peace be upon him, *For me to say* Subḥān'Allāhi, wa' l-ḥamdu lillāhi, wa lā ilāha illa'llāhu, wa'llāhu akbar *is dearer to me than all that is under the sun.*[69] And, *I met Abraham—may peace be upon him—on the night I was made to journey, and he said, 'O Muḥammad! Greet your community with* salām *on my behalf and inform them that the Garden's soil is fragrant and its water sweet, that it is made of plains, and that they are planted with* Subḥān'Allāhi, wa' l-ḥamdu lillāhi, wa lā ilāha illa'llāhu, wa'llāhu akbar.[70] And he said of these four words that he who utters them, for each of them a tree is planted in the Garden. And he said—may God's blessings and peace be upon him—to Abū'l-Dardā'—may God be pleased with him, *Say* Subḥān'Allāhi, wa' l-ḥamdu lillāhi, wa lā ilāha illa'llāhu, wa'llāhu akbar, wa lā ḥawla wa lā quwwata illā bil'llāhi'l-'Aliyyi'l-'Aẓīm, *for these are the subsisting good things, and they cause sins to be cast off just as a tree casts off its leaves,*.[71] He also said of *lā ḥawla wa lā quwwata illa bil'llāhi'l-'Aliyyi'l-'Aẓīm* that it is a treasure from the Garden[72] and a remedy for ninety nine ailments, the least of which is worrying.[73] And he said—may God's blessings and peace be upon him, that he to whom God has granted a favor and he wishes it to endure should repeat with frequency *lā ḥawla wa lā quwwata illa bil'llāhi'l-'Aliyyi'l-'Aẓīm.*

One of the best invocations is *subḥān'allāhi wa biḥamdih.* He said—may God's blessings and peace be upon him, *The best loved words to God are* subḥān'allāhi wa biḥamdih.[74] And when asked which word was best? He answered—may God's blessings and

68. Ibn Ḥibbān, *Ṣaḥīḥ*, (837, 1844).
69. Muslim, *Ṣaḥīḥ*, (4861); Tirmidhī, *Sunan*, (3521).
70. Tirmidhī, *Sunan*, (3384).
71. Rāmhurmuzī, *Al-Amthāl*, (96); Ibn Shāhīn, *Faḍā'il al-A'māl,* (477). The *ḥadīth* without *Lā ḥawla wa lā quwwata illā bi'l-llāh* is in Aḥmad, *Musnad,* (11288, 17630); Al-Ḥākim, *Mustadrak,*(1843, 1943); Ibn Māja, *Sunan*, (3803).
72. Bukhārī, *Ṣaḥīḥ*, (3883, 5905, 6838); Muslim, *Ṣaḥīḥ*, (4873, 4875).
73. Al-Ḥākim, *Mustadrak,*(1948); Ṭabarānī, *Kabīr*, (1274); *Awsaṭ*, (956, 5185).
74. Muslim, *Ṣaḥīḥ*, (4911); Aḥmad, *Musnad,* (20459).

peace be upon him, *That chosen by God for His angels*, subḥān'allāhi wa biḥamdih.[75] And he said *For he who says* subḥān'allāhi'-'aẓīmi wa biḥamdih *a palm tree is planted in the Garden.*[76] *For he who says it a hundred times, a thousand good deeds are recorded and a thousand evil ones cast off.*[77] And, *He who says, morning and evening,* subḥān'allāhi wa biḥamdih *a hundred times, none shall bring a better deed on Resurrection Day save he who has said it an equal or greater number of times.*[78] And he said, *Two words, light on the tongue, heavy in the scales, beloved to the All-Merciful*, subḥān'allāhi wa biḥamdih, subḥāna'llāhi'l-'Aẓīm.[79]

The Mother of the Faithful, Juwayriya—may God be pleased with her—said that the Prophet—may God's blessings and peace be upon him—once went out of her house, then returned at midmorning and found her still sitting glorifying God. He said, "Are you still in the same state I left you in?" She answered, "Yes." He said, "I have said four words three times after leaving you. Were they to be weighed against all that you have said since this morning, they would outweigh it, *subḥāna'llāhi wa biḥamdihi 'adada khalqihi, wa riḍā nafsihi, wa zinata 'arshihi, wa midada kalimātih.'*"[80]

Other invocations that are of great goodness, blessings, and immense merits and reward are *istighfār*, invocations of blessings on the Chosen Prophet, and *du'ā'*.

As for *istighfār* (asking for forgiveness), God says of its merits-and August is the Speaker, *God shall never torment them so long as you are amidst them and He shall never torment them so long as they ask for forgiveness.* [8:33] And, *And ask forgiveness of your Lord, then repent to Him, and He will grant you good things to enjoy until a designated time, and He will give of His favor to every person of grace. But if you turn, I fear for you the torment of a momentous day.* [11:3] And He recounts—Exalted is He—on behalf of

75. Muslim, *Ṣaḥīḥ*, (4910); Aḥmad, *Musnad,* (20549); Tirmidhī, *Sunan*, (3517).

76. Ibn Ḥibbān, *Ṣaḥīḥ*, (827); Tirmidhī, *Sunan*, (3386,3387); Al-Ḥākim, *Mustadrak,*(1801,1842).

77. Muslim, *Ṣaḥīḥ*, (4866); Tirmidhī, *Sunan*, (3385); Aḥmad, *Musnad,* (20746).

78. Muslim, *Ṣaḥīḥ*, (4858); Tirmidhī, *Sunan*, (3391); Aḥmad, *Musnad,* (8479, 8480).

79. Bukhārī, *Ṣaḥīḥ*, (5927, 6188); Muslim, *Ṣaḥīḥ*, (4860).

80. Muslim, *Ṣaḥīḥ*, (4905).

His Prophet Noah—may peace be upon him, *So I said, 'Ask forgiveness of your Lord, for He is ever forgiving, and He will loose the sky upon you in torrents, and give you wealth and sons, and give you gardens and give you rivers.* [71:10, 11,12] And, *And he who does evil or wrongs himself, then asks forgiveness of God, he shall find God forgiving, Compassionate.* [4:110]

The Prophet—may God's blessings and peace be upon him—said, *He who perseveres in asking forgiveness, God shall grant him relief from all worries, a way out from every difficulty, and shall send him provision from whence he never expected it.*[81] And, *Blessed is he in whose record shall be found abundant pleas for forgiveness.*[82] He also said that he *who says, 'I ask God for forgiveness' seventy times a day, seven hundred sins will be forgiven him; and those men and women are failures indeed who commit more than seven hundred sins a day.*[83] And he said—may God's blessings and peace be upon him, *By God! I ask God for forgiveness and repent to him more than seventy times every day.*[84] And, *Shall I inform you of your ailment and your remedy? Your ailment is but your sins, and your remedy is the remembrance of God.*[85] And, *Iblīs has said, 'By Your might and majesty O lord, I shall never cease to tempt Your servants so long as their spirits remain in their bodies.' God said, 'By My might and majesty, I shall never cease to forgive them so long as they ask Me for forgiveness.'*[86]

'Abdallāh ibn 'Umar said, We used to keep count and found that the Messenger of God—may God's blessings and peace be upon him—said more than a hundred times each session *rabbi'ghfir li wa tub 'alayya, innaka anta't-tawwābu'r-raḥīm.*[87] This is why you must—may God have mercy on you—repeat with great frequency this blessed invocation that the Messenger of God—may God's blessings and peace be upon him—considered of such a high degree.

81. Abū Dāwūd, *Sunan*, (1297); Ibn Māja, *Sunan*, (3809).
82. Ibn Māja, *Sunan*, (3808).
83. Bayhaqī, *Dalā'il al-Nubuwwa*, (2960); Abū Nu'aym al-Aṣbahānī, *Ma'rifat al-Ṣaḥāba*, (3459, 3699,6451).
84. Bukhārī, *Ṣaḥīḥ*, (5832); Tirmidhī, *Sunan*, (3182).
85. Bayhaqī, *Shu'ab al-Īmān*, (10244).
86. Aḥmad, *Musnad,* (10814, 10940); Al-Ḥākim, *Mustadrak,*(7782).
87. Abū Dāwūd, *Sunan*, (1295); Ibn Māja, *Sunan*, (3804).

It has reached us that Imām Aḥmad ibn Ḥanbal—may God have mercy on him—was seen after his death in a dream vision saying that God had granted him to profit much from a few words he had heard from Sufyān al-Thawrī—may God have mercy on him, "O God! O Lord of all things, by Your power over all things, forgive me everything, and ask me to account for nothing." Therefore, do repeat with frequency these blessed words too.

It has also been handed down that he who asks God twenty seven times every day for forgiveness for all men and women believers becomes one of those servants by whose *baraka* people find mercy, rain is sent down upon them, and their provisions reach them. These are the attributes of the *Abdāl* among men of God and virtuous servants.

As for invoking blessings upon the Messenger of God—may God's blessings and peace be upon him—its merits are immense and its benefits for those who do it with frequency are abundant in this world. God—Exalted is He—says, *God and His angels bless the Prophet. O believers! Invoke blessings upon him and salute him with peace.* [33:56] How greatly does God honor and exalt His Prophet in this verse, and how emphatically does He encourage His believing servants to invoke blessings and peace upon him.

He said—may God's blessings and peace be upon him, *He who invokes blessings upon me one time, God blesses him ten times.*[88] A certain authoritative scholar—may God have mercy on him—said, "Were God to bless a servant once only in his lifetime, it would be sufficient honor and dignity. How much more so should He bless him ten times for each single invocation of blessings upon His Prophet?" May God be praised for the immensity of His favor and the abundance of His gifts. He said—may God's blessings and peace be upon him, *He who invokes blessings upon me once, God blesses him ten times, raises him by ten degrees, inscribes ten good deeds in his record, and removes ten evil ones.*[89] And, *Those who shall have the most rights upon me on Judgment Day are those who invoke blessings upon me most.*[90] And, *He who says, 'O God! Bless*

88. Muslim, *Ṣaḥīḥ*, (616); Abū Dāwūd, *Sunan*, (1307); Nasā'ī, *Sunan*, (1279).

89. Aḥmad, *Musnad*, (15759); Bayhaqī, *Shu'ab al-Īmān*, (1519); Nasā'ī, *Sunan*, (1280); Ṭabarānī, *Kabīr*, (17961).

90. Tirmidhī, *Sunan*, (4426); Ibn Ḥibbān, *Ṣaḥīḥ*, (913); Abū Ya'lā, *Musnad*, (4881); Bayhaqī, *Shu'ab al-Īmān*, (1526); Ṭabarānī, *Kabīr*, (9679).

Muḥammad and grant him the seat nearest to You on Judgment Day,' he has deserved my intercession.[91] And, *'He who says, "May God reward Muḥammad on our behalf as befits Him,' he shall have tired out seventy scribes for a thousand mornings.*[92] And, *Invoke blessings upon me wherever you are, for your blessings shall reach me.*[93]

It has been handed down that God has angels roaming the earth to convey to the Prophet—may God's blessings and peace be upon him—the greetings of those of his community who invoke blessings upon him,[94] and that none of his community salutes him without God returning his noble spirit back to him so that he may answer them. Shaykh ibn Ḥajar says in *al-Durr al-Manḍūḍ*, "It has been handed down that the Prophet said, *None shall ever salute me with peace without God returning my spirit to me so that I may salute him back.*"[95] It has also been handed down that God salutes with peace ten times he who salutes the Prophet, just as for he who has invoked blessings upon him. He said—may God's blessings and peace be upon him, *He will be disgraced he before whom I am mentioned and who does not invoke blessings and peace upon me.*[96] And, *He before whom I am mentioned, but who fails to invoke blessings upon me, he has missed his way to the Garden.*[97]

He has bid us—may God's blessings and peace be upon him—invoke blessings upon him in great abundance on Fridays in particular, saying—may God's blessings and peace be upon him, *Invoke blessings upon me in abundance on Fridays, for the blessings of my community shall be presented to,*[98] And, *Invoke blessings upon me*

91. Aḥmad, *Musnad*, (16377); Bazzār, *Musnad*, (2030); Ṭabarānī, *Kabīr*, (4353, 4354); *Awsaṭ*, (4313).
92. Ṭabarānī, *Kabīr*, (11347); *Awsaṭ*, (240).
93. Ṭabarānī, *Kabīr*, (2663); *Awsaṭ*, (372).
94. Aḥmad, *Musnad*, (3993, 4093); Ibn Ḥibbān, *Ṣaḥīḥ*, (961); Nasā'ī, *Sunan*, (1265).
95. Abū Dāwūd, *Sunan*, (1745); Aḥmad, *Musnad*, (10395).
96. Aḥmad, *Musnad*, (7139); Tirmidhī, *Sunan*, (3468).
97. Ṭabarānī, *Kabīr*, (2818); *Awsaṭ*, (372).
98. Abū Dāwūd, *Sunan*, (883, 1308); Aḥmad, *Musnad*, (15575); Ibn Māja, *Sunan*, (1075, 1626); Nasā'ī, *Sunan*, (1357).

during the noble night and radiant day.[99] Meaning Friday eve and day.

Therefore, every believer should invoke blessings in abundance upon the Messenger of God—may God's blessings and peace be upon him—but even more so on Friday eve and Friday. He should join salutations of peace to the blessings, for God has enjoined both upon us. A *ḥadīth* states that God—Exalted is He—addressed the Prophet—may God's blessings and peace be upon him—thus, *He who invokes blessings upon you, I shall bless him, and he who salutes you with peace, I shall salute him.*[100]

He who invokes blessings and peace upon his Prophet should also include his family, for the Prophet—may God's blessings and peace be upon him—desires this for them and *ḥadīth*s have been handed down to this effect. A weak transmission states that the invocation of blessings upon the Prophet but not his family is called the 'incomplete invocation'. And God knows best.

As for prayer (*du'ā'*), God has prescribed, commanded, and encouraged it. He says—August is the Noble Speaker, *Call upon your Lord imploringly and fearfully, He likes not the aggressors. Corrupt not the earth after it was made good and call upon Him in fear and hope. The mercy of God is near to those who act with excellence.* [7:55,56] And, *To God belong the most beautiful names, so call upon Him using them.* [7:180] And, *Your Lord says, 'Call upon Me and I will answer you.'* [40:60] And, *He is the Living, there is no God but He, so call upon Him, making religion His with sincerity. Praise belongs to God, Lord of the worlds.* [40:65]

The Prophet—may God's blessings and peace be upon him—said, *Prayer (du'ā') is all of worship.*[101] And, *Prayer is the weapon of the believer, the pillar of religion, and the light of the heavens and earth.*[102] And, *Destiny is overcome only by prayer; and nothing lengthens life save benevolence.*[103] And, *Prayer is the marrow*

99. Bayhaqī, *Shu'ab al-Īmān*, (2898); Ṭabarānī, *Kabīr*, (260); *Awsaṭ*, (246).

100. Aḥmad, *Musnad*, (1574, 1575); Al-Ḥākim, *Mustadrak,* (770, 1977).

101. Abū Dāwūd, *Sunan*, (1264); Aḥmad, *Musnad*, (17229, 17660); Ibn Māja, *Sunan*, (3818); Tirmidhī, *Sunan*, (2895, 3170).

102. Abū Ya'lā, *Musnad*, (419); Al-Ḥākim, *Mustadrak,* (1766).

103. Aḥmad, *Musnad*, (21379); Tirmidhī, *Sunan*, (2065); Ibn Māja, *Sunan*, (87, 4012).

of worship.[104] And, *Do not be feeble in prayer, for none shall ever perish who prays.*[105] And, *Prayer is of benefit for things that are happening and things that are yet to happen.*[106] And, *Call upon God while certain of being answered, and know that God does not answer the prayer of a heart that is distracted and oblivious.*[107]

The Prophet—may God's blessings and peace be upon him—commanded us to pray emphatically and forcefully, not to say, "O God! Forgive me if You wish." But to ask assertively, eagerly, insistently, with the certainty of being answered, presence of heart with one's Lord, fearful of being denied the answer because of one's distraction and shortcomings in fulfilling the rights of one's Lord, yet hopeful to be answered and obtain one's wishes in the knowledge that God's generosity is complete and His promise true. It has been transmitted that God is shy and generous. He is shy of the servant who raises his hands to Him, to send him back empty handed. And also that none ever asks God without being answered. He may receive his request immediately, or greater hardship is prevented from reaching him, or his prayer is saved for him to receive in the life to come in a better and more perfect form.

Thus a person should be constantly praying and imploring, whether in times of affluence or need, ease or hardship. He should never think that the answer is too slow appearing, nor should he despair. God the Exalted may have a hidden purposes and benefits in delaying certain matters, and the person may be destined to obtain even more profit from whence he did not expect it. Let him pray and commit the matter to God. Also, whenever he asks his Lord for anything, let him ask simultaneously for gentleness, well-being, and a good ending. Let him ask God for every single thing he wants-provided it should be pleasing to Him-of the affairs of this world or the next, whether important or insignificant. He should not neglect to make his food *ḥalāl*, for it is one of the most important conditions for prayers to be answered. A *ḥadīth* describes a *man who travels for long periods, is unkempt and dusty, who raises his hands to heaven, 'O Lord! O Lord!' yet his food is illicit, his clothes illicit, he is sus-*

104. Tirmidhī, *Sunan*, (3293); Ṭabarānī, *Awsaṭ*, (3324).
105. Al-Ḥākim, *Mustadrak,*(1772); Ibn Ḥibbān, *Ṣaḥīḥ*, (872).
106. Aḥmad, *Musnad*, (21033); Tirmidhī, *Sunan*, (3471).
107. Aḥmad, *Musnad*, (6368); Al-Ḥākim, *Mustadrak,*(1771); Tirmidhī, *Sunan*, (3401).

taining himself on the illicit, how can he possibly be answered?[108] One of the predecessor once said, "Prayer is like a key, the teeth of which are licit morsels of food."

A person should never neglect to pray, whether in times of hardship or ease. The Prophet—may God's blessings and peace be upon him—said, *Make yourself known to God in times of affluence that He may know you in times of hardship.*[109] And, *He whom it would please to be answered by God when hardships and afflictions strike, let him pray in abundance in times of ease.*[110]

On the whole, prayer is one of the greatest favors of God upon His servants. He enjoined it upon than and encouraged them to do it, to the extent that He—August and Majestic is He—becomes angry with those who do not ask of Him. As he said—may God's blessings and peace be upon him, *He who fails to pray God the Exalted, He becomes angry with him.*[111]

A person should pray for goodness and safety from evils for himself, his two parents, his loved ones, and all Muslims. Let him beware to the extreme from praying against himself, his children, his wealth, or any servant of God. Should someone wrong him, let him leave him to God and be content with God's support for him. A *ḥadīth* says, *He who prays against he who has wronged him, he has already taken what is due to him.*[112]

There is no good in evil prayers against an iniquitous person, or any other for that matter. On the contrary, one should pray for him, for this is the attribute of God's compassionate servants.

'Ā'isha—may God be pleased with her—said that the Prophet—may God's blessings and peace be upon him—always preferred comprehensive, complete prayers, using no other. Among such comprehensive Prophetic prayers are the following:

O God! I ask You for well-being in this world and the next.

O God! Make good the endings of all our affairs, and protect us from humiliation in this world and torment in the next.

---

108. Muslim, *Ṣaḥīḥ*, (1686); Tirmidhī, *Sunan*, (2915).

109. Aḥmad, *Musnad*, (2666); Al-Ḥākim, *Mustadrak,*(6364); Bayhaqī, *Shu'ab al-Īmān*, (1089).

110. Al-Ḥākim, *Mustadrak,*(1955); Tirmidhī, *Sunan*, (3304).

111. Tirmidhī, *Sunan*, (3295).

112. Tirmidhī, *Sunan*, (3475).

O God! Make my provision licit and beneficial, and my behavior righteous.

O God! Inspire me with my right-guidance and protect me from the evil in myself.

O God! I ask You for right-guidance, piety, continence, and independence from need.

O God! As You have given me an excellent form, give me an excellent character.

O God! Make my inward better than my outward, and make my outward virtuous.

O God! I ask You for knowledge that is profitable, provision that is licit and beneficial, and works that are acceptable [to You].

O God! Make the best of my lifetime its final portion, the best of my works their concluding ones, and the best of my days that on which I meet You.

O God! Show me the truth as true and grant me to follow it, and show me falsehood as false and grant me to avoid it.

O God! Hide us when we slip and assuage our terrors.

O God! Grant us good in this world, good in the next, and protect us from the torment of the Fire.

Begin prayer by praising and thanking God, and extolling Him, then invoke blessings and peace upon the Prophet and his family. Close your prayers in the same manner, then say, '*Amīn*!'

Let every servant be abundant in asking for well-being in this life and the next. The *ḥadīth* says, *God is never asked for anything more pleasing to Him than well-being in this world and the next.*[113] This is one of the best and most comprehensive prayers.

God it is who grants success.

Many invocations and prayers of the Messenger of God—may God's blessings and peace be upon him—have been handed down. Some of these were designated for specific times or situations, others were unconditional. The Prophet—may God's blessings and peace be upon him—bequeathed them to his community, encourag-

113. Al-Ḥākim, *Mustadrak,*(1787); Tirmidhī, *Sunan*, (3437).

ing it to use them, that they may cause them to obtain all goodness and be safe from the evils and afflictions that occur by the will of God the exalted at certain times and situations. Those who persevere in them will be saved and secure. They are those who shall win and obtain everything. Those who neglect them, let them blame only themselves. Your Lord is never unjust to the servants. Imām al-Nawawī—may God have mercy on him—has collected a good number of those in his book *al-Adhkār*, to which he has adduced explanations and clarifications, valuable rules, and important observations, such as to reassure the heart and dilate the breast. May God reward his efforts and recompense him well on behalf of all Muslims. The author of *'Uddat al-ḥiṣn al-ḥaṣīn* has also collected a profitable number of these—may God have mercy on him. We have also arranged for our companions a brief collection-blessed by God the Exalted's will-of the invocations specific to mornings and evenings.

Chapter Eight: On Enjoining Good and Forbidding evil

Know—O brothers, may God make us and you of those who uphold justice and enjoin it—that enjoining good and forbidding evil is one of the greatest pillars of religion and most important responsibilities for believers. Thus does God command, both in His Book and on the tongue of His Messenger—may God's blessings and peace be upon him—urging and encouraging it, and severely forbidding abandoning it. He says—Exalted is He, *Let there be from among you a community who invite to benevolence, enjoining good, and forbidding evil. Those shall be successful.* [3:104] And, *You are the best community brought out for mankind, you enjoin good, forbid evil, and believe in God.* [3:110] And, *Believing men and women are allies of one another. They enjoin good, forbid evil, establish the ritual prayer, pay the* zakāt, *and obey God and His Messenger. Those shall be shown mercy by God. God is indeed August, wise.* [9:71 And, *Those of the Children of Israel who disbelieved were cursed by the tongue of David and Jesus, son of Mary, because of their disobedience and transgressions. They forbade not one another the reprehensible things they committed. Evil indeed was what they used to do.* [5:78,79]

The Messenger of God—may God's blessings and peace be upon him—said, *When one of you sees something reprehensible, let him change it with his hand, if he cannot then with his words, if he cannot, then with his heart, and this is the weakest degree of faith.*[1] And, *O people! Enjoin good and forbid evil, before you pray but are not answered, and ask forgiveness, but are not forgiven.*[2]

Enjoining good and forbidding evil does not prevent your sustenance from reaching you, nor does it bring nearer your appointed time. When the Jewish rabbis and Christian monks abandoned enjoining good and forbidding evil, they were cursed by their Prophets, after which they were flooded with afflictions. He said—may God's blessings and peace be upon him, *The best* jihād *is a word of*

---

1. Muslim, *Ṣaḥīḥ*, (70); Abū Dāwūd, *Sunan*, (963); Ibn Māja, *Sunan*, (1265); Tirmidhī, *Sunan*, (2098).
2. Ibn Māja, *Sunan*, (3994); Tirmidhī, *Sunan*, (2095).

truth to a tyrannical ruler.[3] And when he was asked who the best of people were, he answered, *Those who fear their Lord most, preserve their kinship bonds best, and are most active in enjoining good and forbidding evil.*[4]

It has reached us that God once punished a whole town, the population of which was eighteen thousand whose works were akin to those of Prophets, except that they never became angry for God.

It has now become clear why there is no permission to neglect enjoining good and forbidding evil so long as it is practically possible. He who neglects it and takes it lightly will have scorned one of the rights of God and shown disrespect toward what He has declared sacrosanct. Such a person's faith is weak and he is scarcely afraid or shy of God. If his silence is caused by his eagerness for worldly things, greed for wealth or social eminence, or fear that should he enjoin good and forbid evil his position will be weakened and influence lost with those sinners and wrongdoers that he speaks to, then his own sin is great. But if his silence is due to his belief that he would expose himself to harm, whether this will affect his own person or his possessions, then it is permissible for him to keep silent, but on condition that this expected harm is seriously damaging and certain to occur. Should he proceed to enjoin good and forbid evil despite this, his wage would be immense and his reward abundant. It would constitute proof of his love for God, his giving Him priority over his own self, and his extreme zeal in serving His religion. As He says—Exalted is He, *And enjoin good and forbid evil, and bear what is afflicting you with patience. These are among the hardest of things.* [31:17]

How excellent is the state of a person who is beaten, imprisoned, or insulted for upholding the rights of his Lord, enjoining His obedience, and forbidding His disobedience. This used to be the pattern of the Prophets and Messengers, virtuous saints, and practicing scholars, as is recorded in their stories and described in their biographies. There is no good in cowardice or weakness that prevent one from supporting religion and opposing the unjust and the corrupt, to drive them back toward the obedience of the Lord of the worlds. Anger for God and jealousy when His commands are flouted and that is committed which He has forbidden and rebuked from are

3. Abū Dāwūd, *Sunan*, (3781); Ibn Māja, *Sunan*, (4001); Nasā'ī, *Sunan*, (4138); Tirmidhī, *Sunan*, (2100).

4. Bayhaqī, *Shu'ab al-Īmān*, (7718).

the attributes of Prophets and *Ṣiddīqūn*. This is how they were described, how they were known to be, what they became famous for. It has been handed down that the Prophet—may God's blessings and peace be upon him—never became angry for personal reasons, rather it was when the sacrosanct limits of God were trespassed that nothing stood before his anger. He said—may God's blessings and peace be upon him—concerning 'Umar ibn al-Khaṭṭāb, *He speaks the truth, and among people he has no friend.* God—Exalted is He—says in describing His loved ones among believers, *Humble towards the believers, proud towards the disbelievers, struggling in the way of God, fearing not the reproaches of those who would reproach them.* [5:54]

It has now become clear how the complete believer cannot control his feelings whenever he witnesses reprehensible things being committed, but must change them, unless prevented from doing so by an overpowering cause. As for the hypocrites and those whose faith is very weak, whenever they witness blameworthy things, they come up with feeble excuses that are unacceptable to God and His Messenger—may God's blessings and peace be upon him. Yet when they are insulted or unjustly deprived of some of their possessions, you see them reacting violently and remaining resentful for long periods. None of this is ever shown toward those who are persistently unjust, corrupt, and neglectful of the rights of God the Exalted. On the other hand, the behavior of sincere believers is quite the opposite. They become angry for God, not for their own selves, they stop their dealings with those who are disobeying God and neglecting His orders, and they dispute with them when they deny the truth, but they forgive and let go when the insult or wrong affects them personally. Observe how the two parties are different from each other, then join the better and more upright of the two. *Seek God's help and be patient. The earth belongs to God and He bequeaths it to whom He will among His servants. The ultimate end belongs to the God-fearing.* [7:128]

Enjoining good and forbidding evil is a collective (*kifāya*) obligation, which means that when some Muslims do it, the others are relieved of the obligation and no blame is attached to them. However, the reward goes only to those who were engaged in it. When the obligation is not fulfilled, all those will share in the sin and censure who were aware of blameworthy things being committed and were capable of stopping them, either by direct action or by exhortation, but did not do so.

Once a blameworthy thing is witnessed the first thing to do is to explain how wrong it is to the perpetrators, then to exhort them with gentleness, tact, and compassion to desist. If they do not respond then they should be admonished, frightened [with God's punishment], spoken harshly to, and rebuked. Finally one resorts to physical intervention to put an actual end to the evil being committed.

The first two degrees, that of teaching with gentleness, and that of admonishing, and frightening, concern everyone and are generally possible. He who pretends he is incapable of them usually comes up only with untenable excuses. As for the third degree, that of putting a stop to evil by force and physical intervention, it can be done only by he who has given himself over to God the Exalted, struggles with his wealth and self in the way of God, and fears no reproaches, or by those who are so authorized by the government.

In brief, a person should do what he can, should not neglect to support God's religion, and should not seek a way out by coming up with unacceptable excuses that do not relieve him from the obligation imposed upon him by God the Exalted.

Know that gentleness, tact, mercy, and compassion are most important when enjoining good and forbidding evil, so keep to them and never swerve away from them so long as you believe that the intended goal can thus be achieved. The *ḥadīth* states, *Gentleness never comes into anything without embellishing it, nor is it removed from anything without blemishing it.*[5] And it has been transmitted that only those should enjoin good and forbid evil that are gentle in enjoining, gentle in forbidding.

A person should always comply with what he is enjoining and refrain from what he is forbidding, for this is how his words will have an effect on hearts and will be taken seriously. This is the better and more worthy course of action. Severe threats have been proffered against those who enjoin good but do not practice it and forbid evil but commit it. However, one should enjoin good and forbid evil even when one does not practice what one preaches, for he who knows but neither practices what he knows, nor teaches

5. Muslim, *Ṣaḥīḥ*, (4698); Abū Dāwūd, *Sunan*, (2119).

it, is worse and deserves more punishment than he who teaches without practicing. And God knows best.

Beware—O brothers—of compromise (*mudāhana*) in religious matters. This is to refrain from enjoining good and forbidding evil, and from proclaiming the truth or supporting justice, because anxious to please others in the expectation of obtaining something from them, money, influence, or any other worldly profit. Seldom has anyone done this without God abasing and humiliating him, causing others to wrong him, and depriving him of that which they possess and he covets. On the other hand, maneuvering (*mudārā*) is permissible. This is that a person may give away something of his worldly possessions to protect his religion, worldly affairs, or his honor from the slander of evil people. A *ḥadīth* says, *That which a man expends to protect his honor is for him a charity.*[6] Thus there is neither harm nor censure for a person to protect himself from the evil of evil persons by giving away whatever he needs to give, provided it causes him no religious harm. However, keeping away from evil people is better and more cautious. The above mentioned things apply only when one becomes afflicted with such people without having brought it on himself, for otherwise a God-fearing believer is not permitted to keep company with people of evil and falsehood, on the contrary he should avoid them and be wary of them.

Also beware of spying, which is seeking to know the hidden shameful private affairs of others. God—Exalted is He—says, *Do not spy*, and the Prophet—may God's blessings and peace be upon him—said, *He who seeks to bring out the shameful things of his brother, God shall bring out his shameful things, and he whose shameful things God brings out, He will expose him, even were he in the innermost part of his house…*"[7]

You should keep hidden the shameful things of Muslims, not talk about them or spread the news around. God—Exalted is He—says, *Those whom it pleases to see indecency spread among believers, theirs shall be a painful punishment in both this world and the hereafter.*[24:19] And he said—may God's blessings and peace be upon him, *He who shields a Muslim* [from scandal], *God will shield him in this world and the hereafter.*[8]

6. Al-Ḥākim, *Mustadrak,*(2272); Bayhaqī, *Shu'ab al-Īmān*, (10309).
7. Aḥmad, *Musnad*, (18963, 21368); Tirmidhī, *Sunan*, (1955).
8. Bukhārī, *Ṣaḥīḥ*, (2262); Muslim, *Ṣaḥīḥ*, (4677,4867).

Only a hypocrite, loathed by God, will always be talking of the faults, failings, and shameful things of other people.

Should he witness a fault in his brother, the duty of a Muslim is to keep it hidden and to counsel him in private, gently and tactfully. For, *God shall keep helping the servant so long as the servant is helping his brother.*[9]

He who witnesses a blameworthy thing that he has no power to change or forbid should detest he who is committing it and detest his act in his heart. As he said—may God's blessings and peace be upon him, *if he cannot, then with his heart.*[10] He should detest those of his relatives who persistently commit sins and he should leave their place, for to witness evil things by choice is not permissible. He who is told to refrain from a blameworthy act but does not respond and persists in it must be boycotted until he desists and repents to his Lord. He said—may God's blessings and peace be upon him, *One of the strongest bonds of faith is to love for God and hate for God.*[11]

Let those who are being enjoined good and forbidden evil beware to the extreme from arrogance, haughtiness, and rejecting the truth; or of saying to he who is counseling them, "See to yourself first!" or any other similar utterance explicitly rejecting the truth. It is to be feared for such persons that God shall loathe them, that His wrath will afflict them, and that their state shall be similar to him whom God describes thus, *And when he is told fear God, arrogance seizes him in his sin. Hell shall be enough for him and an evil ending place it is.* [2:206] As for him who is offering the counsel, this does not affect him at all, on the contrary, when he is rejected his reward will be greater, so let him be patient and bear with fortitude. Let his intention be to deliver both himself and his brother from sin. Let his attitude be that of one whose brother Muslim is in peril, threatened with drowning or burning for instance, when he is capable of saving him. He should be even more committed, for damaging one's religious affairs and exposing oneself to the wrath of the Lord of the Worlds is immensely more perilous than to lose worldly goods or even one's life. The consequence of the latter is only to leave this ephemeral life, this evanescent abode. There is no comparison whatsoever between

9. Bukhārī, *Ṣaḥīḥ*, (2262); Muslim, *Ṣaḥīḥ*, (4677,4867).

10. Muslim, *Ṣaḥīḥ*, (70).

11. Bayhaqī, *Shu'ab al-Īmān*, (12, 13).

ruining one's religion and ruining one's worldly affairs. He who is enjoining good and forbidding evil is striving to save himself, whether his exhortations are accepted or not. It has reached us that on Judgment Day some men will cling onto others who, not knowing them, will say, "What is it with you? We do not know each other!" To which they will reply, "You saw us doing wrong but never counseled us." The *ḥadīth* says, *The likeness of he who upholds the limits of God and he who trespasses them is that of a boat on which are people. They drew lots, some got to stay on deck, others below. Whenever those below wished to draw water they were forced to pass between those on deck. They said, 'Shall we drill a hole in our section* [of the boat] *so that we can draw water without annoying those above?' Should they then allow them to proceed with what they want, they would all perish. But if they prevent them forcefully from doing so, the two groups will be saved.*[12] The meaning is that he who enjoins and forbids does so for his own good, for he strives to save himself from the burden of sin that God would make him carry should he refrain to do so while capable of it. He hopes for God's reward and the generous promise He made to those who would support His religion and uphold it. He says, Exalted is He, *God shall surely support he who supports Him. God is indeed Strong, August.* [22:40] And, *O believers! If you support God, He will support you and make your feet firm.* [47:7]

Among the most incumbent and important good manners of enjoining good and forbidding evil are to avoid arrogance, harshness, derision, and gloating over the sinners [should something afflict them], for these things cancel reward and attract punishment. They may cause the truth to be rejected and may prevent people from accepting and responding to it. So beware of them to the extreme! Be gentle, affectionate, flexible, compassionate, humble, and modest. God it is who grants success and support. Trust should be placed in Him and dependence should be upon Him.

We have already discoursed on enjoining good and forbidding evil at the beginning of this book when commenting on His saying—Exalted is He, *Let there be a group from among you who invite to benevolence, enjoin good, and forbid evil. Those are the successful.* [3:104] We may have repeated some of that in this chapter, for it is the appropriate time to do so and may lead to increasing conviction. This is also because of our earnest wish to

12. Bukhārī, *Ṣaḥīḥ*, (2313).

influence hearts in a beneficial way, for this matter is essential and bears much elaboration and even repetition, so immense is its place in religion and so general its benefit which extends to all Muslims, and in such a dire need are they for it. This is even more so because so may people have taken to treating the matter lightly for no good excuse, people who would have exposed themselves to no harm doing it. This is what has prompted us to discourse at length and repeat ourselves. Deeds are valued according to the intentions and to each person what he has intended.

Chapter Nine: On *Jihād*

We have thought it appropriate to quote here some of the Qur'ānic verses and *ḥadīths* concerning *Jihād* and its merits in order to complete the benefit to be derived from the subject, for *Jihād* is a division of enjoining good and forbidding evil, but it is the highest, and the most noble and superior division, because it is enjoining the highest good, which is *Tawḥīd* and Islam, and forbidding the worst evil, which is disbelief and associating others with God.

Jihād begins with an invitation to Islam, before progressing to fighting with the sword.[1] So many verses and *ḥadīths* exist concern-

---

1. When Imām al-Haddād discourses on *Jihād*, it is implicitly assumed that people know they are required to take arms against external aggressors, under the banner of a legitimate ruler, and in conformity with the injunctions of the Qur'ān and *Sunna*. This taken for granted, he freely encourages people never to hesitate whenever taking up arms is required, quoting much of the textual evidence concerning the merits of fighting for the sake of God. Moreover, in his days, the old state of affairs still subsisted whereby everyone who thought himself able to was busy invading other people, seizing their riches, and creating empires. Nowadays, however, texts are quoted out of context so frequently both by Muslim extremists and non Muslim adversaries that one is forced to make explicit what used to be implicit which is that Islam does indeed enjoin *jihād* against enemies, but according to a set of rules that those who fight must abide by on pains of forsaking their status as God-fearing men and falling into major sin. One such rule is to resort to war only when attacked or threatened with impending aggression. Another is that the moment the enemy desists from aggression and sues for peace it is granted. The third is that civilians are not to be harmed. A review of the verses of the Qur'ān which mention fighting make this abundantly clear. The first verse which commands Muslims to fight also makes it clear that it should be against those who fight them and that aggression is forbidden. *Fight for the sake of God those that fight against you, but aggress not.... God loves not the aggressors.* [2:190] When the aggressors cease hostilities, the instructions become as follows, *But if they give over, then let there be no hostility except against violators.* [2:193] In *sūrat al-Nisā'* the instructions are as follows, *So if they keep away from you and wage not war against you and offer you peace, then God allows you no way against them... If they keep not away from you, nor offer you peace, nor cease their hostilities against you, then seize them and kill them wherever you come upon them. Against these We have granted you a clear authority.* [4:90, 91]

In case of impending conflict, Muslims are commanded to prepare as best as they can. This preparation may deter the enemy from attacking, in which case if they wish for peace it must be granted them. *And prepare for them whatever force and strings of horses you can, that you may put fear into the enemy of God, your enemy... But if they incline toward peace, incline to it, and place your trust in God, for He is the Hearing the Knowing.* [8:60,61] Permission is granted to fight those who do not honor their treaties with the Muslims. *If they break their oath after their treaty and thrust at your religion, then fight the leaders of disbelief—for they have no binding oaths—that they may give over. Will you not fight a people who broke their oaths and wished to drive out the Messenger and attacked you first?* [9:12,13] War is a hateful thing and Muslims must be forced into it, not undertake it with relish. The Prophet said, *O Men! Desire not to meet the enemy and ask God for safety; but if you do encounter them, then be steadfast and know that the Garden is under the shadows of the swords.* [Bukhārī, *Ṣaḥīḥ*, 2965] He repeatedly forbade them to harm women, children, the elderly and the sick, as well as monks and hermits. Whenever he sent a force on expedition he commanded them to fear God and forbade them to steal from the booty, then he forbade them, among other things, treachery, mutilation, and killing children, or hermits in their cells. [Abū Dāwūd, *Sunan,* 2614; Aḥmad, *Musnad,* 2728; Muslim, *Ṣaḥīḥ*, 1731] Abū Bakr, the first caliph, gave the following instructions to his commanders as he sent them out, "I enjoin ten things upon you: never kill a child, a woman, or an old man, never cut down a fruit bearing tree, do not bring ruin to places that are alive, do not hamstring a sheep or a camel except to eat, do not drown or burn palm trees, do not appropriate any of the spoils illegally, and do not behave cowardly." [Ibn Abī Shayba, *Muṣannaf,* 33121] When sending an army into agricultural territory, 'Umar, the second caliph, remembered to forbid them to harm the farmers, since they were not fighting men. [Ibn Abī Shayba, *Muṣannaf,* 33120] Islam forbids attacking those who respect their treaties. *So long as they are true to you, be true to them; for God loves the God-fearing.* [9:7] There is no question of forcing anyone to accept Islam. *There is no coercion in religion. Rectitude has become distinct from error.* [2:256] Those who are at peace with the Muslims are to be treated according to the Islamic code of courtesy and justice. *God does not forbid you to be kind and equitable to those who neither make war on your religion, nor expel you from your homes. God loves those who are equitable. God only forbids you to take for friends those who fight against you in religion's cause and expel you from your homes, or help others do so.* [60:8,9] The Prophet said, *He who kills a person with whom there is a treaty shall never smell the fragrance of the Garden, even though its fragrance can be*

ing *Jihād* that they would be too numerous to exhaust. Therefore, we shall briefly quote some, simply for the *baraka* of discoursing on this noble principle of religion, one with which God has honored Islam and Muslims and humiliated idolatry and idolaters. God—Exalted is He—says, *Prescribed for you is fighting, though it be hateful to you. Yet you may hate a thing when it is better for you, or love a thing when it is worse for you. God knows and you know not.* [2:216] And, *Fight them until there is no persecution and religion becomes all God's.* [2:193] And, *God has preferred those who fight over those who stay with an immense reward; degrees from Him, forgiveness, and mercy. God is ever Forgiving, Compassionate.* [4:95, 96] And, *Take them, confine them, and lie in wait for them at every place of ambush. Should they repent, perform the prayer, and pay the* zakāt, *then let them go their way.* [9:5] And, *Those who have believed, emigrated, and fought in the way of God with their possessions and their selves are greater in rank with God. Those they are the winners. Theirs are glad tidings from their Lord of mercy from Him, good pleasure, and gardens where they shall find permanent bliss, immortal therein. With God indeed is an immense wage.* [9:20-22] And, *Go forth, light and heavy, and struggle with your possessions and selves in the way of God. This is better for you, if you but knew.* [9:41] And, *Permission is given to those who fight because they have been wronged, and God is indeed capable of helping them.* [23:39] And, *God has bought from the believers their selves and their possessions against the gift of the Garden, that they fight in the way of God, slay and be slain. That is a promise binding upon God in the Torah, the Gospel, and the Qur'ān, and who fulfills his promises more truly than God? So rejoice in the transaction you have made with Him, that is the immense triumph.* [9:11]

The Messenger of God—may God's blessings and peace be upon him—said, *Fight the idolaters with your possessions, your selves, and your words.*[2]

When asked which works are best, he answered—may God's blessings and peace be upon him, *Belief in God and* Jihād *in the*

---

experienced at a distance of forty years. [Bukhārī, *Ṣaḥīḥ*, 3166, 6914] *The wealth of those with whom there is a treaty is forbidden....* [Abū Dāwūd, *Sunan,* 3806] *He who has a treaty with a people, let him not tie a knot, or untie it, unless they break it or he warns them that he is about to do it.* [Abū Dāwūd, *Sunan*, 3806]

2. Aḥmad, *Musnad*, (11798, 12097,13146); Nasā'ī, *Sunan*, (3045,3141).

way of God.[3] When asked the same question on another occasion, he answered, *Belief in God and His Messenger*. They asked, "Then which?" He answered, Jihād *in the way of God*. They asked, "Then which?" He answered, *An accepted pilgrimage.*[4] He also said—may God's blessings and peace be upon him, *Go forth in the way of God. To him who fights in the way of God for a time equal to that between twice milking a she-camel, the Garden becomes due.*[5]

Abū Sa'īd al-Khudrī—may God be pleased with him—said, "A man once came to the Messenger of God—may God's blessings and peace be upon him—asking, 'Who are the best among people?' He answered, *A believer who struggles with his person and his possessions in the way of God.* The man asked, 'Then whom?' He answered, *Then a believer who worships God in a remote glen, sparing the people his evil.*[6]

He also said—may God's blessings and peace be upon him, *A day standing guard in the way of God is better than this world and what is in it. A piece of the Garden the size of one of your whips is better than this world and what is in it. For the servant to go on a sortie in the way of God, morning or evening, is better than this world and what is in it.*[7] And, *God has given His guarantee to he who goes out for His sake that: should he go out purely for My sake, for his faith in Me and belief in My Messengers, I shall either admit him to the Garden, or return him to his house from which he set out laden with whatever wage or spoils he has obtained. By He in whose hand the soul of Muḥammad is, none of you shall ever be wounded in the way of God without coming on Resurrection Day with the blood looking the color of blood, but the odor that of musk. By He in whose hand the soul of Muḥammad is, were it not for my reluctance to distress the Muslims, I would never have stayed behind an expedition setting out in the way of God the exalted, but I find not the means to provide them all with mounts, nor are they able to provide them for themselves, and it would distress them that I should leave them behind. By He in whose hand the soul of Muḥammad is, I wish*

3. Muslim, *Ṣaḥīḥ*, (119).
4. Bukhārī, *Ṣaḥīḥ*, (25, 1422); Muslim, *Ṣaḥīḥ*, (118).
5. Tirmidhī, *Sunan,* (1574).
6. Bukhārī, *Ṣaḥīḥ*, (2578, 6013); Muslim, *Ṣaḥīḥ*, (3501, 3502).
7. Bukhārī, *Ṣaḥīḥ*, (2678); Tirmidhī, *Sunan,* (1587).

I could fight in the way of God, be slain, fight and be slain again, then fight and be slain again.[8]

When asked, "O Messenger of God, is there anything that equals *Jihād*?" He answered, *You will not be able to bear it.* They asked him again and received the same answer. The third time he answered, *The likeness of one who fights in the way of God is that of one who is constantly fasting, praying, humbly reciting the verses of God, never slackening in his prayers and fasts until the fighter in the way of God comes back.*[9]

And he said—may God's blessings and peace be upon him, *There are in the Garden a hundred degrees prepared by God the Exalted for those who fight in the way of God, the distance between each two degrees being equal to that between the sky and the earth.*[10] And, *Never will the Fire touch a servant whose feet have become dusty in the way of God.*[11] And he said—may God's blessings and peace be upon him, *He who has wept for the fear of God will never enter the Fire unless milk returns into the udder; and the dust raised in the way of God is never coupled with the fumes of Hell in the nostrils of a Muslim.*[12] And, *Two eyes will not be touched by the Fire: an eye that has wept for the fear of God and another who has kept vigil, standing guard in the way of God.*[13] And, *To shoot an arrow in the way of God is equivalent to setting free a slave.*[14] And, *He who keeps a horse to ride in the way of God because he has faith in God and believes in His promise,* [the horse's] *fodder, water,* [and even] *dung, and urine shall be in his scales on Judgment Day.*[15] Which means that these shall be considered good deeds to his credit.

There are immense merits and rewards in expending in the way of God and assisting the fighters. He said—may God's blessings and peace be upon him, *He who equips a warrior fighting in the way of God, he has fought; and he who takes care of an absent war-*

8. Muslim, *Ṣaḥīḥ*, (3484); Aḥmad, *Musnad,* (6860); Bayhaqī, *Shu'ab al-Īmān*, (4071).
9. Muslim, *Ṣaḥīḥ*, (3490).
10. Bukhārī, *Ṣaḥīḥ*, (2581).
11. Bukhārī, *Ṣaḥīḥ*, (2600).
12. Aḥmad, *Musnad,* (10156); Nasā'ī, *Sunan*, (3056,3062).
13. Tirmidhī, *Sunan,* (1563); Al-Ḥākim, *Mustadrak,* (2388); Bayhaqī, *Shu'ab al-Īmān*, (809, 4070).
14. Nasā'ī, *Sunan*, (3092); Tirmidhī, *Sunan,* (1562).
15. Bukhārī, *Ṣaḥīḥ*, (2641); Nasā'ī, *Sunan*, (3526).

rior's family, he has fought.[16] A man once came to the Messenger of God, may blessings and peace be upon him, bringing a bridled she-camel, saying, "This is in the way of God." The Prophet said, *You will be given for it on Judgment Day seven hundred she camels, all bridled.* [17] And he said, *He who expends in the way of God, it shall be recorded for him seven hundredfold.*[18] And he said that, *He who expends on a fighter without himself taking part in the battle, he will receive seven hundred* Dirhams *for each* Dirham *spent; and he who expends to equip himself for battle, he will receive seven hundred thousand* Dirhams *for each* Dirham.[19]

Standing guard in the way of God has immense merits. He said—may God's blessings and peace be upon him, *Standing guard one day in the way of God is better than a thousand days anywhere else.*[20] And it has been handed down that he who dies standing guard continues to receive his wage until Judgment Day and is spared the questioning in the grave.[21]

As for the merits of martyrdom in the way of God, they are so tremendous that they cannot be counted and so honorable and great that their limits and quantities are beyond encompassing. God—Exalted is He—says, *Think not that those who were slain in the way of God are dead, on the contrary they are alive with their Lord, by Him provided, rejoicing in what God has given them of His favor, and joyful in those who have not joined them, but remained behind, that no fear shall be on them, neither shall they grieve.* [3:169, 170] And, *Those who are slain in the way of God, He will not send their works astray. He will guide them, and assuage their minds, and admit them to the Garden that He has made known to them.* [47:4-6] And the Prophet—may God's blessings and peace be upon him—said, *The martyr is given six special things by God: He is forgiven with the first gush of his blood, sees his seat in the Garden, is adorned with the beautiful attributes of faith, is protected from the torment of the grave, is safe from the Greater Terror, has the Crown of Dignity placed upon his head, each of its rubies being better than this world and what it contains, is given seventy two wide eyed maidens for*

16. Bukhārī, *Ṣaḥīḥ*, (2631); Muslim, *Ṣaḥīḥ*, (3511).
17. Muslim, *Ṣaḥīḥ*, (3508); Nasā'ī, *Sunan*, (3136).
18. Nasā'ī, *Sunan*, (3135); Tirmidhī, *Sunan,* (1550).
19. Ibn Māja, *Sunan*, (2751).
20. Nasā'ī, *Sunan*, (3118); Tirmidhī, *Sunan,* (1590).
21. Nasā'ī, *Sunan*, (2116); Tirmidhī, *Sunan,* (1546).

his wives, and is granted to intercede for seventy of his relatives.[22] And he said—may God's blessings and peace be upon him, *There is nothing that God loves more than two drops and two traces: a tear-drop spilled for the fear of God and a drop of blood spilled in the way of God. As for the two traces, they are a trace in the way of God and another in an obligation prescribed by God.*[23] And he said—may God's blessings and peace be upon him, *The martyr feels the pain of being slain no more than one of you feels an insect bite.*[24]

A *ḥadīth* says that the spirits of martyrs are within green birds, eating from the fruits of the Garden, drinking from its rivers, then retiring to lanterns hanging from the Throne.[25] Another says that the martyr wishes to return to the world to be slain again ten times over, because of the merits of martyrdom that he is witnessing.[26]

When the Prophet—may God's blessings and peace be upon him—was asked, "Why are all people questioned in the grave except the martyr?" He answered, *The flashing of swords over his head is sufficient as a trial for him.*[27]

One of the most important and incumbent things for the fighter in the way of God is sincerity in fighting for God, intending nothing but His sake—Exalted is He—the support of His religion, and the supremacy of His Words. No other purpose should enter into this, such as being seen by others, being talked about by them and respected, the spoils that might be won, or any other worldly purpose. He said—may God's blessings and peace be upon him, *He who goes on a sortie in the way of God intending no more than to obtain a camel hobbling cord, he will receive no more than what he intended.*[28] A man once asked, "O Messenger of God! I stand in the rank intending it to be for the sake of God, but also that I may be seen there." He received no answer until the following verse was revealed, *He who looks forward to the meeting with his Lord, let him do good works and associate no other in his Lord's worship.*

22. Aḥmad, *Musnad,* (16553); Tirmidhī, *Sunan*, (1586).
23. Tirmidhī, *Sunan,* (1592).
24. Ibn Māja, *Sunan,* (2792); Nasā'ī, *Sunan*, (3110); Tirmidhī, *Sunan,* (1591).
25. Muslim, *Ṣaḥīḥ*, (3500); Abū Dāwūd, *Sunan*, (2158); Tirmidhī, *Sunan,* (2937).
26. Nasā'ī, *Sunan*, (3109); Aḥmad, *Musnad,* (11892).
27. Nasā'ī, *Sunan*, (2026).
28. Nasā'ī, *Sunan*, (3087, 3088); Aḥmad, *Musnad,* (21634, 21669).

[18:110][29] It was also asked, "O Messenger of God! A man may fight for the spoils, a man for renown, and a man so as to be noticed. Which of those is in the way of God?" He answered, *He who fights to make the Word of God supreme, he is in the way of God.*[30] And in the *ḥadīth* where the Prophet—may God's blessings and peace be upon him—mentions the three who shall be the first of God's creatures to feed the Fire, he said, *and a man who having been slain in the way of God is brought* [on Judgment Day] *and God enumerates his favors upon him, then asks him what he had done with them. He replies, 'I have fought in Your way until I was slain.' God will say, 'You lie! All you wanted is for it to be said: "He is valiant," and it was said.' Then he is ordered to be dragged on his face and thrown into the Fire.*[31] And he said—may God's blessings and peace be upon him, *Most of the martyrs of my community die in their beds. How many a man was slain between the ranks, but his intention is known only to God.*[32]

The fighter should beware to the extreme from ostentation and desiring anything other than the sake of God. Let him restrict his intention to God and be careful to make it even purer when in battle. Let him be greatly concerned with setting his intention right, lest he be slain while his sincerity is tainted, which thing will cause his works to fail, his wage to be revoked, and his end to be evil—may God protect us-and his situation to be extremely perilous.

Another thing that the fighter should be extremely wary of is to flee from battle at a time when it cannot possibly be permissible. The Prophet—may God's blessings and peace be upon him—considered this a ruinous thing, one of the greatest of major sins. He said—may God's blessings and peace be upon him, *There are three things in the presence of which good works avail nothing: Associating with God, disloyalty to the two parents, and fleeing from battle.*[33]

He should also beware of illegally appropriating something of the spoils, for the sin of this is immense. The Messenger of God—may God's blessings and peace be upon him—cautioned strongly against it. Illegally appropriating something is to take something

29. Al-Ḥākim, *Mustadrak,* (2481, 8057); Bayhaqī, *Shu'ab al-Īmān,* (6588).

30. Bukhārī, *Ṣaḥīḥ*, (2599, 2894); Abū Dāwūd, *Sunan*, (2156).

31. Tirmidhī, *Sunan,* (2304).

32. Aḥmad, *Musnad,* (3584).

33. Ṭabarānī, *Kabīr*, (1404).

from the spoils to oneself, to the exclusion of the other fighters, without their knowledge or approval. And God knows best.

Every Muslim should intend *Jihād* and think about it in his mind, so as to escape the threats proffered against those who do not. He said—may God's blessings and peace be upon him, *He who dies without having taken part in a sortie or having desired to do so, he will die with some hypocrisy in him.*[34]

One should also ask insistently for martyrdom. He said—may God's blessings and peace be upon him, *He who asks God for martyrdom with sincerity, God will cause him to attain to the degrees of the martyrs even if he dies in his bed.*[35]

O God! Cause us to be of those who fight in Your way with their possessions and their selves, desiring Your good pleasure, Your favor and gifts, O Generous One!

We have discoursed on this subject briefly for the *baraka* and good augury of discoursing on *Jihād*, for our reluctance to leave the book without any mention of it, and our wish that some Muslims will read it and see virtuous desire for it aroused in himself, we shall thus have gained some of the reward reserved for the fighters. The authentic *ḥadīth* says, *He who points out a good thing is as he who does it,*[36] *and he who enjoins right guidance shall receive a wage similar to that of those who obeyed him, without this diminishing their own wages in any way.*[37] My success comes only from God, upon Him do I rely and to Him do I turn repentant.

You are now aware O brother—may God have mercy on you—of the merits of struggling in the way of God and its place in religion. He who is able to should therefore hasten to participate in *Jihād*. Let him be resolute and determined, and avoid indolence and neglect. He who is unable to, let him make the intention, be abundant in his prayers for those who fight, help them as much as he can, and occupy himself with struggling against his ego and passions to make them obedient to his Lord and Guardian, for this is part of *Jihād*. He said—may God's blessings and peace be upon him, *The fighter is he who fights his passion for the sake of God, and the emigrant is he*

---

34. Muslim, *Ṣaḥīḥ*, (3533); Abū Dāwūd, *Sunan*, (2141).

35. Muslim, *Ṣaḥīḥ*, (3532); Abū Dāwūd, *Sunan*, (1299); Tirmidhī, *Sunan,* (1577).

36. Abū Dāwūd, *Sunan*, (4464); Tirmidhī, *Sunan,* (2594).

37. Muslim, *Ṣaḥīḥ*, (4831); Abū Dāwūd, *Sunan*, (3993); Tirmidhī, *Sunan,* (2598).

who leaves that which God has forbidden him.[38] And it has reached us that he said to one of his Companions as they returned from an expedition, *You have returned from the smaller* Jihād *to the greater* Jihād, *the struggle against the ego.*[39]

Among the most perilous of major sins and most formidable of ruinous crimes is for Muslims to fight each other for power and kingship, worldly goods, and the fanaticism and sectarianism that belong to the Age of Ignorance. God—Exalted is He—says, *He who slays a Muslim intentionally, his punishment shall be Hell, immortal therein. God shall cast His wrath upon him, curse him, and prepare for him a formidable torment.* [4:93]

And the Prophet—may God's blessings and peace be upon him—said, *When two Muslims cross swords, the slayer and the slain shall both be in the Fire.* They asked, "This is the slayer, but why the slain?" He answered, *He was intent on slaying his man.*[40] And he said in his sermon on the Day of Sacrifice on his Farewell Pilgrimage, *God has forbidden you your blood, possessions, and honor, just as this day of yours is forbidden, in this month of yours, in this town of yours. Woe to you! Be careful and do not revert, after I am gone, to being disbelievers, cutting each others' necks.*[41] And he said—may God's blessings and peace be upon him, *To insult a Muslim is corruption, and to fight him is disbelief.*[42] And, *A believer shall remain at ease within his religion so long as he does not spill forbidden blood.*[43] And, *For the world to perish is of less consequence to God than for a single believer to be killed without justification.*[44] And, *Were the inhabitants of His heavens and earth to share in killing a single believer, He would cast them all into the Fire.*[45] And, *Whosoever shares, even with half a word, in the killing*

---

38. Ibn Ḥibbān, *Ṣaḥīḥ*, (4952); Al- Ḥākim, *Mustadrak,* (24); Ṭabarānī, *Kabīr*, (15191).

39. Bayhaqī, *Kitāb al-Zuhd al-Kabīr*, (384); Fakhr al-Dīn al-Rāzī, *Tafsīr Mafātīḥ al-Ghayb*, vol. 11, p. 157; Zamakhsharī, *Tafsīr al-kashshāf*, (715); Ghazālī, *Iḥyā' 'Ulūm al-Dīn*, vol. 2, p. 210; p. 266.

40. Bukhārī, *Ṣaḥīḥ*, (30, 6367); Muslim, *Ṣaḥīḥ*, (5139, 5140).

41. Bukhārī, *Ṣaḥīḥ*, (4051, 6278); Muslim, *Ṣaḥīḥ*, (3179).

42. Bukhārī, *Ṣaḥīḥ*, (46, 5584); Muslim, *Ṣaḥīḥ*, (97).

43. Bukhārī, *Ṣaḥīḥ*, (6355).

44. Ibn Māja, *Sunan*, (2609); Nasā'ī, *Sunan*, (3922); Tirmidhī, *Sunan,* (1315).

45. Tirmidhī, *Sunan,* (1318).

of a believer, will meet God with: 'Has despaired of God's mercy!' inscribed between his eyes.[46]

There are so many awesome warnings concerning this matter, so let a Muslim beware greatly and avoid exposing himself to God's wrath, loathing, curse, formidable torment, and despairing of His mercy. We ask God for safety and protection from all kinds of abasement and temptation in this world and the next, for us, our loved ones, and all Muslims.

46. Ibn Māja, *Sunan*, (2610).

Chapter Ten: On Duties and Rights

It is perhaps appropriate that we should include here a brief discourse on assuming public office.

Know O brothers—may God grant us and you constant success-that there are perils in assuming public office and that the pursuit of them is arduous and wearisome. The believer who is concerned for his religion and keen to steer himself to deliverance and safety should avoid such offices as much as possible.

The Duties of Political Power

Among the most important public offices are those of leadership and political power, followed by judiciary positions, then responsibility for the properties of orphans, *awqāf*, and other similar things, in all of which there are perils. Concerning leadership, the Prophet—may God's blessings and peace be upon him—said, *Its beginning is blame, its middle is regrets, and its end is torment on Judgment Day.*[1] And, *None shall accept charge for ten or more people without being brought on the Resurrection Day with his hands tied to his neck, after which either his justice will set him free, or his tyranny will ruin him.*[2] It has been transmitted that rulers will be stood on the bridge that crosses over Hell. Those who had been doing good will be saved, but if they had been doing evil, the bridge will break beneath them and they will plummet in Hell for seventy autumns.[3] It has also been transmitted that certain men shall come to wish that they had been hung by their hair to the Pleiades rather than to have assumed responsibility for the Muslims.[4]

And he said—may God's blessings and peace be upon him—concerning judges, *He who is made a judge will have had his throat cut without a knife.*[5] And he said that he who judges ignorantly or unjustly shall end up in the Fire, while he who judges justly will

---

1. Bazzār, *Musnad,* (2391); Ṭabarānī, *Kabīr*, (14558).
2. Aḥmad, *Musnad,* (21268); Ṭabarānī, *Kabīr*, (7622, 7626).
3. Ṭabarānī, *Kabīr*, (1203, 1204); Abū Nu'aym al-Aṣbahānī, *Ma'rifat al-Ṣaḥāba,* (1099, 4808).
4. Abū Ya'lā, *Musnad,* (6088); Aḥmad, *Musnad,* (8273, 10341); Al-Ḥākim, *Mustadrak,* (7116).
5. Abū Dāwūd, *Sunan*, (3101); Tirmidhī, *Sunan,* (1247); Ibn Māja, *Sunan*, (2299).

have deserved to break even, which means that the good deeds in his record will equal the evil ones and he will thus be saved.

On the whole, avoiding public office is wiser and more appropriate. However, if a servant is tried with it, let him acquaint himself with what is due to God therein and what to His servants, then let him strive zealously to fulfill and uphold these obligations, neither exceeding the limits, nor falling short of them, showing neither neglect nor shortcomings. Only in this manner will he escape the severe threats and obtain the abundant reward. He said—may God's blessings and peace be upon him, *A single day of a just ruler is better than sixty years' worshipping, and a single statutory punishment implemented justly on earth gives it more blessings than forty mornings of rain.*[6] It has been transmitted that *the prayers of a just ruler are always accepted,*[7] that *none shall treat such a man with contempt but a hypocrite,*[8] and that *he will be one of the seven who will be shaded by God on the day when there will be no shade but His.*[9] He said—may God's blessings and peace be upon him, *On Judgment Day the just shall be on pulpits of lights, to the right of the All-Merciful.*[10]

As for he who assumes power in a tyrannical and iniquitous manner, woe to him from the punishment and torment of God. So many *ḥadīth*s have been handed down detailing how abased and loathed he will then be. Even though he may enjoy some pleasures for a while in this world, the consequences will be so evil and he will be forced to endure such torture that he will wish he had never been created, nor ever been a being with a name. He said—may God's blessings and peace be upon him, *O God! He who assumes charge of any of my community's affairs and treats them harshly, treat him harshly! But he who is gentle on them, be gentle on him!*[11] And another *ḥadīth* states that *no servant shall be entrusted by God*

6. Bayhaqī, *Shu'ab al-Īmān*, (7128); Ṭabarānī, *Kabīr*, (11764).
7. Aḥmad, *Musnad,* (7700, 9348); Nasā'ī, *Sunan*, (1742); Tirmidhī, *Sunan,* (2449).
8. Ṭabarānī, *Kabīr*, (7724).
9. Bukhārī, *Ṣaḥīḥ*, (620); Muslim, *Ṣaḥīḥ*, (1712).
10. Muslim, *Ṣaḥīḥ*, (3406); Nasā'ī, *Sunan*, (5284).
11. Abū 'Awāna, *Mustakhraj*, (5674); Ṭabarānī, *Awsaṭ*, (367).

with people, then dies having wronged his subjects, without God forbidding the Garden to him.[12]

Strive then-O ruler enjoying providential support- to be just to your subjects. Treat them gently, look into their affairs fairly, find out how they are faring and take good care of them, do not be so distracted or preoccupied as to lose sight of their interests, for God shall ask you to account for those He places in your charge. Every responsible person shall be asked to account for the object of his responsibility.

Beware twice over of treating your subjects with injustice and iniquity, you will thus ruin your life in both this world and the next. Just as you are forbidden to wrong your subjects, you are forbidden to allow them to wrong each other. You are also forbidden to neglect inquiring after their interests. 'Umar ibn al-Khaṭṭāb—may God be pleased with him—said, "Were a small goat to die out of neglect on the banks of the Euphrates, I would fear to be asked to account for it." How much more does this apply to neglecting the interests of orphans, widows, and the weak and destitute among Muslims.

The Duties of Judges

As for you—O blessed judge-you must be cautious and alert to the extreme in order to perceive the truth in each case and judge accordingly. Beware of feeling an inclination toward one of the litigants. Should you notice any such thing within yourself, withhold judgment until they both come to be equal in your sight and it no longer matters to you which one is right and which one wrong.

Beware of accepting bribery, for it is an abomination. The Prophet—may God's blessings and peace be upon him—has cursed he who bribes, he who accepts it, and he who has mediated between them.

Judge by what God has revealed to His servants, for He says-and August is the Noble Speaker, *And he who judges not according to what God has revealed, those are the disbelievers.* [5:44] Or as in other clear and unequivocal verses of the Glorious Book which is never attained by falsehood, neither from before or behind it, a revelation of one who is Wise, Praiseworthy: *those are the unjust* and *those are the corrupt.*

---

12. Ṭabarānī, *Kabīr*, (16869); Al-Shihāb al-Quḍā'ī, *Musnad al-Shihāb*, (749).

Managing the Properties of Orphans and *Awqāf*

As for responsibility for the properties of orphans, it is a dangerous thing fraught with difficulties and hardships. It is most important and incumbent upon he who is afflicted with it to be extremely cautious and careful and strive to the utmost to preserve their property and increase it. Let him beware of neglecting or damaging it, or appropriating or squandering any of it. God- Exalted is He—says, *Give the orphans their possessions. Do not exchange the corrupt for the good and do not expend of their possessions with yours, this indeed is a formidable wrong*. [4:2] And, *Those who devour the possessions of orphans unjustly, devour fire in their bellies, and they shall suffer a blaze*. [4:10] And the Prophet—may God's blessings and peace be upon him—mentioned appropriating the possessions of orphans among the most ruinous seven major sins.

Not far removed from this in sin and deserving blame is to appropriate *waqf* properties unjustly and unfairly. Let he who assumes such responsibility beware to the extreme. It is safer to avoid it altogether in order to escape the perils and blame attached to it. And God knows best.

Just as it is incumbent upon the man in office to treat those in his charge fairly, avoiding injustice, excess, or neglect in all their affairs, so it is incumbent upon the head of a family to treat everyone with justice and equity, avoiding injustice or neglect, for they are his subjects and he is legally responsible for them. A *ḥadīth* says that a man may be written down a tyrant when he is in charge of no more than his family. This is when he treats them unfairly.

We ask God—Exalted is He—to be treated with gentleness and granted well-being, and for the realization of *taqwā* and rectitude. There is neither power nor ability save by God, the High, the Formidable.

The Duties of Parents

Know O brothers—may God make us and you of those who are loyal and good, upholding the rights of God and those of His servants, seeking His good pleasure-that loyalty to one's parents, the preservation of kinship bonds, discharging with excellence one's duties towards one's family, dependents, and slaves, and treating well one's neighbors, friends, and all other Muslims, all belong to what God has prescribed and recommended, encouraged and urged, while forbidding abandoning or ignoring them, and threatening those who neglect and waste them.

As for the parents, God commands that we treat them with loyalty and benevolence, and forbids that we treat them badly. He enjoins this with utmost severity and strongly warns against contravention in His formidable Book and by the tongue of His noble Messenger. He says—Exalted is He, *Your Lord has decreed that you shall worship none other than Him and be good to your parents. Should they attain old age with you, one or both of them, never show your impatience with them, neither chide them, but speak to them gently, and lower the wing of humility out of compassion, and say, 'My Lord! Have mercy on them as they raised me up when I was little*. [17:23, 24] And, *And We have recommended to man his two parents. His mother bore him in weakness upon weakness, and his weaning was in two years. Be thankful to Me and your two parents. To Me is the return*. [31:14] Observe—may God have mercy on you—how He couples the injunction to be good to the parents to that of His *Tawḥīd* and worship, and how He couples thanking them to thanking Him. And He says—Exalted is He, *Worship God, associate nothing with Him, and be good to your parents*. [4:36] And, *We have charged man that he be kind to his parents. His mother bore him with pain and gave birth to him with pain, and his bearing and weaning were thirty months. Until when he is fully grown and reaches forty years he says, 'My Lord! Dispose me that I be thankful for Your favor with which You have blessed me and my two parents, and that I may do good well pleasing to You, and make my seed righteous. To You do I repent and I am one of those who have surrendered. Those are they from whom We shall accept the best of what they have done and overlook their sins. They are among the people of the Garden, the true promise which they were promised*. [46:15, 16]

'Abdallāh ibn Mas'ūd—may God be pleased with him—said, I asked the Messenger of God—may God's blessings and mercy be upon him—which works were best loved by God? He answered, *The ritual prayer in its proper time*. I asked, "Then which?" he answered, *Loyalty to one's parents*. I asked, "Then which?" He answered, Jihād *in the way of God*.[13] And he said—may God's blessings and mercy be upon him, *The good pleasure of God lies in the*

13. Bukhārī, *Ṣaḥīḥ*, (496, 2574); Muslim, *Ṣaḥīḥ*, (120, 122).

good pleasure of the parents, and His displeasure lies in theirs.[14] And, *There are three things in the presence of which good works avail nothing: Associating with God, disloyalty to one's parents, and fleeing from battle.*[15] And, *The most serious of major sins are three: Associating with God, disloyalty to one's parents, and bearing false witness.*[16] And, *May he be humiliated, he whose parents have grown old, one or both of them, but who is not admitted to the Garden.*[17] The meaning is that he is not admitted to the Garden because he has not served them with kindness. Loyalty when they grow old deserved special mention because elderly people are in need for someone to look after them, manage their affairs, and serve them. And God knows best.

It has been transmitted that God—Exalted is He—says, "He upon whom morning comes with his parents satisfied with him, while I am displeased with him, I am satisfied with him. On the other hand, he upon whom morning comes and he has satisfied me, while his parents are displeased with him, I am displeased with him." And the Prophet said—may God's blessings and mercy be upon him, *Serve your parents loyally and your children will serve you loyally. Be chaste and your women will be chaste.*[18] When a man sought his permission to go to *Jihād*, he asked him, *Are your parents alive*? And when he answered, "Yes." He told him, *Let your* Jihād *be in them.*[19] Which means: Strive arduously to serve them well, this shall be your way of struggling in the way of God. Another man asked him, "What rights do the parents have on their children?" He answered—may God's blessings and mercy be upon him, *They are either your Garden or your Fire.*[20] And he said—may God's blessings and mercy be upon him, *He whom it would please to have his life prolonged and his provision increased, let him serve his parents*

---

14. Tirmidhī, *Sunan*, (1821); Al-Ḥākim, *Mustadrak*, (7358); Bayhaqī, *Shu'ab al-Īmān*, (7584).
15. Ṭabarānī, *Kabīr*, (1404).
16. Bukhārī, *Ṣaḥīḥ*, (2460); Muslim, *Ṣaḥīḥ*, (126).
17. Muslim, *Ṣaḥīḥ*, (4627).
18. Al-Ḥākim, *Mustadrak*, (7368); Ṭabarānī, *Kabīr*, (252); *Awsaṭ*, (1014, 6477).
19. Bukhārī, *Ṣaḥīḥ*, (2782, 5515); Muslim, *Ṣaḥīḥ*, (4623).
20. Ibn Māja, *Sunan*, (3652).

loyally and preserve his kinship bonds.[21] And, *Three will never enter the Garden: he who is disloyal to his parents, the alcohol addict, and he who brags about his charity.*[22] It has been transmitted that loyalty to one's parents is better than *Ḥajj*, *'Umra*, and *Jihād* in the way of God, that he who is disloyal to his parents, God will not look at him on Resurrection Day and he will never catch a whiff of the scent of the Garden.

On the whole, the rights of parents are the greatest following those of God and those of His Messenger. Therefore, do serve them graciously, treat them kindly, obey them, and be humble in their presence. Give them priority over yourself, your wife, and your children, when it comes to service, gifts, and gracious treatment. Never show them that you expect them to show gratitude, and never perceive their service as tedious. Count their need for you and expectations that you will serve them and be good to them among the greatest of God's gifts to you and the best of the good works He has granted you to perform.

And know that gracious service to one's mother should exceed that to one's father many times over. Perhaps it is because of the hardships that the mother endures during pregnancy, delivery, lactation, and bringing up, and because of her overflowing affection and compassion. And God knows best.

A man once asked the Prophet—may God's blessings and mercy be upon him, "Who deserves most my keeping his company with good grace?" He answered, "Your mother." The man asked, "Then whom?" He answered, "Your mother." Again he asked, "Then whom?" And again he was answered, "Your mother." When he asked yet again, he was answered, "Your father."[23]

Just as a person should serve his parents graciously during their life, so should he continue to do so after they pass away. This consists in praying and asking forgiveness for them, giving charity on their behalf, settling their debts, executing their wills, preserving their kinship bonds, and treating kindly their friends and those they used to love. These are all included under loyalty to one's parents, as stated in many *ḥadīths*.

---

21. Aḥmad, *Musnad*, (12922, 13309); Bayhaqī, *Shu'ab al-Īmān*, (7610); Ibn Ḥibbān, *Ṣaḥīḥ*, (440).
22. Nasā'ī, *Sunan*, (2515).
23. Bukhārī, *Ṣaḥīḥ*, (5514); Muslim, *Ṣaḥīḥ*, (4621).

There are great benefits in praying and asking forgiveness for the dead and in giving out charity on their behalf. Therefore, no person should neglect doing so for the two parents in particular, then relatives, those with rights upon one, and all Muslims in general.

Parents should help their children be loyal to them. They should be forgiving, not subject their children to too much pressure when demanding their rights, nor insist overmuch that it be done to perfection, especially these days when benevolence and loyalty have become scarce, and rebellion and disloyalty have become rife. When the parents are forgiving to their children, they save and deliver them from the sin of rebellion and the punishment it should attract in this world and the next, and they themselves obtain a reward from God, a generous wage that is better, more perfect, superior, and longer lasting than their children's loyalty. He said—may God's blessings and peace be upon him, *May God have mercy on a parent who assists his child being loyal to him.*[24]

Let parents beware to the extreme from praying against their disloyal child, for this can only increase him in harm, corruption, and disloyalty. Some of this damage is bound to cause more harm to the parents in this world. Since the prayers of parents [for or against their children] are always accepted [by God], they should pray for, not against them. God may very well reform them through the *baraka* of their prayers, they may then revert to being loyal. The result will be that their parents will again benefit from their loyalty and be greatly pleased with them, while the children will obtain the reward for being loyal and escape the sin of disloyalty. God it is who grants success and assistance.

The Rights of Children

Children also have rights over their parents. They should be provided for so long as they need to be, educated with excellence, taught praiseworthy traits of character, excellent attributes, and beautiful moral qualities, and protected from the contrary of these. They should receive good names, and prior to all this, their mothers should have been chosen from blessed, virtuous origins. The Prophet—may

24. Abū 'Abdal-Raḥmān al-Sulamī, *Ādāb al-Suḥba*, (90).

God's blessings and peace be upon him, said, *Choose well for your sperm, marry those who match,*[25] *for the origins penetrate*[26].

Parents should be fair in providing for their children and not prefer one over the other simply because of his natural inclinations or other whimsical reasons.

The most important duty for parents as concerns their children is to teach them virtue and courtesy, so that they may grow up loving goodness, accepting the truth, respectful of religious matters, but disdainful of worldly ones, always giving priority to things of the hereafter. Those who fail to bring up their children in a disciplined and virtuous manner, but plant in their hearts the love of this world and its appetites, and render them careless as concerns religion, then they see them rebelling against them, let them blame only themselves. Loss is more likely to affect the neglectful. Much of the disloyalty witnessed these days is due to neglecting what we have mentioned earlier. This becomes evident to anyone who observes and reflects on how things are. Power and ability are only by God, the High and Formidable.

Nurturing Kinship Bonds

As for nurturing one's kinship bonds, which is being good to one's relatives, God enjoins it in His saying, *Give your kinsman his due.* [17:26] And He says—Exalted is He—praising those whom He has chosen and is pleased with, *And those who join what God has bid them join, fear their Lord, and dread an evil reckoning…* [13:21] Among the things that God had bid them join are kinship bonds. And He says—Exalted is He—warning and rebuking others from severing their kinship bonds, *Those who break their pact with God after it was pledged, who sever what God bid them join, and who work corruption in the earth, theirs shall be the curse and theirs shall be the evil abode.* [13:25] And He says—Exalted is He, *Should you turn away, would you then work corruption in the land and sever you kinship bonds? These are they whom God has cursed, and so made them deaf and blinded their eyes.* [47:22, 23] Thus does

25. Ibn Māja, *Sunan,* (1858); Al-Ḥākim, *Mustadrak*, (2637); Dāraquṭnī, *Sunan*, (3834). The word "match" here refers to the legal concept of *Kafā'a*, which means that spouses should be of equal social status and lineage.

26. Al-Shihāb al-Quḍā'ī, *Musnad*, (599). The "origins" are the genetic constitution of a particular family. Genetic traits penetrate across generations and are likely to appear in children and grandchildren.

the Book explicitly state that he who severs his kinship bonds is accursed.

'Alī ibn al-Ḥusayn—may God be pleased with both- counseled one of his children thus, "Beware of keeping company with one who has severed his kinship bonds, for I have seen such a one being cursed in three different places in the Book of God the Exalted."

The Messenger of God—may God's blessings and peace be upon him—said, *He who believes in God and the Last day, let him treat his guest honorably; he who believes in God and the Last Day, let him nurture his kinship bonds; and he who believes in God and the Last Day, let him speak words of goodness or else keep silent.*[27] And, *He whom it would please to have his life prolonged, his provision increased, and be protected from an evil death, let him fear God and nurture his kinship bonds.*[28] And, *God—August and Majestic-says, 'I am the All-Merciful. I have created the womb (*raḥim*) and derived a name for it from Mine. He who nurtures it, I shall nurture him, but he who ruptures it, I shall cut him off* [from My mercy].'[29] And he said—may God's blessings and peace be upon him, *None shall enter the Garden who has severed his kinship bonds.*[30] And, *Mercy never descends on people among whom is one who has severed his kinship bonds.*[31] Now if mercy never descends on people in the midst of whom is one who has severed his kinship bonds, how much more does the man himself deserve this? How immense shall God's loathing for him be and His cutting him off from all kinds of goodness?

Be careful—may God have mercy on you—to preserve your kinship bonds. Beware of severing them, for it is one of the greatest sins and its punishment is hastened in this life, after which there shall be severe punishment and painful torment prepared by God in the hereafter.

Similarly, the reward for benevolence and nurturing kinship bonds is hastened in this life, after which there shall be immense reward and an honorable return.

---

27. Bukhārī, *Ṣaḥīḥ*, (5673).
28. Aḥmad, *Musnad,* (1150); Al-Ḥākim, *Mustadrak,* (7389); Bayhaqī, *Shu'ab al-Īmān*, (7716).
29. Tirmidhī, *Sunan,* (1830); Aḥmad, *Musnad,* (1594); Al-Ḥākim, *Mustadrak,* (7378).
30. Bukhārī, *Ṣaḥīḥ*, (5525); Muslim, *Ṣaḥīḥ*, (4636).
31. Bayhaqī, *Shu'ab al-Īmān*, (7729); Bukhārī, *Al-Adab al-Mufrad*, (64).

He said—may God's blessings and peace be upon him, *The swiftest of rewards is that for loyalty and nurturing kinship bonds, and the swiftest of punishments is that for iniquity and severing kinship bonds.*[32] And, *There are no sins more deserving of swift punishment in this life, before what is in store in the hereafter, than iniquity and severing kinship bonds.*[33] I say: The reward for loyalty and nurturing kinship bonds is thus both hastened in this life and awaiting in the hereafter, and so is the punishment for disloyalty and severing kinship bonds. We ask God for safety.

A person should nurture the bonds between him and his kin, even if they do not reciprocate. He should treat them kindly even if they show no such kindness to him. He said—may God's blessings and peace be upon him, *The one who is nurturing* [his kinship bonds] *is not the one who is reciprocating, but the one who when these bonds are ruptured, he rejoins them.*[34]

One should also bear whatever harm comes to him from them with patience and not retaliate. On the contrary, he should forgive and pardon, keep speaking to them, and treat them kindly. The more severely they injure and wrong him, the more important it becomes to treat them kindly, and the more meritorious donations to them become." He said—may God's blessings and peace be upon him, *The best charity is that given to a relative who harbors rancor.*[35] Such a relative is one who feels enmity towards he who does him good. A man once complained to the Prophet—may God's blessings and peace be upon him, "I have relatives whom I treat well but who sever the bonds between us." At the end of the *ḥadīth* the man is told, *You will continue to be supported by God so long as you carry on behaving thus.*[36] Meaning nurturing kinship bonds and treating them with benevolence, even though they keep rupturing these same bonds and doing wrong.

One should not overlook his needy relatives and kin, while giving to others. He said—may God's blessings and peace be upon him, *He who overlooks* [his needy relatives] *is as he who withholds*

32. Abū Dāwūd, *Sunan*, (4256); Ibn Māja, *Sunan*, (4201); Tirmidhī, *Sunan*, (2435).

33. Ibn Māja, *Sunan*, (4202).

34. Bukhārī, *Ṣaḥīḥ*, (5532).

35. Aḥmad, *Musnad,* (14781, 22430); Al-Ḥākim, *Mustadrak,* (1427); Bayhaqī, *Shu'ab al-Īmān*, (3274, 7721).

36. Muslim, *Ṣaḥīḥ*, (4640); Aḥmad, *Musnad,* (6413, 8975).

his charity.[37] It has been transmitted that he who gives charity to strangers while aware that some of his relatives are in need, God the Exalted will not accept his charity. And he said—may God's blessings and peace be upon him, *Charity to the indigent is charity, but charity to relatives is both charity and nurturing of kinship bonds.*[38] I say: This applies when relatives are not in dire need, for if they are then it is rightfully theirs. Should there be enough charity to suffice both one's kinsmen and others, only then would it be charity for strangers and both charity and nurturing of kinship bonds for relatives. But if the relatives are overlooked and charity goes elsewhere, while the giver is aware of their need, then this would be sinful and unjust, and this charity would be unacceptable, as stated earlier.

The nearer the relative the more rights he has and the more deserving of benevolence. The weak, destitute next of kin are more deserving of help and kind treatment than more affluent ones. This is because the poor relative has two rights, that of blood relations and that of poverty. God coupled together the commands to do good to blood relations and the poor in the verses of His Book. One example is His saying—Exalted is He, *Give the kinsman his right, and the indigent, and the traveler...*[30:38] Another is His saying—Exalted is He, *And give of your wealth, however much you love it, to kinsmen, orphans, and the indigent.* [2:122] And there are others. There is no doubt that treating kindly he who has two rights takes precedence over treating kindly he who has one right only.

Let the servant who is providentially assisted strive to nurture his ties of kinship in whatever manner he is able to: kindness, service, gifts, donations, visits, and comforting. He should make the appropriate choice as to which of these is suitable with each of his relatives, so he will have discharged his duties toward them, nurtured his kinship bonds, and comforted them. He should never fail to nurture his kinship bonds out of indolence or avarice, treating lightly those bonds to which God has attributed so much importance and severely threatened those who sever them. It is the servant's to do his best, according to his means, and it is God's to assist and forgive. He said—may God's blessings and peace be upon him, *Treat your kin with kindness, even if by simply greeting them with* salām.[39]

---

37. Abū Dāwūd, *Sunan*, (1352).

38. Ibn Māja, *Sunan*, (1834); Nasā'ī, *Sunan*, (2535); Tirmidhī, *Sunan*, (594).

39. Bayhaqī, *Shu'ab al-Īmān*, (7740, 7741).

These days, severing kinship bonds and lack of concern for helping and treating them kindly has become rife. It may be that this is why the land has become afflicted with poverty and scarcity of provision, for it has been handed down that preserving kinship bonds lengthens lives and increases wealth, and that God has increased certain people's provisions and accrued their wealth, although He has never looked at them since he created them, and this for their preservation of their kinship bonds. Severing bonds and abandoning kindness will have the opposite effect. And God knows best.

The Rights of Wives and Dependents

As for wives and all those whom a person is responsible for providing for and looking after, he should cover their expenditure, provide for them, fulfill their rights, and teach them their religious duties and everything they need to know for their salvation and safety in the hereafter. He must also impose upon them obedience to the commands of God and avoidance of what He has forbidden.

God—Exalted is He—says, *They* [the women] *have the same rights* [as men, to be fulfilled] *in mutual kindness*. [2:228] And, *Live with them in kindness*. [4:19] And, *When they obey you, do not seek ways to wrong them*. [4:35]

The Prophet—may God's blessings and peace be upon him—said, *Treat women well.*[40] He frequently instructed the men to treat the women with kindness and benevolence. He said, *The best among you are the best to their women.*[41] And, *The best among you are the best to my family, and I am the best of you to my family.*[42] Therefore, a man should treat his women well, be gentle, solicitous for their welfare, compassionate, and patient whenever they are harsh or behave discourteously. He should not be too demanding of his rights upon them. As for the rights of God, he should insist that they be fulfilled. No laxity in this is permissible. Also, he should not surrender the management of all his affairs to the woman, giving her power over himself and his wealth, as some heedless fools do. This is reprehensible both in terms of *Sharīʿa* and rationality. The woman is in the same position as a bondmaid or a follower. He who makes his bondsmaid or follower his master has turned things upside down and headed the wrong way. He said—may God's blessings and

40. Muslim, *Ṣaḥīḥ*, (267); Ibn Māja, *Sunan,* (1841).
41. Ibn Māja, *Sunan,* (1968); Aḥmad, *Musnad,* (9725).
42. Tirmidhī, *Sunan*, (3830); Ibn Māja, *Sunan,* (1967).

peace be upon him, *No people shall succeed who surrender their leadership to a woman…*[43] And al-Ḥasan al-Baṣrī—may God have mercy on him—said, "No man shall obey his wife in all her whims without God casting him into the Fire."

A man who has two or more wives is obliged to be fair. If he fails to treat them equally, he will be accountable for his sin and deserving of censure. The Prophet—may God's blessings and peace be upon him—said, *He who has two wives and does not treat them equally, he will come on Judgment Day with one of his sides drooping.*[44]

The Rights of Husbands

The rights of a husband over his wife are among the greatest. If she fulfils them she will obtain abundant rewards, whereas if she neglects them she will earn great sins. The Prophet said—may God's blessings and peace be upon him, *Were I to command a person to prostrate himself before another, I would have commanded the wife to prostrate herself before her husband.*[45] So great is his right upon her. And, *Any woman whose husband is satisfied with her at the time she dies will be admitted to the Garden.*[46] And, *The woman who performs her five [prayers], fasts her month, guards her private parts, and obeys her husband, it will be said to her, 'Enter from any of the doors of the Garden you choose to.'*[47] And, *God-Blessed and Exalted is He—never looks at a woman who does not thank her husband, when she can never do without him.*[48] And, *When a man invites his wife to his bed and she refuses, so that he spends the night angry with her, the angels will curse her until morning breaks.*[49]

A wife should then obey her husband, not oppose him. She should not dispose of anything in his house, give charity out of his money, or leave the house without his permission. Should she do any of this without permission she will have sinned. When he in-

43. Bukhārī, *Ṣaḥīḥ*, (4073, 6570); Nasā'ī, *Sunan,* (5293); Tirmidhī, *Sunan*, (2188).
44. Ibn Māja, *Sunan,* (1959); Tirmidhī, *Sunan*, (1060).
45. Ibn Māja, *Sunan,* (1842); Tirmidhī, *Sunan*, (1079).
46. Ibn Māja, *Sunan,* (1844); Tirmidhī, *Sunan*, (1081).
47. Aḥmad, *Musnad,* (1573); Ibn Ḥibbān, *Ṣaḥīḥ*,(4237); Ṭabarānī, *Kabīr*, (991); *Awsaṭ*, (4745, 9050).
48. Al-Ḥākim, *Mustadrak,* (2721, 7443); Bazzār, *Musnad,* (2057).
49. Bukhārī, *Ṣaḥīḥ*, (2998, 4794); Muslim, *Ṣaḥīḥ*, (2594).

vites her to his bed, she is not allowed to refuse except for a legally acceptable excuse.

On the whole, the rights of a husband over his wife are immense, to the extent that the Prophet said—may God's blessings and peace be upon him, *If a man happens to have an ulcer and his wife licks it, she would still not have fulfilled his rights*.[50] Women should therefore strive to fulfill their husbands' rights and avoid neglecting any of them, that they may obtain God's reward and good pleasure, and escape his punishment and wrath. On the other hand, a husband should forgive his wife some of her shortcomings and avoid demanding his rights too meticulously, so as not to drive her into failing in her duties. Women are imperfect in both their understanding and their religion. They often take lightly their duties toward their husbands and act neglectfully. He who is indulgent, God will treat him with indulgence. He who overlooks mistakes, God will overlook his.

The Merits of Marriage

Know—may God have mercy on you—that marriage has many merits, advantages, and benefits, both in this life and the next. There is much encouragement toward it in the Book and *Sunna*. God—Exalted is He—says, *Marry those women you please, two, three, or four…*[4:3] And, *Marry the single among you, and the righteous among your bondsmen and bondmaids. If they are poor, God will enrich them of His favor. God is Vast, Knowing*. [24:32] The Messenger of God said—may God's blessings and peace be upon him, *O young people! He who is able, let him marry, for it helps one lower his gaze and protect his private parts. He who is unable to, let him fast, for it diminishes lust*.[51] And, *Whosoever wishes to meet God pure and purified, let him marry free women*.[52] And, *Four things are among the* Sunnas *of the Messengers: Modesty, perfume,* siwāk, *and marriage*.[53] And, *Marry, for by your numbers I shall outrival the other communities on Resurrection Day*.[54] And, *When the servant marries, he has completed half his religion, let him fear*

50. Al-Ḥākim, *Mustadrak,* (2717); Ibn Ḥibbān, *Ṣaḥīḥ*,(4238).
51. Bukhārī, *Ṣaḥīḥ*, (4677, 4678); Muslim, *Ṣaḥīḥ*, (2485, 2486).
52. Ibn Māja, *Sunan,* (1852).
53. Tirmidhī, *Sunan*, (1000).
54. Ibn Māja, *Sunan,* (1853); 'Abdal-Razzāq, *Muṣannaf*, (10391).

God in the other half.[55] Ibn 'Abbās—may God be pleased with them both-said, "There is no reason for not marrying save incapacity or debauchery." I say: Marriage frees the heart from the whisperings of the Devil concerning women, such as may occur to a man during ritual prayer as he stands before God, during reciting the Qur'ān, or remembering God, which thing makes him discourteous toward Him. Marriage helps keeping one's gaze down and protecting one's private parts. The merits of such benefits have been detailed in the Book and *Sunna* in such a manner as not to escape the notice of any knowledgeable, insightful person. God—Exalted is He—says, *Tell the believers to lower their gaze and guard their private parts. This is purer for them. Indeed, God is aware of what they do.* [24:30] And he said—may God's blessings and peace be upon him, *The gaze is one of the poisoned arrows of Iblīs.*[56]

Marriage requires patience in treating women with kindness, fulfilling their rights, and providing for them and the children. There is great merit in this, in addition to the merit of being the cause of procreating righteous offspring that will worship God the Exalted, pray for their parents, and ask forgiveness for them during the latter's lifetimes and after their deaths. Some of the children may die before puberty, which thing attracts immense reward for the parents.

There are great merits and abundant rewards in raising children and looking after them well, especially if they are girls. He said—may God's blessings and peace be upon him, *If you spend a* Dīnār *in the way of God, a* Dīnār *to free a slave, a* Dīnār *in charity to a poor person, or a* Dīnār *on your family, the greatest reward will be for that spent on your family.*[57] And, *That which you feed yourself is for you a charity, that which you feed your child is for you a charity, that which you feed your wife is for you a charity, and that which you feed your servant is for you a charity.*[58] And, *Once the son of Adam dies all his works cease except three: a running charity, knowledge that is made use of, or a righteous progeny who pray for him.*[59]

He also said—may God's blessings and peace be upon him, *No Muslim loses three of his children who die before puberty without*

55. Bayhaqī, *Shu'ab al-Īmān*, (5246).
56. Al-Ḥākim, *Mustadrak,* (7988); Ṭabarānī, *Kabīr*, (10211).
57. Muslim, *Ṣaḥīḥ*, (1661).
58. Aḥmad, *Musnad,* (16550); Nasā'ī, *Al-Sunan al-Kubrā,* (9204).
59. Nasā'ī, *Sunan,* (3591); Tirmidhī, *Sunan*, (1297).

God admitting him to the Garden because of his grief over them. In one version a woman is said to have asked, "Or two?" And he answered, *Or two.*[60] And he said—may God's blessings and peace be upon him, *To send forward* [to the hereafter] *a miscarried fetus would be more pleasing to me than to beget a hundred fully armed men.*[61] It has been handed down that children shall be given vessels full of the beverage of the Garden to give their parents to drink on Resurrection Day, when people will be suffering hardship and thirst such as God only knows. They shall stand at the gates of the Garden and refuse to enter until their parents are admitted, so that God shall order their parents to the Garden along with them by His mercy.

He also said—may God's blessings and peace be upon him, *He who is tried with girls and raises them well, they will be a barrier between him and the Fire.*[62] And, *He who is begotten three girls, brings them up well, treats them kindly, and provides for them, the Garden becomes inevitably his.*[63] They asked, "O Messenger of God! What if they were only two?" He answered, *Even if they are only two.* Some of those who were present remarked that had they said, "And only one?" He would have said, "And even if only one." And he said—may God's blessings and peace be upon him, *He who begets a female, does not bury her, nor humiliate her, nor prefer his other* [male] *children over her, God shall admit him to the Garden.*[64] The words, *does not bury her*, refer to the practice of the Age of Ignorance of burying alive their female offspring.

When informed that they have begotten a female, or even that someone else has, certain stupid people utter abominable things such as they should not, to show their hatred for girls. This is ugly and detestable, not far removed from the way God describes the people of the Age of Ignorance, *And when any of them is given the glad news of a female, his face is darkened and he suppresses his anger. He hides from the people because of the evil of the glad news that had been given to him. Should he keep it and be ashamed or bury it into the dust? Evil indeed is how they judge!* [16:58, 59]

Let the God- fearing believer beware of this, of aversion to his female children, of offending them, or of preferring his male chil-

60. Bukhārī, *Ṣaḥīḥ*, (1172, 1292); Muslim, *Ṣaḥīḥ*, (4766).

61. Bayhaqī, *Shu'ab al-Īmān*, (9421).

62. Bukhārī, *Ṣaḥīḥ*, (1329); Tirmidhī, *Sunan*, (1838).

63. Aḥmad, *Musnad,* (8071, 10957, 11488).

64. Abū Dāwūd, *Sunan*, (4480); Al-Ḥākim, *Mustadrak,* (7456).

dren over them, for he does not know in which of his children the *baraka* will be, nor which of them will deserve a good ending to their lives.

He who wishes to marry should seek a woman who is religious, good, and virtuous, even if poor or not very comely. The Prophet—may God's blessings and peace be upon him—has exhorted and encouraged us to seek the religious woman. He said—may God's blessings and peace be upon him, *Win a religious woman, may your hands be blessed.*[65] Therefore, a man should never marry a woman only for her wealth or her beauty, for this is detestable. He said—may God's blessings and peace be upon him, *Do not marry women for their beauty, for that very beauty may cause their perdition. Do not marry them for their wealth, for that very wealth may make them overbearing. But marry them for their religion…*[66]

Then there is he who wishes not to marry in order to devote himself to acquiring knowledge and worshipping activities, and to be free from worldly preoccupations and attachments. If his heart is free from any desire for women, there is no harm and no sin in not marrying. A number of our virtuous predecessors—may God have mercy on them—and also latecomers have done this. One of them was asked, "Will you not marry?" He answered, "I have failed to reform my own ego, how can I burden myself with another?" When asked the same question, another replied, "Were I able to divorce my own ego, I would have." As for Bishr ibn al-Ḥārith—may God have mercy on him—when they said to him, "People are talking about you, they say you have forsaken the *Sunna*." He answered, "Tell them, 'He is fully occupied with the obligatory." I say: He who wishes to marry should do so intending it to be of assistance to him in both his religious and worldly affairs, while he who abstains should intend thereby to protect his religion and opt for caution so as to be safe. Thus should both marriage and abstention be according to a righteous intention that will draw one nearer to God. As for he who intends, in either case, nothing but worldly aims and gains and the satisfaction of his natural inclinations and appetites, he is far removed from right conduct and the emulation of our virtuous ancestors. God is the One to grant success and assistance, there is no Lord other than He.

65. Bukhārī, *Ṣaḥīḥ*, (4700); Muslim, *Ṣaḥīḥ*, (2661, 2662).
66. Ibn Māja, *Sunan,* (1849).

The Rights of Slaves

It is enjoined and encouraged to treat slaves very well. God—Exalted is He—says, *Worship God and associate nothing with Him. Treat the two parents well, as also relatives, orphans, the indigent, the neighbor who is of kin, the neighbor who is a stranger, the companion in your vicinity, the traveler, and that your right hands own.* [4:36] And the Prophet—may God's blessings and peace be upon him—said, *The slave should be given, and with kindness, his food and clothes, and he should not be charged with more work than he is capable of.*[67] And, *Fear God in what your right hands own.*[68] *Feed them of what you eat, clothe them of what you wear, and do not charge them with more work than they are capable of. Those you like, keep, those you do not, sell, but do not torment God's creatures.*[69] For, though God—Exalted is He—has made them your property, had He so wished, He would have made you theirs. To a man who once asked, "O Messenger of God, how many times should we forgive the servant?" He answered, *Forgive him seventy times every day.*[70] He also said—may God's blessings and peace be upon him, *He shall not enter the Garden who is evil in his ownership.*[71] He who is evil in his ownership is he who is evil to his slaves, which means failing to give the slave sufficient food and clothes, imposing on him such tasks as are beyond his capacity, and insulting or beating him unjustly. These shall all be avenged in the hereafter, as many *ḥadīth*s state. Should the slave be beaten or insulted for an act that deserves such treatment, it should be done with moderation, never becoming excessive. However, to forgive and pardon is better and more excellent, and deserves a great reward from God—August and Majestic is He.

The Rights of Animals

He who owns any animals or cattle should look after them well, treat them with solicitude, and always remain aware of their condi-

67. Imām Mālik, *Muwaṭṭa'*, (1552); Bayhaqī, *Shu'ab al-Īmān*, (8320).

68. Aḥmad, *Musnad*, (552); Bayhaqī, *Shu'ab al-Īmān*, (10612).

69. Aḥmad, *Musnad*, (15813, 20509, 20538); Bayhaqī, *Al-Sunan al-Kubrā*, vol. 8, p. 36

70. Abū Dāwūd, *Sunan*, (4496); Tirmidhī, *Sunan*, (1872).

71. Bayhaqī, *Shu'ab al-Īmān*, (8333, 8334, 8335); Ṭabarānī, *Awsaṭ*, (11368).

tions, whether he does so himself or delegates these tasks to one of his trustworthy children or servants. If he fails to do so he will have sinned and deserved censure. A *ḥadīth* states that, *A woman was sent to the Fire because of a cat she had tied, neither feeding it, nor allowing it to feed itself on the small beings of the earth.*[72]

The Rights of Neighbors

God has enjoined us to treat our neighbors well in His saying—Exalted is He, *Worship God and associate nothing with Him. Treat the two parents well, as also relatives, orphans, the indigent, the neighbor who is of kin, the neighbor who is a stranger,...*[4:36] And the Messenger of God—may God's blessings and peace be upon him—laid great emphasis on the rights of neighbors, exhorting people to treat them well, strongly forbidding them to offend them, so much so that he said—may God's blessings and peace be upon him, *Gabriel kept recommending the neighbor to me until I thought he was about to allow him to inherit.*[73] Meaning he was about to grant the neighbor a share in the inheritance of his neighbor. He said—may God's blessings and peace be upon him, *He who believes in God and the Last Day, let him honor his neighbor...*[74] And he said that whoever offends his neighbor will have offended him, and he who offends him would have offended God. He also said, *By God! He is not a believer whose neighbor is not safe from his harm.*[75] Harm here means evil, injury, and exasperating behavior. And God knows best.

The rights of neighbors are immense and treating them well is a most important religious duty. This can be achieved only by refraining from offending them, bearing their offences if any, doing them good, and treating them as kindly as possible. These are the attributes of believers whose faith is complete. As he said—may God's blessings and peace be upon him, *Be good to your neighbor and you will be a Muslim.*[76]

The neighbor with most rights upon you is he whose door is nearest to you, then the next, and so on. A *ḥadīth* says, *The neigh-*

72. Bukhārī, *Ṣaḥīḥ*, (3071, 3223); Muslim, *Ṣaḥīḥ*, (4160, 4751).
73. Bukhārī, *Ṣaḥīḥ*, (5555, 5556); Muslim, *Ṣaḥīḥ*, (4757).
74. Bukhārī, *Ṣaḥīḥ*, (5560); Muslim, *Ṣaḥīḥ*, (67).
75. Bukhārī, *Ṣaḥīḥ*, (5557); Muslim, *Ṣaḥīḥ*, (66).
76. Ibn Māja, *Sunan,* (4207); Bayhaqī, *Shu'ab al-Īmān*,(5510); Ṭabarānī, *Kabīr*, (203).

bors are three: some have three rights, some have two, and some have one. He who has three rights is the Muslim neighbor who is also a relative, for he has the right of a neighbor, that of a Muslim, and that of a relative. He who has two rights is the Muslim neighbor: his is the right of the neighbor and the right of Islam. As for he who has one right, this is the non-Muslim neighbor; his is the right of the neighbor.[77] Observe how he confirms the rights of neighborliness for the non-Muslim neighbor despite his disbelief, and you will understand how great the rights of neighbors are and how important in religion. So strive—may God have mercy on you—to do good to your neighbors as much as you can, having first refrained from offending them in any way and patiently endured their injuries if any. Seek God's help and be patient. *And none shall receive it save those who are patient, and none shall receive it save those who are immensely fortunate.* [41:35] Imām al-Ghazālī quotes in the *Iḥyā'* and other works an all-inclusive *ḥadīth* concerning how one should behave toward one's neighbor. He says—may God have mercy on him: He said—may God's blessings and peace be upon him, *Do you know what rights a neighbor has? When he asks for your help you should help him, when he asks for loan you should loan him, when he is poor you should give him, when he is sick you should visit him, when he dies you should escort his funeral, when something good happens to him you should congratulate him, and when he is stricken with affliction you should console him. You should not elevate your building so high as to obstruct the wind from reaching him save with his permission, neither should you offend him with the vapors of your cooking pot, unless you give him a serving. Whenever you buy fruits you should offer him some as a gift. If you do not, then bring it inside discreetly and let not your child take it out to spite his. Do you know what rights a neighbor has? By He in whose hand my soul is, only he upon whom God has mercy will be able to fulfill his neighbor's rights.*[78]

Our virtuous predecessors used to go to extremes to be good to their neighbors and never offend them. We have been told that once, when mice proliferated in the house of one of them and he was told,

77. Bayhaqī, *Shu'ab al-Īmān*, (9238); Ṭabarānī, *Musnad al-Shāmiyyīn*, (2401).

78. Bayhaqī, *Shu'ab al-Īmān*, (9237); Ṭabarānī, *Musnad al-Shāmiyyīn*, (2373).

"Why do you not buy a cat?" He answered, "I fear lest the mice flee into my neighbors' houses, which is sure to irritate them."

The Rights of Companionship

We are enjoined, exhorted, and encouraged to treat our companions well. Companions have rights that are important to observe. God—Exalted is He—says, *Worship God and associate nothing with Him. Treat the two parents well, as also relatives, orphans, the indigent, the neighbor who is of kin, the neighbor who is a stranger, the companion in your vicinity…* [4:36] The Prophet—may God's blessings and peace be upon him—said that no person shall befriend another, even for part of a day, without being asked to account for his company on Judgment Day: did he uphold God's rights in that or not? And, *The best of companions are those who behave best toward their companions, and the best of neighbors are those who behave best toward their neighbors.*[79] And, *No two shall love one another without he whose love for his companion is greater being more beloved to God.*[80]

The essence of companionship is sincere love and unblemished affection. When this is in God and for God, its reward is immense. He said—may God's blessings and peace be upon him, *God—Exalted is He—said, 'My love is due to those who love one another for Me, sit with one another for Me, and offer gifts to one another for Me.'*[81] And he said—may God's blessings and peace be upon him, *God—Exalted is He—shall say on Resurrection Day, 'Where are those who loved one another for My majesty? Today I shall shade them in My shade on a day when there shall be no other shade.*[82] And he said—may God's blessings and peace be upon him, *He will experience the sweetness of faith who loves other people for no reason other than God.*[83] And, *Seven shall be shaded by God under His shade on a day when there shall be no other shade…* He mentioned

79. Tirmidhī, *Sunan*, (1867); Aḥmad, Musnad, (6278).
80. Al-Ḥākim, *Mustadrak,* (7431); Bayhaqī, *Shu'ab al-Īmān*, (8758,); Ibn Ḥibbān, *Ṣaḥīḥ*, (567); Ṭabarānī, *Kabīr,* (1798); *Awsaṭ*, (3009, 5437).
81. Aḥmad, *Musnad*, (21021); Al-Ḥākim, *Mustadrak,* (7422); Imām Mālik, *Muwaṭṭa'*, (1503).
82. Muslim, *Ṣaḥīḥ*, (4655); Imām Mālik, *Muwaṭṭa'*, (1500).
83. Bukhārī, *Ṣaḥīḥ*, (15, 20, 5581); Muslim, *Ṣaḥīḥ*, (60, 61).

them one after the other until he said, *and two men who loved each other in God, meeting and separating on this…*[84]

When a person loves another, becomes his friend and companion for his love of God and obedience to him, this is love in God the Exalted.

If he loves and befriends him because he helps him uphold his religion and obey his Lord, he loves him in God.

If he loves and befriends him because he helps him manage those worldly affairs which are necessary for him in his journey to the hereafter, he loves him in God the Exalted.

If he loves and befriends him because he has a personal inclination to him and finds solace in his company, or because he is of assistance to him in his worldly affairs and means of sustenance, this is personal inclination, unrelated in any manner to love in God. It is ego centered friendship based on one's natural disposition. It is permissible and may not be-God willing-devoid of good.

But if he loves and befriends him because he helps him commit sins and injustice, and facilitates for him the means to corruption and reprehensible behavior, then this is an ugly and blameworthy kind of love and friendship. It is in the way of the Devil and has nothing to do with God. In the hereafter it will turn into enmity, if this has not already happened in this life. God—Exalted is He—says, *Intimate friends shall be enemies to one another on that day, save the God-fearing*. [43:67]

Therefore you should-O brother-only love and keep company with God-fearing people, people of knowledge, and those of God's virtuous servants who are detached from this world, who are His protégés among believers. For a man shall be with whom he loves[85] in this life and the next, as stated in authentic *ḥadīth*s and as he said—may God's blessings and peace be upon him, *A man's religion is that of his intimate friend, so let every man be careful who he becomes intimate with.*[86] And, *solitude is better than an evil companion, but a virtuous companion is better than solitude.*[87]

Thus, keeping company with God-fearing and virtuous people draws one nearer to God. This is the praiseworthy, benevolent companionship, as is stated in so many Prophetic and other traditions. It

84. Bukhārī, *Ṣaḥīḥ*, (620, 1334); Muslim, *Ṣaḥīḥ*, (1712).
85. Bukhārī, *Ṣaḥīḥ*, (5702, 5703); Muslim, *Ṣaḥīḥ*, (4779).
86. Abū Dāwūd, *Sunan*, (4139); Tirmidhī, *Sunan*, (2300).
87. Al-Ḥākim, *Mustadrak,* (5475); Bayhaqī, *Shu'ab al-Īmān*, (4784).

is love for God and in God, the rewards of which are immense, and the importance in religion and rank of which are high.

On the other hand, the company of evil people and those whose company brings nothing good, such as the heedless who are distracted away from God and the Last Abode, is a blameworthy detestable company, for evil and corrupt people should be detested in God and it is incumbent to avoid and stay away from them. This is one of the important matters in religion. He who loves in and for God those of God's servants who are righteous and God-fearing must necessarily detest those who rebel against Him and turn away from His obedience. For love in God and detestation in God go together, neither can be sound without the other, and both rank high in religion. The Messenger of God—may God's blessings and peace be upon him—said, *Among the strongest ties of faith are to love in God and detest in God.*[88] And, *The best of works are to love in God and detest in God…*[89] And he said that religion was but love and detestation.

God revealed to Jesus—may peace be upon him, "Were you to worship Me as much as all the inhabitants of the heavens and the earth, but without loving for My sake and detesting for My sake, it would avail you nothing with Me." And Jesus himself—may peace be upon him—said, "Seek God's love by detesting those who commit sins. Draw nearer to God by keeping away from them. And seek God's good pleasure in their displeasure." Al-Ḥasan al-Baṣrī—may God have mercy on him—said, "Boycotting the corrupt brings you nearer to God."

It has now become clear that it is incumbent upon the believer to love the people of goodness, religion, knowledge, and virtue, both the living and the dead. So should he detest the people of falsehood, corruption, iniquity, and transgression, both the living and the dead. He should choose for companions the virtuous and righteous and avoid the evil and the corrupt. The *ḥadīth* says, *Keep no company save that of a believer, nor let anyone eat your food but a God-fearing person.*[90] He who is able to find no God-fearing, virtuous, benevolent believer to keep company with, then seclusion and solitude are better and nearer rectitude than to mix with evil, corrupt people. Associating with corrupt people is of immense harm and tremendous

88. Aḥmad, *Musnad,* (17793); Bayhaqī, *Shu'ab al-Īmān*, (12, 13).
89. Abū Dāwūd, *Sunan*, (3983).
90. Aḥmad, *Musnad,* (10909); Al-Ḥākim, *Mustadrak,* (7273); Al-Ḥākim, *Mustadrak,* (9064).

evil. It is fraught with perils and difficult trials, both immediate and future. Among these are acquiring their attributes unaware, watching them and so coming to find comfort in their presence, inclining toward their evil states, easing the impact of sins on the heart, being led to imitating them and approving of their words and deeds.

The poet said,

> Ask not about a man, but about his companions,
> For one is bound to imitate one's companions

Another said,

> Mangy animals are not cured by proximity to the healthy
> But it is the healthy that become mangy

Now you know how the company of superior, virtuous people is full of benefits and of both immediate and long-term profits. He said—may God's blessings and peace be upon him, *The good companion is like the musk vendor. Either he gives you of it, or you may purchase some, or you will smell from him a fragrant smell. But the evil companion is like the bellows blower. Either he burns your clothes or you smell from him a foul smell.*[91]

You may ask, "Should one befriend a good person given to obedience who then shifts behavior and becomes one who is distracted and sinful, what should one do then?" I say, "You should counsel him gently and compassionately and try to make him return to God. If he does not respond, you should admonish him harshly and try to put the fear of God into him. If this gives no result, stay away from him and wait for God's decision. Should he revert to his previous good state, you can resume your friendship; if not, there is no good in befriending a person in which there is no good."

If you ask, "One is obliged to detest sinners, avoid them, and abandon befriending and mixing with them, but is one also not obliged to counsel the Muslims in general and to summon those people who are evil and sinful to good and obedience?" I say, "It is so. But counseling and inviting to goodness does not necessitate keeping their company and mixing with them. It may take place either when you meet them and feel that they would be willing to accept counseling and inviting them to goodness, or if you are qualified you may go to them wherever you know you are likely to find them without becoming their companion or mixing with them much.

91. Bukhārī, *Ṣaḥīḥ*, (1959, 5108); Muslim, *Ṣaḥīḥ*, (4762).

This is commendable and required of those who are qualified. Know this and let not the Devil confound you, for the road is clear and right is distinct from wrong.

Know now that when you wish to befriend someone so that he may be your companion, that you may find comfort in his company, and that he may be of assistance to you in both your worldly and religious affairs, you should choose carefully beforehand, test him, and inquire about his behavior. If he turns out to be suitable, so be it. If not, you should not proceed, for not everyone is suitable to become a friend and companion. Such companionship that is not preceded by deliberate choice often quickly turns into enmity and estrangement.

The Proof of Islām—may God have mercy on him—says, "Whenever you wish to befriend someone, look for five things in him, intelligence, good character, virtue, some degree of detachment from worldly things, and that he is not a liar." This is comprehensive and sufficient.

When friendship comes into being and affection is born between your companion and yourself certain rights become incumbent upon you without the fulfillment of which this friendship will remain an image without reality, devoid of benefit, useless.

The rights of companionship are many. In sum they are to desire for your companion the same good you desire for yourself and dislike to see him subjected to any evil you would have disliked to suffer yourself, to attribute the same importance to his affairs as to yours, strive to serve his interests and fulfill his needs, feel happy when his situation is satisfactory and anxious when it is not, try to bring him happiness in any way you can, preserve his interests whether he is present or absent, during his lifetime and after he dies, look after his wife, children, and relatives during his life and after his death, and help him with your money whenever he needs help. If you can bring yourself to give him preference over yourself it would be better and more excellent. This is how the virtuous predecessors behaved—may God have mercy on them—and their behavior toward their companions was praiseworthy as is well known. They would enter their friends' houses in their absence, eat of their food, and take whatever they needed. Their friends did the same with them. One of them was asked, "Do you have more love for your brother or for your friend?" He answered, "I love my brother when he is my friend." Another asked a man he was visiting, "Does one of you put his hand into his brother's pocket and take whatever he needs?" He said, "No." He said, "Then you are not brothers." Whenever one of them died, his companion would take such complete care of his wife and children that the only thing the children missed was to see their father's face. Numerous well known stories have been handed down concerning this. However, this is something that we have lost a long time ago, so that nothing remains of brotherhood in God and friendship save appearances and formalities that are of no use. The Imām, the Proof of Islam has written comprehensively on the conditions of companionship, its rights and courtesies, in the Book of Companionship in the *Iḥyā'*, and has discoursed on it briefly but usefully in *Bidāyat'al-Hidāya*.

On the whole, every behavior that is either obligatory or recommended toward Muslims in general becomes more incumbent and recommended toward friends and companions.

The Rights of Muslims in General

Every Muslim has numerous rights over other Muslims. We have mentioned some of them in the Book of Assistance, so you may look them up there if you wish.

The Messenger of God—may God's blessings and peace be upon him—said, *The rights of one Muslim on another are six.* They asked, "What are they, O Messenger of God?" He answered, *Whenever you meet him, greet him with* salām, *whenever he calls you, answer him, whenever he asks you for counsel, counsel him, whenever he sneezes, bless him, whenever he is ill, visit him, and whenever he dies, escort his funeral.*[92]

Among the most incumbent rights of one Muslim over another are to counsel him in religious matters, assist him in acts of benevolence and God-fearing, and exhort him to obey God, Lord of the Worlds.

Other important rights are to keep concealed what would shame him, relieve his distress, assist him whenever he needs assistance, fulfill his needs, save he who is in peril, support the oppressed, help the weak, grant respite to the one in difficulty, respect the elderly, show compassion to the small, avoid causing harm, avoid treating him disdainfully or despising him, avoid letting him down, deriding, or mocking him. You should never cheat a Muslim, nor resent, harbor rancor, or think ill of him. You must be concerned with the situation of Muslims in general, feel happy when something good happens to them and aggrieved when something evil befalls them, desire

92. Muslim, *Ṣaḥīḥ*, (4023); Aḥmad, *Musnad,* (8490, 8973).

for them all what you desire for yourself and dislike for them what you dislike for yourself. He said—may God's blessings and peace be upon him, *None of you is a believer until he desires for his brother what he desires for himself.*[93] And, *A believer is to other believers as one edifice each part of which supports the others.*[94] And, *He who is unconcerned with the affairs of the Muslims is not one of them.*[95] And, *He is not one of us who has no compassion for our young and no respect for our elders.*[96] And, *He who cheats us is not of us.*[97] And, *Support your brother whether he is wrong or being wronged.* They asked, "Support him when he is being wronged we know, but how do we support him when he is the one committing the wrong?" he answered, *If you prevent him from wronging others you will have supported him.*[98] And he said may-God's blessings and peace be upon him, *Resent not one another, bid not higher to deceive one another, detest not one another, turn not your backs on one another, try not to outbid one another in commerce, and -O servants of God- be brothers! The Muslim is a brother to the Muslim; he does not wrong him, nor let him down, nor despise him, nor lie to him. Piety is here.* At this he pointed his noble hand at his chest three times. *It is sufficient evil for a man to despise his brother Muslim. Everything in the Muslim is forbidden, his blood, his property, and his honor.*[99] And, *He who relieves a believer's distress in this world, God shall relieve his distress on Resurrection Day. He who grants a person in difficulty respite, God shall ease his difficulties in this life and the next. He who shields a Muslim from shame, God shall shield him from shame in this life and the next. God will always assist the servant so long as the servant is assisting his brother.*[100] And, *He who is striving to fulfill his brother's need, God shall fulfill his.*[101]

God says the truth and He guides to the path.

---

93. Bukhārī, *Ṣaḥīḥ*, (12); Muslim, *Ṣaḥīḥ*, (64).
94. Bukhārī, *Ṣaḥīḥ*, (459, 2266); Muslim, *Ṣaḥīḥ*, (4684).
95. Al-Ḥākim, *Mustadrak,* (7273); Ṭabarānī, *Awsaṭ*, (7686).
96. Abū Dāwūd, *Sunan*, (8002, 8016), Tirmidhī, *Sunan*, (478, 1842).
97. Muslim, *Ṣaḥīḥ*, (146); Ibn Māja, *Sunan*,(2216).
98. Bukhārī, *Ṣaḥīḥ*, (6438); Tirmidhī, *Sunan*, (2141).
99. Bayhaqī, *Shu'ab al-Īmān*, (6385); Bukhārī, *Ṣaḥīḥ*, (2262); Muslim, *Ṣaḥīḥ*, (4650).
100. Muslim, *Ṣaḥīḥ*, (4867); Abū Dāwūd, *Sunan*, (4295); Tirmidhī, *Sunan*, (1345).
101. Bukhārī, *Ṣaḥīḥ*, (2262, 6437); Muslim, *Ṣaḥīḥ*, (4677).

Chapter Eleven: On Ruinous Things

Ḥalāl or Lawful Provision

Know O brothers—may God suffice us with what is lawful from needing the unlawful, with His obedience from His disobedience, and with His favor from other than Him- that one of the most important religious duties and best things with which a servant may seek to draw nearer to God, the Lord of the Worlds, is carefully to keep away from the unlawful and the suspect, and seek the lawful and expend of it. God—Exalted is He—says, *O Men! Eat of what is in the earth, lawful and good, and follow not the steps of the Devil, he is to you a manifest enemy.* [2:168] And, *Eat of what God has provided you, lawful and good, and fear God in whom you are believers.* [5:88] And, *O believers! Devour not your wealth between you wrongly, except there be trading by mutual agreement; and kill not one another. Truly God is compassionate to you. But he who does that in transgression and injustice, him We shall certainly roast at a fire, and that for God is an easy matter.* [4:29, 30]

The Messenger of God—may God's blessings and peace be upon him—said, *The best of your religious practices is circumspection* (*wara'*).[1] And, *O Abū Hurayra! Be circumspect and you will be the best of worshippers…*[2] And, *Seeking lawful provision is incumbent upon every Muslim.*[3] And, *Seeking lawful provision is an obligation to every Muslim in addition to his other obligations.*[4] And, *God is good and He accepts only that which is good; and God has enjoined upon the believers what He had enjoined upon the Messengers, saying—Exalted is He, O Messengers! Eat of what is good and do good works, I know well what you do.* [23:51] And He said—Exalted is He, *O believers! Eat of the good things We have provided you.* [2:172] Then the Prophet mentioned a man unkempt, dusty, traveling long distances, raising his hands to heaven, *"O Lord! O Lord!" but his food is unlawful, his beverage unlawful, his clothes unlawful, and he had been sustaining himself on the unlawful, how*

---

1. Al-Ḥākim, *Mustadrak,* (288,289); Bayhaqī, *Shu'ab al-Īmān*, (1665, 1667); Ṭabarānī, *Awsaṭ*, (4170).
2. Ibn Maja, Sunan, (4207); Bayhaqī, *Shu'ab al-Īmān*, (5510, 10683).
3. Ṭabarānī, *Awsaṭ*, (8848).
4. Bayhaqī, *Shu'ab al-Īmān*, (8482); Ṭabarānī, *Kabīr*, (9851).

can such a one possibly be answered?[5] And he said—may God's blessings and peace be upon him, *He shall not be admitted to the Garden whose flesh has grown on the unlawful.*[6] And, *Every flesh that has grown on the unlawful, the Fire is more worthy of it.*[7] And, *For you to fill your mouth with dust is better than to put into it unlawful food.*[8] And, *When one acquires money from an unlawful source, then gives it away in charity, it is not accepted from him. If he spends it, it will never be blessed, and if he leaves it behind, it will be his provision* [on his journey] *to the Fire.*[9] And, *He who buys a garment for ten* Dirhams, *one of which is unlawful, God shall accept no ritual prayer of him so long as he wears it.*[10] If this is what happens when one tenth of the price of the garment is unlawful, how will it be if the whole price was so? And if this is what happens with a garment on the outside of the body, what about the food which enters into the body and flows into the flesh, blood, veins, bones, and all the rest of the body? Reflect upon this with deliberation, fear God, and beware.

Ibn 'Abbās—may God be pleased with him and his father—said, "God does not accept the ritual prayer of a man inside whom is one unlawful morsel of food." And ibn 'Umar—may God be pleased with him and his father- said, "Were you to keep praying until you become [bent] like a bow, and fast until you become [thin] like a bowstring, none of this will be accepted in the absence of protective circumspection." It is said that the Torah says, "He who cares little where his food comes from, God cares little from which of the doors of the Fire He shall admit him." And Sufyān al-Thawrī—may God have mercy on him—said, "He who expends unlawful gains in acts of obedience is as he who washes his polluted clothes with urine." Obviously, the clothes will never be purified in that manner, but only increase in impurity. And ibn al-Mubārak—may God have mercy on him—said, "To refuse a single suspect *Dirham* is more

5. Muslim, *Ṣaḥīḥ*, (1686); Tirmidhī, *Sunan*, (2915); Aḥmad, *Musnad*, (7998).

6. Bayhaqī, *Shu'ab al-Īmān*, (5520, 5521, 9081); Dārimī, *Sunan*, (2832); Ibn Ḥibbān, *Ṣaḥīḥ*, (1751); Ṭabarānī, *Kabīr*, (15628, 15640).

7. Tirmidhī, *Sunan*, (558); Aḥmad, *Musnad*, (13919, 14746).

8. Aḥmad, *Musnad*, (7177); Bayhaqī, *Shu'ab al-Īmān*, (5522).

9. Ṭabarānī, *Kabīr*, (10401); Al-Ḥākim, *Mustadrak,* (2096); Bayhaqī, *Shu'ab al-Īmān*, (5285).

10. Aḥmad, *Musnad*, (5473); Bayhaqī, *Shu'ab al-Īmān*, (5851).

pleasing to God than to give a hundred thousand *Dirhams* in charity, then a hundred thousand, then a hundred thousand..." He repeated it until they reached six hundred thousand. And Sahl ibn 'Abdallāh al-Tustarī—may God have mercy on him—said, "He who eats unlawful food, his limbs will disobey, whether he likes it or not and whether he knows it or not. But he who eats lawful food, his limbs will obey, whether he likes or not and whether he knows it or not, and he is granted success in good works." Our predecessors used to say, "Eat what you wish, so will you act." I say: Even if he who eats from unlawful or suspect sources seems outwardly to be performing acts of obedience, they are never accepted, for He says—Exalted is He, *God only accepts from the God-fearing*. [5:27] And the Prophet said—may God's blessings and peace be upon him, that God is good and *He accepts only what is good*.[11] He whose earnings are unlawful inevitably will be afflicted by outward and inward imperfections that will blemish his acts of obedience or even annul them. Whoever reflects on this and observes it in himself and others will recognize the truth of it, unless he is being deceived and lured.

It has now become clear and evident that one should avoid the unlawful to the utmost, guard oneself against it, and keep away from all it in all its forms.

The Suspect

As for the suspect, it is important to avoid it and it may even become obligatory. An authentic *ḥadīth* says, *He who guards himself against suspect things, he has protected his religion and honor, and he who falls into the suspect will fall into the unlawful*.[12] And, *Leave that which arouses your suspicion for that which does not*.[13]

Suspect things are things about which you have doubts and are undecided whether they are lawful or unlawful. These doubts arise from contradictions in the situation. That which is originally lawful, then doubts arise as to whether it still is or not, it is permissible to use it, because at its origin it was lawful. However, avoiding it because it is suspect is eminently virtuous. As for that which is originally unlawful, then doubts arise as to whether it has become lawful, it should be avoided because at the origin it was unlawful.

11. Aḥmad, *Musnad*, (9055).
12. Bukhārī, *Sahīh*, (50); Muslim, *Sahīh*, (2996).
13. Tirmidhī, *Sunan*, (2442); Aḥmad, *Musnad*, (12092).

Suspect things are of many kinds and degrees. Circumspection is strongly recommended here and consists in avoiding them all. However, sometimes suspicions are due to obsessive (*waswās*) or illusory thinking (*awhām*). For example one might say, "All kinds of wealth in this world are suspect, they are never free from invalid transactions at the origin and unjust handling later on, therefore I shall avoid them altogether." Or alternatively, "I shall accept whatever I need of them indiscriminately." These are but obsessions and extremism. The Prophet—may God's blessings and peace be upon him—repeated three times, *Extremists shall perish*![14] There are many kinds of obsessive doubts, they are all due to suspiciousness and illusory things that have no concrete basis in reality. No person should say, "There is nothing lawful left in this world." intending thereby to justify his abandoning circumspection and caution. This statement is false. Imām al-Ghazālī—may God have mercy on him—says, "The lawful is clear and so is the unlawful, as he said—may God's blessings and peace be upon him. This referred to his time—may God's blessings and peace be upon him—but also to all other times. The difference between one epoch and another is but the scarcity or abundance of the lawful, according to whether the epoch is good or corrupt." He goes on to say, "The lawful is abundant and so is the unlawful. The latter is not more abundant. In every epoch the three kinds must exist, the lawful, the unlawful, and the suspect, as the Messenger of God—may God's blessings and peace be upon him—stated when he said, 'The lawful is clear, etc…'"

Now know—may God have mercy on you—that we have drawn attention to suspect things in brief general terms, but they were discussed at length and in detail by the Proof of Islam in the Book of the Lawful and the Unlawful in the *Iḥyā'*, so that he who wishes to satisfy himself more fully concerning these things is advised to refer to that book. A certain scholar—may God have mercy on him—states that no other book was ever written in Islam that is equal to that one. I say: The whole of the *Iḥyā'* is unique in its kind and this becomes clearly evident to any person of knowledge and fair judgment that cares to read and reflect upon it.

14. Muslim, *Ṣaḥīḥ*, (4823); Abū Dāwūd, *Sunan*, (3992), Aḥmad, *Musnad*, (3473).

The Unlawful

Know—may God have mercy on you—that unlawful things are of two kinds, the first is that which is unlawful in itself such as carrion, blood, alcoholic beverages, and those birds, predators, animals, and insects that are forbidden for consumption. This kind never becomes lawful except in extreme necessity, which is for one on the verge of death to find nothing else to consume. Only then does it become permissible. God—Exalted is He—says, *Forbidden to you are carrion, blood, the flesh of swine, what has been consecrated to other than God, that which was strangled, that which was beaten to death, that which fell, that which was gored by horns, that of which predators have eaten-saving that which you make lawful* [by slaughtering before they die]- *and that which has been sacrificed to the idols. Also [forbidden] is the use of divining arrows. That is corruption. Today the disbelievers have despaired of* [ever stifling] *your religion, so fear them not, but fear Me! Today I have perfected your religion for you and chosen Islam for you as religion. But whosoever is forced by hunger, not deliberately inclining to sin,* [for him] *God is Forgiving, Compassionate.* [3:5] And, *He has forbidden you only carrion, blood, the flesh of swine, and that which has been consecrated to other than God. But he who is forced, neither transgressing, nor wronging, no sin shall be on him. God is Forgiving, Compassionate.* [2:173]

To the second kind belong things which are lawful in their selves but owned by another. Things owned by another are unlawful to you save through a legally valid transaction such as buying, vows, gifts, donations, charity, inheritance, and so on. Were you to acquire one of these things other than in a legal manner, it becomes forbidden to you, and if you use it to buy food, beverage, or clothes, these will also be unlawful to you.

There are many forbidden manners of acquiring things, for instance coercion, theft, betrayal, usury, and so on.

Also, if the wealth of the person you are dealing with or taking from is unlawful, it will profit you nothing to take from him, even through a legally valid transaction. For example when a person, about whom you know that most of his wealth or something of that particular portion of his wealth that concerns you is unlawful, gives you something as a gift, or sells it to you by a valid transaction, these lawful transactions will not render the unlawful lawful. This may cause problems to people lacking insight.

It is now clear that a valid transaction does not change something originally unlawful into something lawful. On the other hand an invalid transaction will cause the lawful to become unlawful. For instance, lawful capital may yield unlawful money through an invalid transaction such as usury or something similar.

Now know—may God have mercy on you—that as concerns worldly transactions, people are of three kinds. The first is those who are known to be virtuous, good, and circumspect. It is unconditionally permissible to deal with them without prior inquiry or investigation. The second is those who are unknown to you so that you know nothing of their virtue or otherwise. It is unconditionally permissible to deal with them, but it is better to inquire and investigate whenever possible. This is commendable circumspection, but should be done with tact and without causing offence. The third is those who are known to be inconsistent, lack circumspection, and are reckless in their buying, selling, and other transactions. A God-fearing person should avoid dealing with them altogether. Should he ever be forced to, it becomes incumbent upon him to inquire about what he is about to take from them and investigate its sources. This is necessary circumspection. Should he come to know for certain or believe strongly that a person's wealth is all unlawful it becomes forbidden to deal with him. The same will apply should he come to know that most of his wealth is unlawful and that whatever is there that is lawful is scarce and rare.

Ibn al-Mubārak—may God have mercy on him—was once asked about whether one may deal with a man who deals with the ruler. He answered, "If his dealings are exclusively with the ruler, do not deal with him; but if he deals with others as well, you may deal with him." I say: he who wishes to be circumspect, cautious, and use nothing unlawful, let him be content with little of this world and not wish for more. Let him avoid extravagance, lavish spending, and excessive desire for pleasures. The virtuous predecessors used to say, "The lawful does not bear excess." He who is excessive in seeking the pleasures of this world will inevitably need to use means which cannot be used without indulging in suspect or even forbidden things. This is well known by anyone who has tried it, is of good counsel to himself, and judges fairly, but not to the self-deceived fools and unintelligent ignorant people who deliberately wade into suspect and unlawful things, while pretending to be careful and to accept nothing but what is lawful, then following this with feeble arguments and far fetched explanations to justify their behavior.

God-fearing and circumspection are incumbent and inescapable. Should there be shortcomings, then the least one can do is to be fair and concede that it has happened, then remain humble and ask for forgiveness. One of the virtuous predecessors—may God have mercy on them—was asked, "Where do you eat from?" He answered, "From the same place that you do, but he who weeps as he eats is not as he who laughs." And God—Transcendent is He—knows best.

It is now clear that circumspection is the pivot of religion, the way of the believers who are resolute people of certainty. The virtuous predecessors—may God have mercy on them—were extremely careful to be circumspect and meticulously so. Their stories illustrating this are well known and their pattern of behavior well recorded and familiar to all.

It has reached us that ibn Sīrīn—may God have mercy on him—once bought numerous large jars of oil for much money. In one of them he found a dead mouse. He spilled them all, saying, "I fear that the mouse may have died in the oil press and that all the oil ran over it." As for Sufyān al-Thawrī—may God have mercy on him—when he failed to find purely lawful provision, he ate sand for days. Ibn al-Mubārak once returned from Merv in Khorāsān to Syria because he had borrowed a pen and forgotten to return it. And Ibrāhīm ibn Adham—may God have mercy on him—returned from Jerusalem to Baṣra to return a date that had fallen among his as they were being weighed and that he had forgotten to return at the time. When Dhu'l-Nūn al-Miṣrī—may God have mercy on him—was jailed, a virtuous woman sent him some lawful food which she had bought with the price of her spinning. He sent it back saying it had come to him carried by an iniquitous person, meaning the jailer. One of them attended a moribund patient on a certain night. When he died, he said, "Put out the lamp, for now it has become the property of his heirs." Another said, "Once as I was traveling I lost my way and became extremely thirsty. A soldier who crossed my way gave me some water to drink which caused some hardness to affect my heart for thirty years." There are many more such stories. The few that we have quoted were for the *baraka* of remembering them, for mercy descends when the virtuous are mentioned. But he who is possessed of insight should recognize the difference between the predecessors and the latecomers, understand in what kind of time he lives, and who are the people to whom he belongs and among whom he lives.

Now know—may God have mercy on you—that consuming what is lawful illuminates and softens the heart, instills into it the fear of God and humility before His majesty, activates the bodily members in acts of worship and obedience, causes detachment from this world and desire for the hereafter, and is the means by which one's good works are accepted and prayers answered. As he said—may God's blessings and peace be upon him—to Sa'd ibn Abī Waqqāṣ—may God be pleased with him, *Eat pure food and your prayers shall be answered.*[15]

As for the unlawful and the suspect, they cause the opposite of these good effects. They harden and darken the heart, prevent the bodily members from obedience, instill desire for this world, and cause good works to be rejected and prayers to remain unanswered, as in the *ḥadīth* where the Prophet—may God's blessings and peace be upon him—mentions a man who is unkempt and dusty, who raises his hands toward heaven, "O Lord! O Lord!" But his food is unlawful, etc... We have already quoted the *ḥadīth* in full.

Be careful to the extreme to eat only what is lawful and avoid the unlawful. Circumspection involves not only food, but everything else as well.

Lawful and Unlawful Earnings

You must make your earnings lawful, for it is incumbent upon a person to earn his living and there is merit and abundant reward in doing so when the intention is good. The Prophet said—may God's blessings and peace be upon him, *The best that a man may eat is that which is his own earning.*[16] And, *He upon whom evening comes to find him weary of lawful labor, he will be forgiven.*[17] So let a person work with the intention of protecting his religion, saving himself the embarrassment of depending on others, sufficing himself and his dependents, and giving the surplus away as charity to the needy among the servants of God the Exalted. He would thus be working for the hereafter.

15. Ṭabarānī, *Awsaṭ*, (6683).

16. Abū Dāwūd, *Sunan*, (3061); Nasā'ī, *Sunan*, (4373); Tirmidhī, *Sunan*, (1278).

17. Ṭabarānī, *Awsaṭ*, (7733).

Let him beware to the extreme of becoming so occupied with earning that he neglects God's obligations or falls into what He has forbidden. He would thus lose both this world and the next. There is no clearer evidence of failure. One of our virtuous predecessors—may God have mercy on them—said, "There are three kinds of men, one who is too occupied with the hereafter to attend to this world, he is one of the successful; another who is occupied with this world, but only for the sake of the hereafter, he is one of the lukewarm; and a third who is too occupied with this world to attend to the hereafter, he is one of the unjust." Or he might have said, "one of those who will perish."

If you are one who earns his living from an art or a craft, you must deal honestly with all Muslims[18] and do your job with as much precision and excellence as you can. The *ḥadīth* says, *God loves the believer who is a craftsman.*[19]

Beware of lying or cheating, of breaking your promises, saying, "Tomorrow," or "the day after tomorrow." Beware to the extreme of neglecting to achieve excellence when dealing with someone who is unlikely to recognize the faults in your work, or of using his unfamiliarity with your craft to deceive him. It has been handed down, "Woe to the craftsman and the merchant from, 'No, by God!' and 'Yes, by God!'"[20] And woe to the craftsman from, 'Tomorrow,' and 'the day after tomorrow.'

If you are a merchant, strive in all your dealings to avoid invalid transactions and the kind of contracts that are either forbidden or discouraged. Learn about these things and understand them. There is no way out for you from this and absolutely no permission to neglect it. 'Umar ibn al-Khaṭṭāb—may God be pleased with him—said, "He who has not studied should neither sell nor buy in our market, for he who has not studied may deal in usury unaware." It is as he said—may God be pleased with him.

You must always be fair and generous in your commerce, choose to be indulgent and lenient, rather than rigorous and demanding. This is more likely to increase the *baraka* and accrue your gains. He

18. The author lived in a community composed entirely of Muslims, hence such expressions. Those who live among non-Muslims should be aware that the same legal rules apply to everyone indiscriminately.

19. Bayhaqī, *Shu'ab al-Īmān*, (1233); Ṭabarānī, *Awsaṭ*, (2267).

20. Said by 'Umar during his caliphate and transmitted by Ṭabarī in *Tahdhīb al-Āthār*, (1346).

said—may God's blessings and peace be upon him, *May God have mercy on a servant who is indulgent when he sells, indulgent when he buys, and indulgent when he requests his money.*[21]

Never buy or sell anything without valid formulas of offer and acceptance, for simply handing over something is insufficient to complete the transaction, although some have permitted it in the case of insignificant items, and although the Proof of Islam seemed inclined to accept it when discussing at length in the *Iḥyā'* how to effect exchanges. Nevertheless, buying and selling using explicit agreements is always better and more cautious.

You must refrain from lying altogether. Never say, "I have bought it for so much, I have given for it so much, I will not sell it for less than so much," when you are being untrue, for then you will lose even as you hope to gain. Never swear by God when selling or buying, for the whole world is more insignificant and vile than to deserve a truthful oath, how much more so when you lie? There is no need for oaths. A *ḥadīth* says, *God detests the merchant who constantly swears.*[22] He also said—may God's blessings and peace be upon him, *Oaths may sell the merchandise, but destroy the* baraka (*or profit*).[23] And, *Merchants will be led to the gathering on Resurrection Day as corrupt people, save those who had been God-fearing, loyal, and truthful.*[24]

Beware to the extreme of cheating, deception, fraud, and hiding the faults in what you are selling, for these are severely forbidden and may render transactions altogether invalid. When the Prophet—may God's blessings and peace be upon him—passed by a man who was selling foodstuff and, passing his hand through, felt some of it to be damp, he said, *O owner of the food, what is this*? The man answered, "Rain came down on it." He said, *Will you not place it on top where people can see it? He who cheats us is not of us.*[25] In another version he is said to have observed some low quality food among the rest. He said, *Will you not sell each separately? He*

21. Bukhārī, *Ṣaḥīḥ*, (1934); Ibn Māja, *Sunan*, (2194); Bayhaqī, *Shu'ab al-Īmān*, (7889).
22. Aḥmad, *Musnad,*(20377, 20550); Nasā'ī, *Sunan*, (2529); Bayhaqī, *Shu'ab al-Īmān*, (4659, 7113, 9227).
23. Bukhārī, *Ṣaḥīḥ*, (1945); Muslim, *Ṣaḥīḥ*, (3014).
24. Ibn Māja, *Sunan,* (2137); Tirmidhī, *Sunan,*(1131).
25. Al-Ḥākim, *Mustadrak,* (2114); Ibn Ḥibbān, *Ṣaḥīḥ*, (4996).

who cheats us is not of us.[26] And he said—may God's blessings and peace be upon him, *The two parties retain their freedom of decision until they part company. If they are true and clear, their transaction will be blessed. But if they lie and conceal, the* baraka *in their transaction will be removed.*[27] None is allowed to sell faulty merchandise without pointing out the faults in it. If he conceals them and someone who is present knows about them, the latter is obliged to point them out, as says the *ḥadīth*, for being of good counsel is an obligation. Another kind of forbidden cheating is to mix good with bad merchandise, then sell them together to deceive the buyer. Yet another is to slip a bad dirham among the good ones, which thing is not permissible. If it is given in this manner to someone who is likely to give it to another Muslim in the course of another transaction, it is forbidden. There is no way to dispose of bad coins that do not resemble those in use in the land but to throw them down a well or any other such place, as certain virtuous predecessors used to do, or else take them to the silversmith who is able to extract whatever silver they contain, make it into good coins, and use the copper or any other metal that had been introduced into them in whatever useful manner is possible. He whose ego will not consent to this should be careful never to accept bad illegal *Dirhams*. Should one fall into his hand and his ego does not permit him to destroy it, he should return it forthwith to the person he has taken it from if known to him, but should never give it to another Muslim, for this would be sinful.

Let the merchant fear God in all his affairs, especially in weights and measures, for their peril is great. God—Exalted is He—says, *Woe to the fraudulent, those who, when they measure against the people, take full measure, but when they measure or weigh for others, defraud them.* [83:1-3] The Prophet—may God's blessings and peace be upon him—told the merchants, *You have been given charge of something that has caused previous communities to perish: weights and measures.*[28] Therefore, a merchant must be fair, which means that he must give in the same manner that he takes, and remain careful and cautious. It is better and more cautious for him to give a little more than he should when he gives, and take a little less than he should when taking. One of our virtuous predecessors used to do this, saying, "I am not one to buy 'Woe!' from God for a

26. Aḥmad, *Musnad*, (4867); Ṭabarānī, *Kabīr*, (365); *Awsaṭ*, (2590).
27. Bukhārī, *Ṣaḥīḥ*, (1968); Muslim, *Ṣaḥīḥ*, (2825).
28. Tirmidhī, *Sunan*,(1138); Bayhaqī, *Shu'ab al-Īmān*, (5056).

grain." Meaning by 'Woe!' that in *'Woe to the fraudulent!'* and by grain a little money. Among the virtues of merchants are to accept to annul his bargain with he who has changed his mind, grant respite to those unable to settle what they owe him, deal indulgently with the rest, loan those who need a loan, and fulfill the needs of those in need. He said—may God's blessings and peace be upon him, *He who accepts to annul* [his contract] *with another who is regretting it, God shall annul* [reckoning for] *all his previous stumbling on Judgment Day.*[29] An authentic *ḥadīth* says, *A man who had never done any good used to loan people, saying to his servant, "Collect what is given easily and leave those who are in difficulty. Be indulgent that perhaps God shall treat us indulgently." When he died God—August and Majestic—asked him, "Have you ever done any good at all?" He answered, "No, but I had a servant and I used to loan people, and whenever I sent him to collect I told him to take what is given easily and leave those who are in difficulty, and be indulgent that perhaps God shall treat us indulgently." God, Exalted is He, said, "I shall treat you indulgently."*[30]

He said—may God's blessings and peace be upon him, *Every loan is a charity.*[31] And, *I saw written on the gate of the Garden on the night I was made to journey, 'A charity is multiplied ten times, but a loan is multiplied eighteen times.'*[32]

Let the merchant beware to the extreme of outbidding his brother who has just concluded a purchasing or selling transaction. This means that before the two parties separate he says to the buyer, "I have cheaper than this to offer you." Or to the seller, "I shall give you more for this." Both are forbidden. So is to bid higher with no intention to buy, but to raise the price so as to deceive other Muslims.

Let him also beware of monopolizing food, for it is strictly forbidden. Several *ḥadīth*s rigorously forbid this, such as his saying—may God's blessings and peace be upon him, *He who monopolizes one kind of food for forty nights, he has disavowed God, and God*

29. Ibn Ḥibbān, *Ṣaḥīḥ*, (5119).

30. Nisā'ī, *Sunan*, (4615).

31. Bayhaqī, *Shu'ab al-Īmān*, (5056); Ṭabarānī, *Awsaṭ*, (3631); *Ṣaghīr*, (403).

32. Ibn Māja, *Sunan,*(2422); Bayhaqī, *Shu'ab al-Īmān*, (3405, 3407); Ṭabarānī, *Awsaṭ*, (6908).

shall disavow him.[33] And, *He who brings shall be provided for, but he who monopolizes shall be cursed.*[34] And, *He who practices monopoly is a sinner.*[35] And it has been transmitted that those who engage in monopoly for forty days, then give it all in charity, it will still not be sufficient to save them, and that those who engage in monopoly shall be gathered in the same place with those guilty of murder on Resurrection Day.

Monopoly is to buy food and hoard it when the times are hard, food is expensive, and the people need it, and then hide it until such time as a large profit can be made on it. If it is bought when prices are cheap, with the intention of keeping it until they rise, or if the excess in crops is kept with the same intention, this is not free from being severely reprehensible, and he who does so is in grave danger because of his wish for the prices to rise. Even were he to escape the charge of concealing food, he will not that of desiring the prices to increase which thing will surely cause hardship to the Muslims. The virtuous predecessors used to dislike trading in food altogether because it is trading in necessities, so that the merchant comes to detest ease and affluence for the people and love hard times and dear prices.

Usury (*ribā*)

As for usury, it is an immense sin and a great injustice. God—Exalted is He—says, *O believers! Fear God and give up the usury that is outstanding if you are believers. If you do not, then be warned that God has declared war on you, so has His Messenger.* [2:278, 279] Who can combat God and His Messenger? We seek God's protection from being loathed, afflicted, or wretched. The Messenger of God—may God's blessings and peace be upon him—has cursed he who profits from usury, he whom he profits from, his witness, and his scribe.[36] He counted usury among the seven major sins, together with such things as associating others with God and slaying the soul

33. Aḥmad, *Musnad*, (4648); Al-Ḥākim, *Mustadrak,* (2124).
34. Bayhaqī, *Shu'ab al-Īmān*, (10766); Dārimī, *Sunan*, (2599); Ibn Māja, *Sunan,* (2144).
35. Muslim, *Ṣaḥīḥ*, (3013), Abū Dāwūd, *Sunan*, (2990); Ibn Māja, *Sunan,* (2145); Tirmidhī, *Sunan*, (1188).
36. Muslim, *Ṣaḥīḥ*, (2995); Abū Dāwūd, *Sunan*, (2895); Tirmidhī, *Sunan*,(1127).

that God has forbidden.[37] He said—may God's blessings and peace be upon him, *Usury is of thirty seven kinds, the least of which is equivalent to a man having intercourse with his mother.*[38] And, *Four* [kinds of people] *are forbidden to enter the Garden and taste of its bliss, the alcoholic, the usurer, he who appropriates the property of orphans unjustly, and he who rebels against his parents.*[39]

He said—may God's blessings and peace be upon him, *Gold for gold, silver for silver, wheat for wheat, barley for barley, dates for dates, salt for salt*, [these should be] *like for like, equal for equal, given and taken on the spot. If the kinds differ, then sell as you wish so long as it is on the spot.*[40] He made clear in this *ḥadīth*—may God's blessings and peace be upon him—the legal ruling concerning usury so as to leave no room for disagreement or disobedience. God—Exalted is He—says, *What the Messenger has brought you, take; and what he has forbidden you, desist.* [59:7] And, *Let those beware who disobey his orders lest an affliction befall them or a painful torment.* [24:63] Thus, whoever exchanges gold for gold, silver for silver, wheat for wheat, corn for corn, or dates for dates, must do so like for like, given and taken on the spot. If the kinds differ, for instance wheat for corn, or corn for dates, different measures are permissible and the exchange has to be concluded by each taking what is his immediately. There are many details here the place of which is the books of *fiqh*, this was but a summary.

Beware to the extreme, O brother—may God have mercy on you—of usury, guard yourself against it carefully, for God has forbidden it to His servants, declaring it to be evil and devoid of all good or *baraka*. As He says—Exalted is He, *God destroys usury and increases charity; and God loves not every disbelieving sinner.* [2:276] And, *O believers! Devour not usury, doubled and redoubled, and fear God, that you may succeed. And fear the fire that has been prepared for the disbelievers. And obey God and the Messenger, that you may find mercy.* [3:130-132]

Reflect and consider, and fear God and be cautious, and know that in deferred payment *(nasī'a)* while paying a higher price than that presently required, there is sufficient room to leave usury. This

37. Bukhārī, *Ṣaḥīḥ*, (2560, 6351); Muslim, *Ṣaḥīḥ*, (129).

38. Al-Ḥākim, *Mustadrak,* (2219).

39. Al-Ḥākim, *Mustadrak,* (2220).

40. Muslim, *Ṣaḥīḥ*, (2970); Tirmidhī, *Sunan*,(1161).

is permissible and lawful, so let those who desire the profits of this world take advantage of it.[41]

Beware of the tricks and fraudulent practices that certain self-deceiving fools indulge in. They pretend that usury is not usury, calling things "vows" and circulating them among themselves, thereby imagining that they are safe from its sin and have managed to escape the shame of it in this world and the Fire of it in the next. How unlikely! Tricks in usury are nothing other than usury. A vow (*nadhr*) is something that the servant gives away in benevolent works to please his Lord, only thus can it be valid. What these people do is observably different. He said—may God's blessings and peace be upon him, *No vow* [is valid] *save for something that leads to the good pleasure of God.*[42]

Certain jurists have said that to declare something a vow does alter its legal status in transaction. Even so, this will only affect its external appearance and how it may be viewed in this world, but not its reality and its consequences in the hereafter. He who searches for what those scholars possessed of insight have said will find that they are all agreed in this. The Proof of Islam has said concerning he who vows his wealth to another at the end of the year so that he has to pay no *zakāt* on it and concerning other similar instances, "This all belongs to the deleterious kind of jurisprudence. He who has declared it permissible has meant it to be so only as concerns evading being asked to pay it according to the rules of this world, but when the matter returns to the Wisest of the wise, the Compeller of compellers, it will avail nothing."

The Israelites have suffered many kinds of punishments for indulging in such tricks and deceptions, as well knows anyone who has studied the history of the ancients. Were it not for our concern for brevity we would have quoted some of that. The best of words are those that are brief but informative. *He whom God wishes to tempt, you will avail him nothing with God.* [5:41]

It is a kind of *ribā*[43] to wrongly appropriate other people's property. The manners in which this can be done are numerous and have

41. Deferred payment means taking the commodity now and paying a higher price for it later.

42. Abū Dāwūd, *Sunan*, (2848); Aḥmad, *Musnad*, (6444).

43. The literal meaning of the Arabic word "*ribā*" is to increase. The technical meaning is "usury". However, the term is sometimes used, as the author is doing here, to indicate any kind of illegal increase of one's wealth.

all been forbidden by God—Exalted is He—when He said, *O believers! Devour not one another's wealth wrongly.* [4:29] Among the wrong manners of appropriating other people's money are what iniquitous rulers and their aides extract from the Muslims in terms of taxes, duties, customs, etc. These are strictly forbidden. That which is acquired illegally is undoubtedly unlawful. Levy collectors of all kinds expose themselves to God's wrath and loathing. Several *ḥadīth*s exist censuring them and describing the severity of their punishment. He said—may God's blessings and peace be upon him, *Levy collectors never enter the Garden.*[44] Yazīd ibn Hārūn—may God have mercy on him—said, "He meant excise collectors." And he said—may God's blessings and peace be upon him, *The levy collector is in the Fire.*[45]

Other manners of wrongly appropriating other people's property are to take it unjustly by coercion or brigandage, theft, betrayal of trust, false oaths, and false witness. He said—may God's blessings and peace be upon him, *He who takes a hand-span of land unjustly, God shall wrap it around his neck to the depth of seven earths.*[46] And, *Guard yourselves against injustice, for injustice will be darkness on Judgment Day.*[47] And, *It is unlawful for a Muslim to take his brother's staff without his agreement.* The Companion who transmitted the *ḥadīth* continued, "He said this to demonstrate how severely forbidden the property of a Muslim is."[48] And he said—may God's blessings and peace be upon him—concerning theft, *May God curse the thief! He steals an egg and has his hand cut off, or steals a rope and has his hand cut off.*[49] And he said—may God's blessings and peace be upon him—about betrayal, *The signs of a hypocrite are three, when he speaks, he lies; when he promises, he break his promise; and when he is entrusted with something, he betrays his trust.*[50] And he said—may God's blessings and peace be upon him, *He who cannot be trusted has no faith and he who*

Sometimes it is even used to indicate an increase in one's conceit by belittling or slandering others.

44. Abū Dāwūd, *Sunan*, (2548); Aḥmad, *Musnad*, (16656, 16714).
45. Aḥmad, *Musnad*, (16387); Ṭabarānī, *Kabīr*, (4366).
46. Bukhārī, *Ṣaḥīḥ*, (2273); Muslim, *Ṣaḥīḥ*, (3025).
47. Muslim, *Ṣaḥīḥ*, (4675); Aḥmad, *Musnad*, (5404).
48. Aḥmad, *Musnad*, (22500); Bayhaqī, *Shu'ab al-Īmān*, (5252).
49. Bukhārī, *Ṣaḥīḥ*, (6285, 6301); Muslim, *Ṣaḥīḥ*, (3195).
50. Bukhārī, *Ṣaḥīḥ*, (32, 2485); Muslim, *Ṣaḥīḥ*, (89, 90).

does not keep his pledges has no religion.[51] And, *He who cannot be trusted has no faith, without ritual purification there is no ritual prayer, and without ritual prayer there is no religion.*[52] And, *Three things are clutching at the Throne: Kinship bonds, saying, 'O God! I am by You, so let me not be severed'; trust, saying, "O God! I am by You, so let me not be betrayed; and favor, saying, 'O God! I am by You, so let me not be denied.'*[53]

False Oaths and False Witness

To appropriate other Muslims' wealth by shameless oaths or false witness is a major sin. Well known formidable threats have been proffered against those who commit such things. He said—may God's blessings and peace be upon him, *He who appropriates the wealth of his brother Muslim by a shameless oath, let him take his seat in the Fire.*[54] And, *When he who swears an unjust oath concerning a Muslim's property meets God—Exalted is He—he shall find Him angry with him.* 'Abdallāh ibn Mas'ūd—may God be pleased with him—said, "Then the Messenger of God—may God's blessings and peace be upon him—recited the confirmation for this in the Book of God the Exalted, *Those who sell God's pledge and their oaths for a small price, there shall be no share for them in the life to come. God shall not speak to them, neither look at them on the Day of Arising, nor will He purify them, and for them there shall be a painful torment.* [3:77] [55] And he said—may God's blessings and peace be upon him, *Major sins are to associate others with God, rebel against one's parents, and false oaths* (al-yamīn al-ghamūs).[56] Al-Ḥāfiẓ al-Mundhirī—may God have mercy on him—said, "It was called *al-yamīn al-ghamūs* because it immerses he who swears it into sin in this life and into the Fire in the next." This kind of false oath is that by means of which a person will appropriate something of his brother Muslim's property, however insignificant, to the ex-

51. Aḥmad, *Musnad*, (11935, 12108); Bayhaqī, *Shu'ab al-Īmān*, (5026).
52. Ṭabarānī, *Kabīr*, (19, 353); *Awsaṭ*, (2383); *Ṣaghīr*, (162) .
53. Bayhaqī, *Shu'ab al-Īmān*, (7705).
54. Al-Ḥākim, *Mustadrak,* (7912); Muslim, *Ṣaḥīḥ*, (196); Ibn Māja, *Sunan*, (2315).
55. Bukhārī, *Ṣaḥīḥ*, (2239, 2332); Muslim, *Ṣaḥīḥ*, (197, 198); Ibn Māja, *Sunan*, (2314).
56. Bukhārī, *Ṣaḥīḥ*, (6182, 6362); Tirmidhī, *Sunan*, (2946); Nasā'ī, *Sunan*, (3946).

tent that he said—may God's blessings and peace be upon him, *even a twig of arak.*[57]

As for appropriating other people's property by means of false witness, it is to induce someone to testify falsely, knowingly and deliberately. Both the witness and he whom he has testified for will have sinned. Such a witness will have traded his life to come for the worldly benefit of another. False witness is among the worst of major sins, as stated in authentic *ḥadīths*. He also said—may God's blessings and peace be upon him—repeating it three times, *False witness is equivalent to associating others with God.*[58] And, *Before the feet of a false witness move from their place* [on Judgment Day] *God will have decreed the Fire for him.*[59]

Another form of unjust appropriation of people's property is the bribes and gifts given to the ruler and government officials. These are unlawful. The Prophet—may God's blessings and peace be upon him—cursed he who bribes another, he who accepts a bribe, and he who has mediated between them. He said—may God's blessings and peace be upon him, *Gifts to officials are illegal gains.*[60]

It is also incumbent to beware and preserve oneself from soliciting from others, except in cases of dire need and severe necessity. The Messenger of God—may God's blessings and peace be upon him—said, *It is not lawful for one who has some money to solicit, nor for one who is healthy and strong.*[61] And, *One of you will keep soliciting until he meets God with not a piece of flesh left on his face.*[62] And, *For one who has some money to solicit is equivalent to the Fire. If he is given little, then a little [in the Fire], and if he is given much then much.*[63] When he was asked, "When is a person considered to have some money?" He answered that it was when he had enough for lunch and dinner. And he said—may God's blessings and peace be upon him, *For one of you to take his rope then gather some firewood is better than to solicit from others, whether*

---

57. Muslim, *Ṣaḥīḥ*, (196); Ibn Māja, *Sunan*, (2315).
58. Abū Dāwūd, *Sunan*, (3124); Tirmidhī, *Sunan*, (2222, 2223); Ibn Māja, *Sunan*, (2363).
59. Ibn Māja, *Sunan*, (2364).
60. Aḥmad, *Musnad*, (22495).
61. Tirmidhī, *Sunan*, (590).
62. Bukhārī, *Ṣaḥīḥ*, (1381); Muslim, *Ṣaḥīḥ*, (1724).
63. Bazzār, *Musnad,* (3018); Ṭabarānī, *Kabīr*, (14814).

you are given or not.[64] And, *Stay independent of others, even if you have to use the remains of a* siwāk.[65]

Alcoholic beverages

We now see fit to mention something of how forbidden and blameworthy alcohol is. This part of the book seems most appropriate to do so, since it will constitute the completion of the discourse on circumspection regarding food, beverages, and other things.

Alcoholic beverages are forbidden by God. He commanded the people to avoid them both in His Clear Book and by the tongue of His trustworthy Messenger. He says—Exalted is He, *O believers! Alcohol, gambling, dedicating to idols, and divining arrows are only depravities of the Devil's doing, so avoid them that you may succeed. The devil seeks only to cast among you enmity and hatred by means of alcohol and gambling, and to prevent you from the remembrance of God and ritual prayer. Will you not abstain?* [5:90, 91]

The Messenger of God—may God's blessings and peace be upon him—said, *At the time he commits adultery, the adulterer is not a believer; at the time he steals, the thief is not a believer; at the times he drinks, he who drinks an alcoholic beverage is not a believer.*[66] How utterly forbidden and reprehensible is a thing which causes a man's faith to abandon him when doing it! And he said—may God's blessings and peace be upon him, *God has cursed alcoholic beverages, as well as he who drinks, serves, buys, sells, makes, orders, carries, or receives them.*[67] In a version he adds, *and he who spends of its price*. And he said—may God's blessings and peace be upon him, *He who believes in God and the Last Day let him refrain from alcoholic beverages...*[68] And, *When he dies, the alcohol addict shall meet God—Exalted is He—as an idol worshipper.*[69] And, *Three shall never enter the Garden: the alcohol addict, the severer*

64. Bukhārī, *Ṣaḥīḥ*, (1377); Tirmidhī, *Sunan*, (616).

65. Bayhaqī, *Shu'ab al-Īmān*, (3373); Ṭabarānī, *Kabīr*, (12091).

66. Bukhārī, *Ṣaḥīḥ*, (5150, 6284); Muslim, *Ṣaḥīḥ*, (86, 87).

67. Abū Dāwūd, *Sunan*, (3189); Tirmidhī, *Sunan*, (1216); Ibn Māja, *Sunan*, (3371).

68. Ṭabarānī, *Kabīr*, (11300).

69. Aḥmad, *Musnad,* (2325); Ibn Ḥibbān, (5437).

of kinship bonds, and the believer in sorcery.[70] And, *Avoid alcohol, for it is the key to every evil.*[71] And, *Alcohol includes all other sins; women are the snares of the Devil.*[72] And, *The love of this world leads to every sin.* [73] Ibn ʿAbbās—may God be pleased with him and his father-said, "When alcohol was prohibited, the companions of the Messenger of God—may God's blessings and peace be upon him—took to visiting each other, saying, 'Alcohol has been forbidden and made equivalent to idolatry.'" meaning in its magnitude as a sin. The Prophet—may God's blessings and peace be upon him—said, *He who drinks alcohol, the light of faith leaves his inward.*[74] And, *He who drinks alcohol, God shall give him to drink the boiling water of Hell.*[75] And, *Every intoxicant is forbidden. It is binding upon God that he who drinks alcohol, He shall force him to drink the mud of insanity*. They asked, "O Messenger of God! What is this mud of insanity?" He answered, *That which oozes from the skins of those in Hell.*[76] And, *If they drink alcohol, whip them, if they drink again, whip them again, if they drink again, whip them again, then if they drink again, kill them.*[77] Al-Ḥāfiẓ al-Mundhirī—may God be pleased with him—said, "Several authentic sources mention the execution of the chronic alcoholic, but it was abrogated. And God knows best." And he said—may God's blessings and peace be upon him, *Alcohol is the mother of all filthy things.*[78] And, *He who drinks alcohol in this world shall not drink [the wine of the Garden] in the*

70. Aḥmad, *Musnad,* (18748); Al-Ḥākim, *Mustadrak,* (7343); Ibn Ḥibbān, *Ṣaḥīḥ*, (5436).

71. Ibn Māja, *Sunan*, (3362); Al-Ḥākim, *Mustadrak,* (7340); Bayhaqī, *Shuʿab al-Īmān*, (5345, 5346, 7621).

72. Bayhaqī, *Dalāʾil al-Nubuwwa,* (1994); Ibn Abī Shayba, *Muṣannaf,* vol.8, p. 162.

73. Bayhaqī, *Shuʿab al-Īmān*, (10111);

74. Ṭabarānī, *Kabīr*, (271); *Awsaṭ*, (349).

75. Aḥmad, *Musnad,* (21190); Bayhaqī, *Shuʿab al-Īmān*, (6258); Ṭabarānī, *Kabīr*, (7760).

76. Muslim, *Ṣaḥīḥ*, (3732); Abū Dāwūd, *Sunan*, (3195); Nasāʾī, *Sunan*, (5613).

77. Abū Dāwūd, *Sunan*, (3886); Ibn Māja, *Sunan*, (2563).

78. Nasāʾī, *Sunan*, (5572); Bayhaqī, *Shuʿab al-Īmān*, (5343, 5344); Dāraquṭnī, *Sunan*, (4672); Ibn Ḥibbān, *Ṣaḥīḥ*, (5436).

hereafter.[79] And, *He who drinks alcohol, God does not accept his ritual prayers for forty mornings.*[80]

There is much more that can be quoted with regard to the prohibition of alcohol, its blameworthy state, and the warnings proffered against it. However, that which we have quoted should be sufficient for he to whom God has decreed success. So beware O servants of God of this evil beverage which God has forbidden and made he who drinks it subject to wrath, loathing, and shame both in this world and the next. He who is afflicted with drinking it should repent before he is punished or dies and ends up in the Fire, subject to the wrath of the Compeller. We ask God for us and you for safety and security from all afflictions.

Guarding the Heart and the Bodily Members and Senses

Know, O brothers—may God make us and you of those whose inward and outward are good and upright in believing the truth and acting accordingly-that among the most important things to every believer is to watch his heart and bodily members and senses, look after them, and strive to guard and keep them from that which is hateful to God, and use them in that which is liked by God and pleasing to Him. He says—Exalted is He, *Hearing, sight, and the heart, these shall be asked about this.* [17:36]

The heart and the bodily members and senses are among the greatest favors of God upon His servants. He who uses them in His obedience and adorns them with what is pleasing to Him, and uses them in that for which they were created thus shows gratitude for the favor, guards what should be guarded, and excels in service. For him God shall give the reward of the thankful and the recompense of the excellent, for God never wastes the wages of those who act with excellence. But he who lets loose his heart and bodily members and senses in that which God has forbidden, neglects them and leads them to perdition, and leaves them unguarded, he thus denies the favor of God upon him and deserves to be censured and punished. They shall testify against him before God and reveal whatever acts of disobedience he has used them to commit. He says—Exalted is He, *The day when their tongues, hands, and feet shall testify against them to what they used to do.* [24:24] And, *Today We shall seal their*

79. Muslim, *Ṣaḥīḥ*, (3738); Ibn Māja, *Sunan*, (3364, 3365).

80. Tirmidhī, *Sunan,* (1785); Al-Ḥākim, *Mustadrak,* (901); Bayhaqī, *Shu'ab al-Īmān*, (5338).

mouths, and their hands shall speak to Us, and their feet shall testify to what they used to earn. [36:65]

As for the heart, it is the chief of the bodily members and senses, their commander. Upon it depends whether they are good or corrupt. He said—may God's blessings and peace be upon him, *In the body is a piece of flesh which when good, the whole body is good, but when corrupt, the whole body is corrupt. This is the heart.*[81]

As for the bodily members and senses, we mean by them the seven organs: the eye, the ear, the tongue, the stomach, the private parts, the hand, and the foot.

As for the eye, it is an immense grace bestowed by God upon His servant. He created it so that he may use it to look at His wondrous creatures in His earth and His heavens, that he may increase in knowledge of his Lord and certainty, and also in obedience and service to Him; that he may see through the shadows and may be able to fulfill his needs. If he uses it in what it was created for, he will be one of the obedient and the grateful. But if he releases it to roam in what God has forbidden, such as looking lustfully at forbidden women, then he will have disobeyed and exposed himself to both punishment and afflictions. So let the believer beware of this to the extreme, or of looking at another Muslim with disdain or scorn, or of seeking out the shameful things and faults of other Muslims.

He should also not look persistently at the permissible pleasures of this world and the things that the ego desires, for this would disperse the concentration of the heart and lead it to attend to the improvement of its worldly affairs and hoarding its debris at the expense of the hereafter and preparation for it. To preserve one's eyesight from this is very important, especially for those who wish to concentrate on God and the last abode.

As for looking at forbidden things such as forbidden women and lovely desirable images, this is strictly forbidden. God—Exalted is He—says, *Tell the believers to lower their gazes and preserve their private parts*. [24:30] The Prophet—may God's blessings and peace be upon him—said, *The gaze is a poisoned arrow of Iblīs. He who refrains from it for the fear of God, He shall grant him such acts of worship as will be sweet to his heart.*[82] And Jesus—may peace be upon him—said, "The gaze plants lust in the heart, and a sufficient temptation that is."

81. Bukhārī, *Ṣaḥīḥ*, (50); Muslim, *Ṣaḥīḥ*, (2996).
82. Al-Ḥākim, *Mustadrak,* (7988); Ṭabarānī, *Kabīr*, (10211).

As for the ear, it is also among the greatest graces. It was created for the servant to listen to the words of his Lord and the *Sunna* of his Prophet, and the words of the scholars and sages among the virtuous servants of God. The benefit of this is to behave in such a manner as to please God, and use the ear in the management of those worldly affairs that are a help in the journey to the hereafter. But if he uses it to listen to what God has forbidden, for instance lying, backbiting, and indecencies, he will have denied the grace and shown ingratitude, for he will have used it in other than what it was created for. Imām al-Ghazālī—may God have mercy on him—says, "Never think that only the speaker sins, for the listener is his partner and will be considered one of the backbiters." He who gives ear to something good is a partner to it, and he who gives ear to something evil shares in its sin. And God knows best."

Faults of the Tongue

As for the tongue, it is also among the greatest of God's graces upon His servant. There is in it much good and great benefits for he who preserves it and uses it only in what it was created for. But there will be much evil and immense harm in it for he who neglects to preserve it and uses it in other than what it was created for. God—Exalted is He—created it for the servant to invoke Him abundantly, recite His Book, counsel His servants, invite them to His obedience, teach them His immense rights upon them, and to express whatever thoughts need to be expressed for the fulfillment of his needs, both of this world and the next. If he uses it in this manner, he will have shown gratitude; but if he uses it for other than what it was created for, he will have been one of the iniquitous transgressors.

The affairs of the tongue are most important, for it is the organ with most control over the servant and most influence in leading him to perdition should he fail to control it and prevent it from what God forbids it. The *ḥadīth* says, *Will anything topple the people on their faces (or noses) in the Fire but the doings of their tongues*?[83] And he said—may God's blessings and peace be upon him, *He who believes in God and the Last Day, let him speak words of goodness or remain silent.*[84] And, *May God have mercy on a man who either speaks words of goodness and thus profits, or refrains from*

83. Tirmidhī, *Sunan*, (2541); Ibn Māja, *Sunan*, (3963).
84. Bukhārī, *Ṣaḥīḥ*, (5559, 5670); Muslim, *Ṣaḥīḥ*, (67, 3255).

saying evil, and thus stays safe.[85] And, *He who keeps silent will be saved.*[86] And, *All the speech of the Son of Adam shall be counted against, not for him, save the remembrance of God, enjoining good, or forbidding evil.*[87] And, *A man may speak a word deserving the good pleasure of God, not giving it much thought, yet because of it God grants him His good pleasure until the day he meets Him. And a man may speak a word deserving the wrath of God, not giving it much thought, yet because of it God decrees His wrath upon him in the Fire until the day he meets Him.*[88] And, *A servant may utter a word, not giving it a second thought, but it causes him to plummet in the Fire.*[89]

The perils of the tongue are immense and frightening. Only maintaining silence and speaking only when strictly necessary may save one from them. A person should keep so occupied with reciting the Book of God and remembering Him in abundance as to prevent him from delving into falsehood or what does not concern him.

One of the greatest faults of the tongue is lying, which is to state other than what is, whether by affirming what is not, such as saying, "Such a thing has happened," when it has not, or by denying what is, such as saying, "Such a thing has not happened," when it has. The sin of lying is immense. Lying contradicts faith, and the liar exposes himself to the curse of the All-Merciful. God—Exalted is He—says, *They only forge lies who believe not in the signs of God, and these are the liars.* [16:105] And, *Then We shall cast God's curse upon the liars.* [3:61] The Prophet—may God's blessings and peace be upon him—is reported to have said, *He who wishes to curse himself, let him lie.* And, *Lying leads to corruption and corruption leads to the Fire. A servant may lie and keep on lying until he is written down a liar in the sight of God.*[90] And he was asked, "Does the believer lie?" He answered, *No, they only forge lies who believe not in the signs of God.*[91]

---

85. Bayhaqī, *Shu'ab al-Īmān*, (4730, 4734).
86. Tirmidhī, *Sunan*, (2425); Aḥmad, *Musnad*,(6193, 6367).
87. Bayhaqī, *Shu'ab al-Īmān*, (4747); Ṭabarānī, *Kabīr*, (18996).
88. Aḥmad, *Musnad*,(15291); Ibn Māja, *Sunan*, (3959); Tirmidhī, *Sunan*, (2241).
89. Imām Mālik, *Muwaṭṭa'*, (1563).
90. Bukhārī, *Ṣaḥīḥ*, (5629); Muslim, *Ṣaḥīḥ*, (4721).
91. Ṭabarī, *Tahdhīb al-Āthār*, (1470).

Another great fault of the tongue is backbiting, which is for you to say things about your brother in his absence which he would have resented had he heard them. These things may be faults in his religious practice, body, wife, children, or even the way he walks, dresses, or anything else concerning him. It is the same whether it is done by means of words that are either spoken or written, or by sign language. Thus have such scholars stated—may God have mercy on them—as Imām al-Ghazālī, Imām al-Nawawī, and others.

Backbiting is strictly forbidden. God—Exalted is He—says, *Backbite not one another. Does one of you like to eat his brothers' flesh dead? You would find it loathsome. And fear God, God is indeed Relenting, Compassionate.* [49:12] Thus did God—Exalted is He—liken the backbiter to he who eats the flesh of his dead Muslim brother. How mighty a castigation and rebuke that is! The Messenger of God—may God's blessings and peace be upon him—said, *All of a Muslim is forbidden to the Muslim, his blood, his property, and his honor.*[92] And, *Ribā is of seventy three kinds, the least of which is like a man having intercourse with his mother. The worst ribā is for a man to insult a Muslim.*[93] Once when 'Ā'isha—may God be pleased with her—said to the Messenger of God, "Is it not enough that Ṣafiyya should be such and such?" meaning she was short. He said—may God's blessings and peace be upon him, *You have said such a word that were it to be mixed with the ocean it would alter it.*[94] Meaning it is so repulsive and indecent that if it were to be mixed with the water of the ocean it would pollute the whole of it. And when a woman said of another who had just gone out, "How lengthy is her tail!" he told her to go after her and seek her forgiveness, for she had slandered her.[95] And when he was told that two women fasted all the time but slandered others, he said, "Spit! Spit!" They did and brought out pieces of flesh.[96] This word, so easy to utter, had made her eat of her flesh.[97] See how indecent and repulsive

92. Muslim, *Ṣaḥīḥ*, (4650); Abū Dāwūd, *Sunan*, (4238); Tirmidhī, *Sunan*, (1850).

93. Al-Ḥākim, *Mustadrak,* (2219).

94. Abū Dāwūd, *Sunan*, (4232).

95. Bayhaqī, *Shu'ab al-Īmān*, (6495)

96. Aḥmad, *Musnad,*(22545).

97. This an event where '*Ālam al-mithāl*, the World of Similitude or subtle images, erupts into the physical world thanks to the spiritual power of Prophethood.

backbiting is-O servants of God-and how easy it is to fall into it, save for those upon whom God has mercy and a few they are.

Know that when you notice a fault or a failing in your brother Muslim and think it can be remedied it is incumbent upon you to talk to him about it, but in private. If you are unable to do this, the fault lies in you, therefore do not add another more repulsive one to it by exposing him and informing others of his fault in his absence. You would thus have brought two afflictions upon yourself.

Among the tongue's faults is tale-bearing (*namīma*), which is to inform each party of what the other said about him, so as to cause discord and sedition. God—Exalted is He—says, *Obey not every base swearer, backbiter, going about with tale-bearing.* [68:10, 11] The Prophet—may God's blessings and peace be upon him—said, *The tale-bearer never enters the Garden.*[98] And, *The worst among God's servants are those who go about tale-bearing, sowing dissension among close people.*[99] And, *Tale-bearing and rancor will both go to the Fire, they can never coexist in a Muslim heart.*[100] And, *He is not of me who harbors rancor, who is tale-bearing, or soothsaying, neither am I of him.* Then he recited, *Those who hurt believing men and women for nothing they have committed, they have laid upon themselves slander and manifest sin.* [33:58] One of the virtuous predecessors—may God have mercy on them—said, "The tale-bearer can only be the child of adulterers."

The most repulsive and flagrant kind of tale-bearing is that which reaches the ears of rulers, governors, and so on. It is called (*si'āya*) reporting. He who does this usually intends to induce the ruler to harm the victim, take his wealth, and treat him in an evil manner. Its sin is immense. It is much worse than tale-bearing among ordinary people.

Of the tongue's faults is to insult a Muslim and offend him to his face. He said—may God's blessings and peace be upon him, *To insult a Muslim is corruption, while to wage war on him is disbelief.*[101] And, *Those who insult each other are but two devils abusing*

98. Bukhārī, *Ṣaḥīḥ*, (5596); Muslim, *Ṣaḥīḥ*, (152).

99. Aḥmad, *Musnad,*(17312).

100. Ṭabarānī, *Kabīr*, (625); *Awsaṭ*, (4809).

101. Bukhārī, *Ṣaḥīḥ*, (46, 6549); Muslim, *Ṣaḥīḥ*, (97).

and slandering one another.[102] And, *To return two insults for one is a major sin.*[103]

Of the tongue's faults is to mock and scorn a Muslim, or laugh at him in disdain. God—Exalted is He—says, *O believers! Let no people mock other people who may be better than they, neither let women mock other women who may be better than themselves. Taunt not one another, nor call one another names. It is an evil thing, bad name after faith. Those who do not repent, they are the wrongdoers.* [49:11] He said—may God's blessings and peace be upon him, *It is sufficient evil for a man to despise his brother Muslim.*[104]

Also among the faults of the tongue are false oaths, false witness, cursing, saying to a Muslim, "You disbeliever!" passing judgment on any of the people of the *Qibla* that they are guilty of disbelief, heresy, or corruption without first having ascertained the charge, praying for evil to befall other Muslims, making false promises, double talk, all other forms of repulsive or indecent speech, as well as disputing, arguing contentiously, competing for speech, frequent quarreling, and talking about that which does not concern you. These were all dispraised in numerous verses of the Qur'ān and well known *ḥadīth*s.

The believer who is concerned for himself and his religion should be as he said—may God's blessings and peace be upon him, *He who believes in God and the Last Day, let him speak words of goodness or remain silent.*[105]

The faults of the tongue are many. The Imām, the Proof of Islām mentions twenty of them in that part of the *Iḥyā'* dealing with the faults of the tongue. He has discoursed on them exhaustively, as befits his venerable rank and the immensity of his knowledge. May God be pleased with him and reward him well on behalf of Islam and the Muslims.

Faults of the Stomach

It is most important to preserve and control the stomach. This means that first of all one should prevent unlawful or suspect food from reaching it, then avoid unnecessary appetites, then avoid satiety with lawful food. We have already discussed unlawful and suspect food

102. Aḥmad, *Musnad,*(16836, 16839).
103. Abū Dāwūd, *Sunan*, (4234).
104. Muslim, *Ṣaḥīḥ*, (4650); Abū Dāwūd, *Sunan*, (4238).
105. Bukhārī, *Ṣaḥīḥ*, (5559); Muslim, *Ṣaḥīḥ*, (67).

in the context of circumspection. As for excess in the pursuit of appetites and uninterrupted satiety, they are discouraged (*makrūh*) and lead to many kinds of ailments and harm, among which are hardness of the heart, indolence of the bodily members in obedience, lack of energy during acts worship, reduced capacity to comprehend knowledge and wisdom, and diminished compassion and solicitude for the weak and needy among Muslims.

It is to be feared that excess in the pursuit of appetites and uninterrupted satiety may lead to falling into the suspect or even the unlawful. The Proof of Islam—may God have mercy on him—said, "Eating lawful food to satiety is the origin of all evils, how much more so with the unlawful?"

The Prophet—may God's blessings and peace be upon him—said, *Never does the Son of Adam fill a worse vessel than his stomach. It should suffice the Son of Adam a few morsels to keep his back straight, but if he must, then one third for his food, one third for his beverage, and one third for his breath.*[106] And, *The worst among my community are those who are born in luxury and fed from it. They eat a variety of food, drink a variety of beverages, wear a variety of clothes, and they speak pompously.*[107] And, *Those who are most satiated in this world are those who will be most hungry in the hereafter.*[108] 'Alī—may God honor his face-said, "He whose only concern is that which enters his stomach is worth only as much as that which comes out of it."

A believer should control his appetites out of continence, contentment, and detachment from the world. When he eats he should stop short of satiety, eat whatever lawful food is available without choosing that which is more pleasurable, or more in accordance with his taste. Opting for the cheaper and more frugal kinds is nearer to God-fearing, less burdensome, farther from lust, and more in accordance with the pattern of the virtuous predecessors. The Messenger of God—may God's blessings and peace be upon him—lived mostly on barley which they kneaded and baked for him without prior sifting, since sifts were unknown to them at the time. He and his wives—may God be pleased with them—lived for months on

106. Ibn Māja, *Sunan*, (3340).
107. Al-Ḥākim, *Mustadrak,* (6492); Bayhaqī, *Shu'ab al-Īmān*, (5429); Ṭabarānī, *Kabīr*, (7389); *Awsaṭ*, (2441, 7979).
108. Ibn Māja, *Sunan*, (3341, 3342); Tirmidhī, *Sunan*, (2402).

dates and water, no fire being lit for any of them, either for cooking or any other purpose.

Whenever a believer eats, he should do so observing good manners and according to the *Sunna.* Thus he must say "*Bismillāh,*" at the beginning, and "*Al-ḥamdu lil'llāh,*" at the end, eat with the intention of using it to help him obey God and give him strength to worship Him, and observe all other good manners mentioned in *ḥadīth.*

The Faults of the Private Parts

It is important to preserve one's private parts, for they may lead one into danger. God says in His Book as He praises His believing servants, *And those who guard their private parts, save from their wives or that their right hands own, for that they are not to blame. Those who seek beyond that, these are the transgressors.* [23:5-7] When the Prophet—may God's blessings and peace be upon him—was asked what things are most likely to lead people into the Fire, he answered, *The two hollow things, the mouth and the private parts.*[109] And he said, *He whom God protects from the evil of that which is between his mandibles and that which is between his legs, he shall be admitted to the Garden.*[110]

O believer! You must guard your private parts. This is easier when the heart is prevented from thinking of unlawful things and the eyes from looking at forbidden things.

A *ḥadīth* says, *The adultery of the eye is to look, that of the tongue is to speak, the ego desires and hopes, then the private parts either confirm this or deny it.*[111]

Keep away and beware to the extreme of adultery and homosexuality, for these are perilous indecencies and major sins leading to perdition. God forbids them strictly and categorically. He says—Exalted is He, *Approach not adultery, for it is an indecency and an evil way.* [17:32] And, *Those who call not upon another god with God, nor kill the soul that God has forbidden except by right, neither commit adultery. Those who commit these shall meet the price of sin. Multiplied shall be their torment on the Day of Arising, immortal therein, degraded; save those who repent, believe, and*

109. Aḥmad, *Musnad,* (7566, 8734, 9319); Ibn Māja, *Sunan*, (4236).
110. Al-Ḥākim, *Mustadrak,* (8172, 8173, 8177); Bayhaqī, *Shu'ab al-Īmān*, (4719, 5515); Ibn Ḥibbān, *Ṣaḥīḥ*, (5795); Ṭabarānī, *Awsaṭ*, (5138).
111. Bukhārī, *Ṣaḥīḥ*, (6122); Muslim, *Ṣaḥīḥ*, (4801).

do good works, those God will change their evil into good deeds. God is ever Forgiving, Compassionate. [25:68-70] The Messenger of God—may God's blessings and peace be upon him—said, *At the time when the adulterer commits adultery he is not a believer.*[112] And it has been transmitted that he who persists in committing adultery is like the idol worshipper, and that adulterers shall come on Resurrection Day with their private parts on fire. And he said—may God's blessings and peace be upon him, *Three shall not be spoken to by God on Resurrection Day, nor shall He purify them, nor look at them, and theirs shall be a painful torment: An adulterous elderly man, a king who lies, and an arrogant poor man.*[113] It has also been handed down that a foul smelling wind shall blow upon the People of the Gathering, extremely offensive both to the righteous and the dissolute, and they will be told, "This is the stench of the private parts of adulterers." And an authentic *ḥadīth* states that the Prophet—may God's blessings and peace be upon him—saw the adulterers and adulteresses in something like an oven which sent flames of fire on them from underneath them, so that they screamed and tried to raise themselves up.[114] This is one kind of torment meted out by God to them in the Intermediary World. God—Exalted is He—says of the destruction of the people of Lot following their persistence in committing debauchery, *When Our command came, We turned it upside down and rained on it stones of baked clay, marked by your Lord. These are never far from the wrongdoers.* [11:82, 83] Some commentators said that these stones are never far from the wrongdoers who commit the same act. It has reached us that two men were committing the same evil indecency in a house on the roof of which was one of these stones which had been sent upon Lot's people. The stone pierced the roof and fell on them, killing them. News of this reached one of our predecessors. He remarked, "God has spoken the truth, *these are never far from the wrongdoers.*"

The Prophet—may God's blessings and peace be upon him—said, *What I fear most for my community is the deed of Lot's people.*[115] And, *God has cursed seven of His creatures from above seven*

112. Bukhārī, *Ṣaḥīḥ*, (5150, 6284); Muslim, *Ṣaḥīḥ*, (86, 87).

113. Nasā'ī, *Sunan,* (2528); *al-Sunan al-Kubrā,* (7138); Ibn Ḥibbān, *Ṣaḥīḥ*, (4490).

114. Bukhārī, *Ṣaḥīḥ*, (1297); Aḥmad, *Musnad,* (19236, 19306); Ṭabarānī, *Kabīr*, (6842).

115. Ibn Māja, *Sunan*, (2553); Tirmidhī, *Sunan*, (1377).

heavens. Accursed is he who commits the deed of Lot's people, accursed is he who commits the deed of Lot's people, accursed is he who commits the deed of Lot's people, accursed is he who slaughters for other than God, accursed is he who has intercourse with a beast, accursed is he who rebels against his parents, accursed is he who marries a woman and her daughter, accursed is he who changes the markings of the land, accursed is he who claims to belong to other than his patrons.[116] Thus did he repeat the curse against the first kind thrice, while finding it sufficient to curse each of the other kinds only once. Abū Hurayra—may God be pleased with him—said, The Messenger of God—may God's blessings and peace be upon him—said, *Four are in God's wrath in the morning and in God's displeasure in the evening*. I said, 'Who are they, O Messenger of God?' He answered, *Women who seek to look like men, men who seek to look like women, he who has intercourse with a beast, and he who has intercourse with men.*[117]

Much has been handed down forbidding illegal intercourse and homosexuality, and detailing the punishments of those who commit them. To realize how repulsive, forbidden, and deserving of punishment they are, it suffices to know what God has ordained for them in this world, before the next. Unmarried males and females who are guilty of proven illegal intercourse are to receive a hundred lashes each and be banished from their homelands for a year. Married males and females are to be stoned to death. If one is married and the other not, each is sentenced according to his status. The statutory punishment for homosexuality is as that for illegal heterosexual intercourse according to the strongest opinion. However, some are of the opinion that both partners should be killed and there are some indications to support this in *ḥadīth*. Others are of the opinion that they should be burned. We ask God for safety from every affliction. As for intercourse with an animal, it is a formidable sin, and he who commits it is accursed, as in the *ḥadīth* quoted above. Another *ḥadīth* says, *He who has intercourse with a beast, kill him and kill it.*[118]

As for masturbation, it is repulsive and blameworthy, and leads to many ailments and affliction. Some people are afflicted with it, so

---

116. Al-Ḥākim, *Mustadrak,* (8167); Bayhaqī, *Shu'ab al-Īmān*, (5235); Ṭabarānī, *Kabīr*, (1347); *Awsaṭ*, (8734).

117. Bayhaqī, *Shu'ab al-Īmān*, (5151); Ṭabarānī, *Kabīr*, (867).

118. Ibn Māja, *Sunan*, (2554); Tirmidhī, *Sunan*, (1374).

let them beware. It has been transmitted that God curses he who has intercourse with his hand and that God once destroyed a community who used to play with their private parts.

O God! O Omniscient! O Aware! Purify our hearts from hypocrisy, protect our private parts from indecencies, and treat us and all Muslims with gentleness.

Faults of the Hands

You must let your hands loose in charity, in helping to fulfill other Muslims' needs, in writing down knowledge and wisdom, and in earning lawful money with the intention of using it to assist you in your religion. You must preserve them from causing bodily injury to another Muslim without right, or to appropriate what is not yours of their property by such means as injustice, betrayal, or false transactions.

Faults of the Feet

Beware of using your feet to walk to forbidden or sinful things, assist in a wrong, go to an unjust ruler, to frivolous and distracting ends, or to anything else in which there is neither good nor profit. Walk with them only to what is good and virtuous such as acquiring beneficial knowledge, going to the mosque for congregational prayers, other devotional activities, visiting one's brothers in God, fulfilling the needs of Muslims, and discharging such rights of theirs as visiting the sick, escorting funerals, and other such deeds of goodness and righteousness.

On the whole, your bodily members and senses are among the greatest of God's favors upon you. He created them for you that you may use them in His obedience. If you use them in what they were created for, namely in acts of obedience and conformity, you will have shown gratitude and become one of the people of excellence. But if you use them in other than what they were created for, namely in acts of disobedience and contravention, you will have denied God's favor and betrayed His trust, for the bodily members and senses are among what He has committed to your trust.

We have now completed discussing the seven organs in a comprehensive yet brief manner.

Faults of the Heart

Our purpose now is to discuss briefly something of what concerns the heart, which is the master and king of the bodily members and senses. It is the location of beliefs, traits of character, and intentions, whether these are praiseworthy or blameworthy. There is no possible happiness in this world or the next save for he who purifies and cleans it of vices and all things repulsive, and adorns it with virtues and all things beautiful. God—Exalted is He—says, *By the soul and That which shaped it and inspired it with its wickedness and God-fearing! He has succeeded who purifies it and he has failed who ruins it.* [91:7-10]

Blameworthy traits of character and loathsome attributes are numerous, and so are the praiseworthy traits and agreeable attributes that a believer should embellish his heart with. The Imām, the Proof of Islām wrote on this exhaustively in the second half of the *Iḥyā'* when discoursing first on ruinous, then on saving things. In this art his discourse is the most authoritative and dependable, for he was complete in knowledge, worship, detachment, and gnosis, and because he had collected the discourses of those of the virtuous predecessors and masters of the path who had preceded him. The Muslim scholars and saints of all lands and countries who came after him followed in his footsteps and took of his light. This is well known by anyone who is steeped in these sciences and has plunged into the secrets of the path of God where they were revealed to him.

Now that you know this, know that the blameworthy qualities of the hearts are none other than its ailments. They may lead it to perdition in this world and the next. A believer can never dispense with treating his heart and seeking after its well-being and safety, for only he will be saved who comes to God with a sound heart. You are also well aware that both blameworthy and praiseworthy qualities of the heart are numerous and studying them is lengthy. Since we intend to be brief and concise, we refer those wishing for an exhaustive account to the explanations of the Proof of Islam in the *Iḥyā'*. Here we shall mention briefly those ruinous things which the heart should be purified from and those saving things with which it should be embellished. We shall restrict ourselves to things which are widespread and frequent, and the understanding of which is a necessity.

First of all, a person must purify and free his heart from the vice of doubting God, His Messenger, and the hereafter. This is one of the worst ailments of the heart. It causes perdition in the hereafter and is greatly harmful especially at the moment of death. It may lead—may God protect us-to an evil ending to life. Some people are afflicted with such doubts and it is not permissible for them to keep them to themselves, hide them in their hearts, then meet God still harboring them. On the contrary, they should strive to the utmost to remove these doubts. The best course of action is to ask those who are learned, are people of certainty, God-fearing, and detachment from the world, and who know about God the Exalted and His religion. If they can find none of these, let them study the books they have authored on the science of *Tawḥīd* and certainty.

By doubts I do not mean such thoughts and ruminations as one often has concerning the details of one's faith, but the falsity of which is obvious and one's heart is resolutely set against them, and which the soul finds detestable and repulsive. These are obsessions (*waswās*). It is sufficient to detest and turn away from them, and seek God's protection against them.

One of the worst ailments of the heart and most ruinous attributes is arrogance, which is an attribute of the devils. God—Exalted is He—said concerning Iblīs, *He refused, was arrogant, and became one of the disbelievers.* [2:34] Arrogant persons are detestable to God. He says—Exalted is He, *He likes not the arrogant.* [16:23] And, *God likes not those who are proud and boastful.* [31:18] Pride and boastfulness are attributes of the arrogant person, and the latter is in danger of his heart being stamped upon by God. He says—Exalted is He, *Thus does God stamp upon every arrogant, overbearing heart.* [40:35] Arrogant persons are deflected away from the signs of God. He says—Exalted is He, *I shall deflect away from My signs those who are arrogant in the earth without right.* [7:146] The Messenger of God—may God's blessings and peace be upon him—said, *God said, 'Pride is My upper garment and might My lower garment. He who contests Me one of them, him I shall cast into the Fire.'*[119] And, *The arrogant shall be gathered on Resurrection Day as small as ants but in human form, surrounded by humiliation from every direction.*[120] And, *He who is presumptuous and walks proudly shall find God angry with him when he meets Him.*[121] And, *As a man was*

119. Abū Dāwūd, *Sunan*, (3567); Ibn Māja, *Sunan*, (4164).

120. Tirmidhī, *Sunan*, (2416); Aḥmad, *Musnad,* (6390).

121. Al-Ḥākim, *Mustadrak,* (188); Bayhaqī, *Shu'ab al-Īmān*, (5235); Ṭabarānī, *Kabīr*, (1347); *Awsaṭ*, (8734).

once dragging his clothes proudly, God caused him to be swallowed by the earth wherein he will continue to reverberate until Resurrection Day.[122] And, *He in whose heart is an atom of arrogance shall never enter the Garden.* A man said, "O Messenger of God! A man likes his clothes to look good and his sandals to look good." He said, *God is Beautiful and He loves beauty. Arrogance is to deny the truth and despise others.*[123] He who is haughty and vain, despises others and disdains them, he is the loathsome, arrogant person. Arrogance lies in the heart, but has outward signs indicating its presence. Among these are to love to be given precedence over others, behave toward them superciliously, like to preside over gatherings, proudly strut when walking, being vexed when one's words are not accepted at face value even when wrong, rejecting the truth, and disdaining the weak and the poor among Muslims. Among them are also praising and lauding oneself, vaunting oneself of one's fathers if they happen to be people of religion and virtue, and boasting of one's lineage. This is blameworthy and repulsive. The children of superior people are sometimes afflicted with this when they lack insight and knowledge of the truths of religion. He who vaunts himself of his lineage and his forefathers thereby loses their *baraka*, for they were never boastful, nor arrogant toward others. Had they been so, their superiority would have been annulled. He said—may God's blessings and peace be upon him, *He who is slowed down by his works will not be speeded up by his lineage.*[124] And, *O Ṣafiyya, aunt of the Messenger of God! O Fāṭima, daughter of Muḥammad! I shall avail you nothing with God. Ransom yourselves from the Fire…*[125] And, *There is no superiority for the Arab over the non- Arab, nor for a non-Arab over an Arab, nor black over white, nor white over black, save by the fear of God.*[126] And, *You descend from Adam and Adam is from dust*! *Let certain people stop boasting about their fathers, or they shall be more insignificant than beetles in the sight of God*![127] Superiority and nobility are by God-fearing, not by lineage. God—Exalted is He—says, *The most honorable of you in the sight of God*

122. Bukhārī, *Ṣaḥīḥ*, (3226, 5343); Muslim, *Ṣaḥīḥ*, (3895).

123. Muslim, *Ṣaḥīḥ*, (131).

124. Muslim, *Ṣaḥīḥ*, (4867); Abū Dāwūd, *Sunan*, (3158); Ibn Māja, *Sunan*, (221); Tirmidhī, *Sunan*, (2869).

125. Bukhārī, *Ṣaḥīḥ*, (2548, 4398); Muslim, *Ṣaḥīḥ*, (3895).

126. Ṭabarānī, *Kabīr*, (14444).

127. Abū Dāwūd, *Sunan*, (4452); Aḥmad, *Musnad,* (8381, 10363).

are those who fear God most. [49:13] If a person is exceptional in God-fearing, learning, and worship, then becomes supercilious with others and boasts of his superiority, God inevitably thwarts his piety and annuls his acts of worship. How much more so if he is ignorant and confused, yet prides himself of piety and virtue that are not his, but his forefathers? Is that but immense ignorance and hideous foolishness? All good lies in modesty, humility, and submission to God—Exalted is He. He said—may God's blessings and peace be upon him, *He who is humble, God shall elevate him, but he who is proud, God shall abase him.*[128] To love obscurity and anonymity and detest fame and renown are among the attributes of virtuous believers. Also contentment with a humble place in gatherings, humble clothes, food, and all other worldly things. O Believer! Be careful to implement this.

Among the worst of ruinous things is ostentation (*riyā'*). The Messenger of God—may God's blessings and peace be upon him—called it the "smaller idolatry" and the "hidden idolatry". Ostentation is to seek eminence and respect from others by means of works that are by right for the hereafter. Such is the person who prays, fasts, gives charity, goes to pilgrimage, fights, and recites the Qur'ān so that others respect and honor him, or give him of their possessions. Such a person is ostentatious, his works will be rejected, and his striving will fail, whether he is given what he wants or not. God—Exalted is He—says, *He who hopes to encounter his Lord, let him do good works and not associate in his Lord's worship anyone.* [18:110] *He who desires the tillage of the world to come, We shall increase his tillage, and he who desires the tillage of this world, We shall give him of it, but he will have no share in the hereafter.* [42:20] *So woe to those who pray, but are heedless in their prayers, who make display, and refuse charity.* [107:4-7] And he said—may God's blessings and peace be upon him, *God—Exalted is He—says, 'I am less in need of associates than anyone else. Therefore, he who does something in which he associates another with Me, him I shall disavow, and My share shall go to My* [presumed] *partners.'*[129] And, *He who prays out of ostentation, he has associated* [others with God], *he who fasts out of ostentation, he has associated, and he*

128. Bayhaqī, *Shu'ab al-Īmān*, (7921, 7922); Ṭabarānī, *Awsaṭ*, (5051).
129. Ibn Māja, *Sunan*, (4192); Aḥmad, *Musnad,* (7658, 9246).

who gives charity out of ostentation, he has associated.[130] And, *He who seeks this world with works of the hereafter, God will blot out his face,*[131] *obliterate the memory of him, and write him down to be admitted into the Fire.*[132] And, *He who prays well when observed by others, but prays badly when on his own, he is being contemptuous of his Lord-Blessed and Exalted is He.*[133]

Ostentation is ruinous, its perils are great, and to beware of it is an important duty. The worst kind of ostentation is to have no other motive in performing acts of worship but to be seen by others. Thus one has to make sure one is being observed. A lesser degree is to intend to draw nearer to God—Exalted is He—and obtain recompense in the hereafter, yet still wish to be seen by others so as to obtain their praises and respect. The first kind is more repulsive, more conducive to failure, and more dangerous. However, the second is also repulsive, annuls reward, and is not far from being sinful and deserving of punishment.

The believer must strive to expel ostentation from within himself and to have no other intention or aim in all his acts of obedience or worship but to draw nearer to God and obtain recompense in the hereafter. Only thus will he be free from ostentation and safe from its evil and afflictions-God willing. Whenever he is worried about it, he should conceal his works and perform them in private where no one can see him. This is more cautious and safer. To conceal works is unreservedly better, even for him who is not worried about ostentation, except for him who has achieved perfection of character and sincerity, and hopes that those who observe his works might emulate him.

Some works can only be done in public, for instance acquiring knowledge and teaching, praying in congregation, pilgrimage, *Jihād*, and so on. He who is anxious lest he falls prey to ostentation while doing any of these things should nevertheless not abandon them, but perform them, while striving to expel ostentation from

---

130. Aḥmad, *Musnad,* (16517); Al-Ḥākim, *Mustadrak,* (8056); Bayhaqī, *Shu'ab al-Īmān*, (6576).

131. The expression "blot out his face" means that God will either deprive him of his dignity among people, or make his eyesight and hearing closed to the truth.

132. Ṭabarānī, *Kabīr*, (2085).

133. 'Abdal-Razzāq, *Muṣannaf,* (3738); Bayhaqī, *Shu'ab al-Īmān*, (2973).

within himself, and seeking God's help, for He is the best ally and the best helper.

Among ruinous thing are also resenting other Muslims, wishing any of them evil, harboring enmity, deceit, and rancor, lacking compassion and solicitude, and thinking ill of them. All these are ruinous attributes.

As for resentful envy (*ḥasad*), it is enough disparagement and repulsiveness that God—Exalted is He—enjoined upon His Messenger—may God's blessings and peace be upon him—to seek protection from the evil of the resentful in the same way He enjoined upon him to seek protection from the evil of the Devil. He said—Exalted is He, *And from the evil of the resentful when he is envious.* [113:5] And he said—may God's blessings and peace be upon him, *Beware of resentful envy, for resentful envy consumes good deeds just as fire consumes firewood.*[134] And, *Faith and resentful envy cannot be found together in the heart of a servant.*[135] This is quite severe, so reflect upon it. And he said—may God's blessings and peace be upon him, *Envy not one another, hate not one another, and turn not your back on one another.*[136]

Resentful envy is for one to feel constriction and discomfort in one's breast and heart, and aversion to see God bestow a favor, whether of this world or the next, upon one of His servants, to wish for him to lose it, and sometimes to wish so even if it will not end up with oneself. This is extreme wickedness.

He who observes in himself something of this resentful envy must detest and conceal it, and never manifest it by word or deed, that he may be saved from its evil. A *ḥadīth* says, *Three are inevitably present in my community: belief in evil omens, envy, and thinking ill of others.* A man asked him how to avoid them and he answered, *Whenever you are envious, ask for forgiveness; whenever you think ill, do not inquire; and whenever you fear an evil omen, proceed.*[137] Meaning proceed with what you intend to do and let not the evil omen deter you.

Should the envious person act in a manner opposite to that which should have been induced by envy, should he praise the person he

---

134. Abū Dāwūd, *Sunan*, (4257); Ibn Māja, *Sunan*, (4200).

135. Ibn Ḥibbān, *Ṣaḥīḥ*, (4689); Bayhaqī, *Shu'ab al-Īmān*, (6334); Ṭabarānī, *Kabīr*, (144).

136. Bukhārī, *Ṣaḥīḥ*, (5605, 5606); Muslim, *Ṣaḥīḥ*, (4646, 4649).

137. Ṭabarānī, *Kabīr*, (3153).

envies, and honor and assist him, this would be virtuous on his part and would be one of the most effective remedies for removing or weakening envy.

There is no harm in envy which is free of resentment (*ghibṭa*), which is to wish to obtain, by the grace of God, the same blessing you observe your brother to enjoy [without desiring him to lose it]. If this is a religious blessing, such as knowledge or acts of worship, it is praiseworthy. If it is a worldly blessing, such as money or lawful social eminence, it is permissible.

As for wishing any Muslim evil and harboring deceit, enmity, or rancor for them, it is sufficient rebuke to know that he said—may God's blessings and peace be upon him, *None of you will have believed until he comes to love for his brother what he loves for himself.*[138] And, *He who deceives the Muslims is not of them.*[139] And, *If you can live through every morning and evening harboring in your heart no deceit for Muslims, then do, for it is part of my* Sunna.[140]

As for lack of compassion and solicitude for the Muslims, it indicates hardness of the heart, harshness, and coarseness, all of which are blameworthy and repulsive. The Prophet—may God's blessings and peace be upon him—said, *Have compassion on those on earth and those in heaven will have compassion on you.*[141] *Have mercy and you will find mercy.*[142] *God shows mercy on those of His servants who show mercy.*[143] And, *Compassion is taken away only from he who is wretched.*[144] He who finds in his heart no compassion for Muslims in general, but especially for those suffering hardships and afflictions, or those who are weak and poor, this is because his heart is hard, his faith weak, and he is distant from his Lord.

Thinking evil of Muslims is also blameworthy and repulsive. He said—may God's blessings and peace be upon him—that there were two good attributes that were unsurpassed by any other good, thinking well of God and thinking well of the servants of God; and

138. Bukhārī, *Ṣaḥīḥ*, (12); Muslim, *Ṣaḥīḥ*, (64).

139. Abū Ya'lā, *Musnad,* (896); Ṭabarānī, *Kabīr*, (15309).

140. Tirmidhī, *Sunan,* (2602).

141. Abū Ya'lā, *Musnad,* (4932); Al-Ḥākim, *Mustadrak,*(7739); Ṭabarānī, *Kabīr*, (2439, 10124).

142. Ibn Abī 'Āṣim, *Al-Sunna*, (563). This was stated in this *ḥadīth* to have been said by God to Moses.

143. Bukhārī, *Ṣaḥīḥ*, (1204, 6163); Muslim, *Ṣaḥīḥ*, (1531).

144. Abū Dāwūd, *Sunan,* (4291); Tirmidhī, *Sunan,* (1846).

two evil attributes that were unsurpassed by any other evil, thinking ill of God and thinking ill of the servants of God. The meaning of thinking ill of Muslims is to think ill of such of their words and deeds as are in appearance good, by thinking of them other than what their appearances indicate. It means also to give an evil interpretation to words and deeds the appearance of which is equivocal, thus bearing interpretation in both directions. This second kind is not as bad as the first. Thinking well of Muslims is at the opposite of this. It means that those of their words and deeds the appearance of which is good are accepted as good, while those which are open to interpretation are also taken to be good. Strive to conform to this and seek God's help. Success is only from God.

Greed and Avarice

Among major ruinous things are to love this world and desire it, to be very eager and avid for it, to love eminence and wealth and be very greedy for them, and to be avaricious and niggardly. These are all ruinous attributes and blameworthy traits. He who loves this world, desires it, and is greedy and avid for it, exposes himself to grave dangers and severe threats from God. He says—Exalted is He, *He who desires the life of this world and its ornaments, We shall pay them in full for their works therein and they shall not be defrauded. Those are they who have only the Fire in the hereafter, and their deeds will have failed and their works will be annulled.* [11:15, 16] And, *He who desires this hasty world, we hasten for him therein what we will to whomsoever We desire, then We appoint for him Hell wherein he shall roast, rebuked and abased. But he who desires the hereafter and strives for it as it should, being a believer, those their striving shall be thanked.* [17:18, 19] And He says—Exalted is He—encouraging His servants to detach themselves from this world and reminding them of how perishable and evanescent it is, *And strike for them the analogy of this life of the world: it is as water that We send down out of heaven, and the plants of the earth mingle with it, and in the morning it is straw that the winds scatter. And God has power over all things.* [18:45] And, *Know that the life of this world is but play and diversion and ornaments and boasting among you and rivalry in wealth and children, as the likeness* [of vegetation after rain] *the tillers rejoice in it, but then it withers and turns yellow, soon becoming stubble. In the hereafter there is severe torment, but also forgiveness from God and good pleasure, whereas the life of this world is but the enjoyment of illusion.* [57:20] And, *And as for those who overstep the limits and prefer the life of this world, Hell is the final abode.* [79:37-39] The Prophet—may God's blessings and peace be upon him—said, *Love for this world leads to every sin.*[145] And, *Had this world weighed as much as the wing of a gnat in the sight of God, He would never have given a disbeliever a sip of its water.*[146] And, *This world is the home of he who has no home, the wealth of he who has no wealth, and he amasses for it who is devoid of intelligence.*[147] And, *This world is accursed and accursed is all that is in it, save the remembrance of God, a scholar, or a student.*[148] He also said that he who takes from this world more than his bare necessities will be also taking his ruin unaware. And he said, *Let each of you take no more from this world than the provision of the traveler.*[149] And, *He who is intent on the Hereafter, God makes him inwardly wealthy, gathers for him his affairs, and the world comes to him subdued; but he who is intent on this world, God scatters his affairs, disperses his property, and places his poverty right between his eyes, yet only that will come to him that has been preordained.*[150] And, *Detachment from this world rests the heart and the body, while desire for this world increases worries and sorrows; and idleness hardens the heart.*[151] And he said that the first among this community were saved by detachment and certainty, while the last shall perish through greed and long hopes.[152]

145. Bayhaqī, *Shu'ab al-Īmān*, (10111).
146. Tirmidhī, *Sunan,* (2242).
147. Aḥmad, *Musnad*, (23283); Bayhaqī, *Shu'ab al-Īmān*, (10236). The meaning is that he who has no pleasurable home in Paradise, this world is his only home; and he who has no wealth in the form of good works, material wealth is all he has. He who does not grasp this will waste his time amassing ephemeral wealth for his short life on earth.
148. Tirmidhī, *Sunan,* (2244); Ibn Māja, *Sunan,* (4102).
149. Aḥmad, *Musnad*, (22597); Bayhaqī, *Shu'ab al-Īmān*, (10007. 1009); Ṭabarānī, *Kabīr*, (5946, 6037).
150. Tirmidhī, *Sunan,* (2389); Ibn Māja, *Sunan*, (4095).
151. Al-Shihāb al-Quḍā'ī, *Musnad al-Shihāb*, (268); Bayhaqī, *Shu'ab al-Īmān*, (10141).
152. Bayhaqī, *Shu'ab al-Īmān*, (10430. 10134); Ṭabarānī, *Awsaṭ*, (7865). By first are meant the first three generations of Muslims, the superiority of whom was explicitly stated in *ḥadīth*. By last is meant those who like us come near the end of time and whose golden calf is money.

There are innumerable verses, *ḥadīth*s, and other traditions dispraising both the world and those who love and desire it, as well as those who are greedy for it. Scholars—may God have mercy on them—both early and latecomers have written profusely on this.

By this world is meant every pleasure and appetite on the face of the earth, as well as everything that the ego lusts after, is inclined toward and greedy for. God brought the origins of all this together when He said—Exalted is He, *Made beautiful for mankind is the love of lusts for women and offspring, for heaped up quintals of gold and silver, and for branded steeds, cattle, and plantations. These are the enjoyments of the life of this world, but with God is the best of all returns.* [3:14] Therefore, he who loves and desires all this, is greedy for it, and has no other wish but to enjoy it, he is one of those who love the world and desire it. If he becomes so overwhelmed by such feelings that he no longer cares whether he acquires worldly things in a lawful or unlawful manner, or becomes so occupied with striving for them greedily as to neglect those acts of obedience that God has imposed upon him, and slips into that which God has forbidden, then he has fully deserved the punishments that those who love and desire this world are threatened with. His fate is extremely precarious, unless God rescues him with repentance before he dies and leaves this world.

As for the love of eminence and wealth, and greed for them, they are extremely blameworthy. God—Exalted is He—says, *That is the final abode, we shall assign it to those who seek not supremacy in the earth, nor corruption. The final end belongs only to the God-fearing.* [28:83] And, *O believers! Let not your wealth, nor your children, distract you from the remembrance of God. Those who do this, they are the losers.* [63:9] And, *Your wealth and your children are but temptations.* [64:15] The Prophet—may God's blessings and peace be upon him—said, *Two hungry wolves let loose among sheep will cause no more destruction than the love of eminence and money to a man's religion.*[153]

He who is very greedy for eminence and wealth and the pursuit of rank and respect in the hearts of others exposes himself to numerous ailments, such as arrogance, ostentation, affectation, abandoning humility when faced with the truth and its people, disliking anonymity, and so on. A *ḥadīth* says, *God loves the righteous, God-fearing,*

153. Tirmidhī, *Sunan,* (2298); Aḥmad, *Musnad,* (15224, 15233).

and obscure.[154] Another says, *It may be that an unkempt, dusty man, dressed in two worn out cloths, to whom nobody pays attention, when he beseeches God, He grants him his request.*[155]

He whose greed for money is strong exposes himself to immense dangers and major afflictions, unless God protects and rescues him by His mercy. That which is blameworthy in terms of love and greed for eminence and money is that these be powerful and excessive, so that one will strive to gratify them using in the process whatever means he finds necessary, whether permissible or not, and becomes too occupied to free himself to worship God and remember Him, as happens to many who succumb to temptation and are heedless of God—Exalted is He. But those who pursue these with the right intention of using them as a help for the hereafter, to protect their religion and their own selves from the injustice of the unjust and from the need for others, who are not too distracted to worship God the Exalted and remember Him, who are not abandoned by their fear of God and their piety, then there is no harm in that and no blame-God willing. However, lack of greed for eminence and wealth and forsaking desire for them are safer, more cautious, nearer to God-fearing, and more in line with the pattern of the virtuous predecessors.

As for avarice and miserliness, they are repulsive and ruinous. God—Exalted is He—says, *He who is protected from the greed in himself, those are the successful.* [59:9] And, *Let not those who avariciously withhold what God has given them of His favor think that it is better for them, on the contrary, it is worse for them. That they were avaricious with, they shall have hung around their necks on Resurrection Day.* [3:180] And the Prophet said—may God's blessings and peace be upon him, *Beware of greed, for it has ruined those who were before you. It induced them to spill blood and take what is forbidden.*[156] And, *The miser is distant from God, distant from the Garden, distant from people, but near from the Fire.*[157] And, *Liberality is a tree in the Garden, the branches of which extend into this world. He who holds fast to one of its branches, it will lead him to the Garden. Miserliness is a tree in the Fire, the branches of which extend into this world. He who holds fast to one of its branches, it*

154. Ibn Māja, *Sunan,* (3979); Al-Ḥākim, *Mustadrak,*(4).
155. Tirmidhī, *Sunan,* (3789).
156. Muslim, *Ṣaḥīḥ*, (4675).
157. Tirmidhī, *Sunan,* (1884).

will lead him to the Fire.[158] *For by God none shall enter the Fire but a miser and none shall enter the Garden but the liberal.*[159] And he once said that every generous person is sure to end up in the Garden, that this was incumbent upon God and that he was himself the guarantor of this; whereas every miser is sure to end up in the Fire, this being incumbent upon God, and again he was the guarantor. And he said, *An ignorant but liberal man is more pleasing to God than a learned miser.*[160] You now know how blameworthy and repulsive greed and miserliness are.

Greed is extreme covetousness. As a certain scholar—may God have mercy on him—once said, "It is for a man to be intent on acquiring that which is in other people's possession."

Avarice or miserliness is for a man to wish to retain what he already has. Its maximum is to abstain from settling one's obligations, such as *zakāt*, and so on. He who has reached this point is the true miser who thus exposes himself to the censure and threats concerning miserliness. As for he who abstains from spending in acts of benevolence and good works of which he has the means, his condition is not as bad as the first, but he is still a miser, for he prefers to hold on to his money rather than expend it in that which is more elevating and beneficial to him with his Lord in the way of lofty degrees and good deeds that will subsist in the hereafter. So long as a person prefers keeping his money to spending it in what pleases God, he is never free from some avarice. He becomes generous and liberal only when expending his money in ways pleasing to God becomes preferable and more pleasing to him than withholding it. Know this and act accordingly, may God take charge of your guidance.

Among ruinous things is self-deception, which is for a person to deceive his own soul and present things to it in a manner that is untrue. This is caused by lack of religious insight, lack of knowledge of religion, ignorance of the ailments that affect works and the snares of the Devil, being overwhelmed by the ego's passions and committing oneself to its [vain] hopes and delusions. God—Exalted is He—says, warning His servants against vanity, *O mankind! God's promise is true, so let not the life of this world deceive you, and let not the Deceiver deceive you concerning God.* [35:5] And He says—Exalted is He—describing certain self-deceivers, *Those*

158. Bayhaqī, *Shu'ab al-Īmān*, (10449, 10451).

159. Bayhaqī, *Shu'ab al-Īmān*, (10450).

160. Tirmidhī, *Sunan,* (1884).

whose efforts in the life of this world have gone astray, yet think they have done well. [18:104] And He says—Exalted is He, *But you tempted yourselves, and you awaited, and you doubted, and* [vain] *hopes deceived you, until God's command came, and the Deceiver deceived you concerning God.* [57:14] And the Prophet—may God's blessings and peace be upon him—said, *The sagacious is he who accuses his own soul and works for that which comes after death. The feeble is he who looses his soul in pursuit of his passions, then harbors* [vain] *hopes in God.*[161]

There are many kinds of self-deception and many kinds of self-deceivers, whether among the obedient or the disobedient. One kind of self-deception in people of obedience is to seek knowledge while postponing works, then justify this with textual evidence detailing the merits of knowledge and of seeking it, while ignoring the dispraise and severe threats proffered against those who fail to act in conformity with their knowledge.

Another is to learn, then teach, but for the sake of eminence and greed for what may be obtained from people. Such a person thinks he is learning and teaching for the sake of God, but never passes his own self under scrutiny and never compares his ego with the states of sincere people.

Another is to perform abundant ritual prayers, fasts, and good works, then admire oneself, confine one's perception to one's power and ability, forgetting God's favor in guiding and granting one success. Self-admiration annuls works. One may also fall into ostentation and seek to be highly regarded by other people, yet still think he is sincere and desirous to draw nearer to God. Abu'l-Dardā'—may God be pleased with him—said, "Better is the sleep and not fasting of the sagacious. How they outstrip the vigils of fools and their fasts! An atom's weight from a person of certitude and God-fearing is better than mountains of works from the vain."

As for self-deception on the part of the sinful, one kind is for a person to sin, then repent and ask forgiveness with the tongue, without knowledge of the conditions of repentance and how to make it valid, yet think that he has repented and been forgiven. Another is to sin abundantly and persistently, fail in one's duties, then justify oneself using predestination as an argument, claiming that one is deprived of all choice, as well as of the ability to resist that which has been preordained. This is an immense self-deception. He who

161. Ibn Māja, *Sunan,* (4250); Tirmidhī, *Sunan,* (2383).

says so is a heretic and does not belong to *Ahl al-Sunna*. Yet another is to harbor hopes of forgiveness, even as one is failing to obey commands and avoid forbidden things. Some sinful and neglectful people say, "God is in no need of us or our works, He is neither harmed by sins, nor does He profit from good works." These are words of truth, but deliberately quoted out of context. It is the Devil who has inspired the heart of that vain person with them, then brought them out of his mouth, to cut him off from forgiveness and from striving for it as God commands. Another is for certain sinful and confused people to depend on the virtue of their learned and virtuous fathers and forefathers, but without emulating any of their good characters, deeds, or words. This is blameworthy self-deception and flagrant foolishness. Yet another is for certain sinners to visit the virtuous, serve them, and think-well of them, yet hold back from every kind of good they see them do, every virtue they have, and from their pattern of constant obedience to God.

As we said earlier, the different kinds of self-deception are numerous and only those will be saved from them who return to God and depend only on His favor and generosity, together with exercising firmness and caution, determination in obeying Him, resolution in earnestly worshipping Him, avoiding disobedience, thanking Him for this, while confessing their shortcomings in fulfilling the least of His rights, remaining humble and needy to the utmost, constantly imploring and beseeching Him, and constantly asking for forgiveness, night and day. My success is only from God, upon Him do I depend and to Him do I submit.

Chapter Twelve: On Saving Things

There are numerous saving things that the heart must be embellished with and acquire as its own attributes. We shall discuss briefly some of the more essential and important ones-God willing.

One of the greatest of saving things is repentance to God the Exalted from all sins. God—August and Majestic is He—has commanded His servants to repent, encouraged them to do so, and promised them His acceptance. He says—Exalted is He, *And repent to God, all together, O believers, that you may succeed.* [24:31] And, *O believers! Repent to God, a sincere repentance. [66:8] And, God loves those who are ever repenting and ever purifying themselves.* [2:222] And, *He who repents after his wrongdoing, then does good, God shall relent toward him, God is Forgiving, Compassionate.* [5:39] And, *He it is who accepts repentance from His servants, and forgives evil deeds, and knows what you do.* [42:25]

The Prophet said—may God's blessings and peace be upon him, *He who has repented from a sin is as he who has never sinned.*[1] And, *God extends His hand by day, that he who has done evil by night might repent, and He extends His hand by night, that he who has done evil by day might repent.* [He shall do so] *until the sun rises from where it sets.*[2] And, *O people! Repent to God before you die, and hasten to good works before you become too occupied, and join that which is between you and your Lord by remembering Him in abundance.*[3] And, *God-exalted is He—accepts repentance from a servant so long as he does not gurgle.*[4] Until such time, that is, as his spirit reaches his throat as he is dying. And he said—may God's blessings and peace be upon him, *He who repents, God relents toward him.*[5]

Now know—may God have mercy on you—that repentance is not for a servant to say, "I ask God's forgiveness, I repent to God," without remorse in his heart and without desisting from sin. The scholars—may God have mercy on them—have mentioned the con-

1. Ibn Māja, *Sunan,* (4240); Bayhaqī, *Shu'ab al-Īmān*, (6920, 6939).
2. Muslim, *Ṣaḥīḥ*, (4954); Aḥmad, *Musnad,* (18708, 18793). The sun will rise from the West once in the very last days. This is one of the ten major signs said by the Prophet to precede the Resurrection.
3. Ibn Māja, *Sunan,* (1071); Bayhaqī, *Shu'ab al-Īmān*, (2879).
4. Ibn Māja, *Sunan,* (4243); Tirmidhī, *Sunan,* (3460).
5. Bukhārī, *Ṣaḥīḥ*, (5956, 5957); Muslim, *Ṣaḥīḥ*, (1737, 1738).

ditions necessary for repentance, without which it cannot be valid. These are three: The first is to feel remorse in the heart for previous sins. The second is to refrain from sin; which means that one cannot repent from a sin while still committing it. The third is to resolve never to relapse into sin for the rest of one's life. These three conditions are necessary for sins which are between the servant and his Lord. When the sin is between the servant and other servants, a fourth is added. To explain: If he has injured another human being, whether in his person, honor, or property, he must compensate him by allowing him to exact the legal retaliatory measures in case of personal injury, by returning his property in case this is where he has wronged him, or by asking forgiveness if it is his honor which has been affected. He must strive to the utmost to accomplish this. As for he who has repented from neglecting such obligatory devotions as ritual prayers and fasts, he should requite them as much as time and circumstance will allow.

Once the servant has repented from his sins in the manner described above, he should maintain himself between hope and fear: hope that his Lord will accept his repentance, by His favor and generosity, and fear that He may not, since he may not have repented in the manner that God has commanded him to do and is thus not considered by Him to have repented.

It is a most certain duty upon all Muslims to guard themselves thoroughly against all sins, for in them lies God's wrath and loathing, and furthermore, they are the cause of all the afflictions and catastrophes that befall people both in this world and the next. Should a person fall into sin, he must repent to God immediately and strive neither to persist nor feel comfortable with it.

Every believer should repent continuously to God, renewing his repentance at every moment and in every situation, for sins are numerous, there are minor as well as major ones, manifest as well as hidden ones, and sins that the servant is aware of as well as others he is not. He may be asked to account for not making the effort to learn whether certain acts are sinful or not, as well as their having preliminaries and signs that, had he known them, might have allowed him to do something about them.

It is very important to ask for forgiveness in abundance, for God so commands and encourages, saying—Exalted is He, *Ask God's forgiveness, God is Forgiving, Compassionate*. [2:199] And He says—Exalted is He—to His Messenger—may God's blessings and peace be upon him, *Ask forgiveness for your sins and for the men and women believers.* [47:19] He also says—Exalted is He—describing those of His servants who behave with excellence, *And in the early hours they ask forgiveness.* [51:18]

He said—may God's blessings and peace be upon him, *He who keeps to asking forgiveness, God shall grant him relief from every anxiety, a way out of every difficulty, and provision from whence he does not expect it.*[6] And, *Blessed is he in whose record is found abundant requests for forgiveness.*[7] To realize the merits of asking forgiveness, its profits, and usefulness, it should suffice you to be aware of His saying—Exalted is He, *God was not to torment them so long as they are asking forgiveness.* [8:33] And His saying—Exalted is He—informing about His Prophet Noah—may peace be upon him, *So I said, 'Ask forgiveness of your Lord, for He is Ever Forgiving. He will loose the sky upon you in torrents and will supply you with wealth and sons, and will assign for you gardens, and will assign for you rivers.* [71:10-12]

Repentance and asking forgiveness are treasures of goodness. They are among the greatest gates to good deeds and blessings, and among the most effective means to all good things in this world and the next. Therefore, you must keep to repentance and asking forgiveness—may God have mercy on you—day and night. The Devil—may God curse him—deceives the fools among Muslims by saying, "How can you repent when you well know that you will not uphold your repentance? How can you repent then relapse into sin?" He will keep on whispering such doubts to them. So let the Muslim beware of him, not be deceived, and not be taken by his falsehoods and trickeries. He said—may God's blessings and peace be upon him, *He who asks forgiveness is not persisting [in sin] even should he relapse seventy times a day.*[8] The servant must repent then ask his Lord to assist him and make him steadfast. If his ego defeats him and he relapses into sin, let him defeat it in turn by repeating his repentance. God it is who grants success and assistance.

Hope and Fear

Among saving things are hope in God and fear of Him. Both are noble stations which God has attributed to His Prophets, Messen-

6. Abū Dāwūd, *Sunan*, (1297); Ibn Māja, *Sunan*, (3809).
7. Ibn Māja, *Sunan*, (3808).
8. Abū Dāwūd, *Sunan*, (1293); Tirmidhī, *Sunan*, (3482).

gers, and those among the virtuous believers who followed them with excellence. He said—Exalted is He, *Those they call upon themselves seek the means to come to their Lord, which of them shall be nearer. They hope for His mercy and fear His chastisement. The torment of your Lord is a thing to beware of.* [17:57] And, *They used to hasten to good works and call upon Us out of yearning and awe, and they were humble to Us.* [21:90] And, *Those who have believed and those who have emigrated and fought in the way of God, those hope for God's mercy, and God is Forgiving, Compassionate.* [2:218] And, *And a reminder for the God-fearing who fear their Lord though they have not seen Him and are in dread of the Hour.* [2:48, 49] And, *And those who give what they give while their hearts tremble because they are returning to their Lord.* [23:60]

The Messenger of God said—may God's blessings and peace be upon him, *God—Exalted is He—says, "I am as My servant thinks of Me, and I am with him whenever he remembers Me."*[9] And he said—may God's blessings and peace be upon him, *God—Exalted is He—says, "O Son of Adam! You will never call upon Me and hope in Me and not be forgiven by Me, whatever you may have done, and I shall care little. O Son of Adam! Were your sins to reach up to the clouds in the sky, then you ask My forgiveness, I shall forgive you. O Son of Adam! Were you to come to Me with sins to fill the earth, but meet Me associating nothing with Me, I shall meet you with as much forgiveness."*[10] And, *God—Exalted is He says, "By My eminence! I shall never subject My servant to two fears or two securities. If he fears Me in this world, I shall make him secure on Resurrection Day, but if he feels secure in this world, I shall cause him to fear on Resurrection Day."*[11] And he said—may God's blessings and peace be upon him, *The beginning of wisdom is the fear of God.*[12] The Prophet—may God's blessings and peace be upon him—once visited a young man who was dying. He asked him, *How do you feel*? He answered, "I fear my sins and hope for mercy from my Lord." He said, *These two never unite in the heart of a servant in such a situation without God granting him what he hopes for and securing him from what he fears.*[13]

9. Bukhārī, *Ṣaḥīḥ*, (6856); Muslim, *Ṣaḥīḥ*, (4832, 4851).

10. Tirmidhī, *Sunan*, (3463).

11. Bayhaqī, *Shu'ab al-Īmān*, (794); Ibn Ḥibbān, *Ṣaḥīḥ*, (642) .

12. Bayhaqī, *Shu'ab al-Īmān*, (763).

13. Ibn Māja, *Sunan*, (4251); Tirmidhī, *Sunan*, (905).

Know that fear is a rebuke that restrains people from sins and contraventions, while hope is a leader that leads the servant to acts of obedience and conformity. He who is not rebuked by his fear from disobeying God—August and Majestic is He—nor led by his hope to obey Him, both his hope and fear are but ineffective ruminations of the soul that are of no consequence, for they have failed to lead to their intended goal and benefit.

It is better for the upright believer to remain between fear and hope, so that they are like the wings of the bird, or the pans of the scales. It has been transmitted that "Were the fear of the believer and his hope to be weighed, they would balance each other." But for the believer who mixes [good with evil deeds] and is afraid he might neglect acts of obedience or commit sins it is better and more appropriate for him to remain fearful most of the time, for fear restrains the ego and rebukes it from its transgressions and unruliness. He whose ego is strong and whose lusts are overpowering, but who nevertheless remains hopeful [in forgiveness] most of the time, may be led by his hope to his ruin, for whenever he reminds his inciting-to-evil soul of the immensity of God's mercy and how He easily overlooks sins, he grows bolder in transgressing God's limits, farther away from His obedience, and increasingly sinful. Thus, unaware, he will perish. This has indeed happened to many common Muslims who have been wont to deceive themselves concerning God. This kind of hope is but false hope and self-deception. It bears no resemblance whatsoever to praiseworthy hope, for the latter leads the servant to remain obedient to God and behave in such a manner as to please Him. So let the believer beware of this kind of hope, for it is but a lure from the Devil and an evil which he passes as a good. However, when a person is nearing death, it is better for him to be full of hope and of thinking well of God, whatever his prior condition had been. He said—may God's blessings and peace be upon him, *Let none of you die save thinking well of God.*[14]

Let the believer beware of both extremes: Feeling secure from God's ruses on the one hand, or despairing of His mercy on the other. He says—Exalted is He, *None feels secure from God's ruse save those who are losers.* [7:99] He also says, *None despairs of the mercy of his Lord but those who are astray.* [15:56]

---

14. Muslim, *Ṣaḥīḥ*, (5125); Abū Dāwūd, *Sunan*, (2706); Ibn Māja, *Sunan*, (4157).

For a person to feel secure from God's ruse is to have so much hope and so little fear of Him as to think it highly unlikely that He will chastise and torment him. As for despair, it is to have so much fear and so little hope in God as to feel it highly unlikely to be shown mercy and forgiven. Both are major sins, so beware of them O believer. Remain between fear and hope. Do not deceive yourself concerning your Lord and do not be too bold with Him, for your Lord is swift in chastisement, but He is also Forgiving and Compassionate.

Fortitude, Gratitude, and Detachment

Among the greatest of saving things are to bear God's trials with fortitude, receive His favors with gratitude, and detach yourself from this world, for it is distracting you away from Him.

As for fortitude, its merits are immense and the believer needs it at all times and in all circumstances. The injunctions of God the Exalted and His Messenger—may God's blessings and peace be upon him—concerning fortitude are numerous and well known. He says—Exalted is He, *O believers! Seek help in fortitude and prayer, God is with those who have fortitude.* [2:153] And, *Give glad news to those who have fortitude.* [2:155] And, *God loves those who have fortitude.* [3:146] And He said to His Prophet, *Have fortitude, your fortitude is but by God.* [27:127] And, *Be patient under the decree of your Lord, for you are under Our gaze.* [52:48] And, *And We made from among them leaders guiding by Our command, when they had fortitude.* [32:24] And, *Those who have fortitude will be paid their wages in full, without reckoning.* [39:10] The Messenger of God said—may God's blessings and peace be upon him, *He who has fortitude, God assists him in his fortitude. None was ever given a gift better or vaster than fortitude.*[15] It has been said that fortitude was the mattock of the believer, as well as the commander of his hosts. And the Prophet said—may God's blessings and peace be upon him, *In patiently enduring that which you dislike lies much good.*[16]

It has been handed down that faith has two halves, fortitude and gratitude. The believer needs fortitude when calamities strike, in times of hardships, afflictions, or injuries, so that he does not panic, but retains his inner peace and dignity, does not feel anxious and impatient, but returns to God humbly and submissively, with supplications and implorations, thinking well of his Lord, in the certain

15. Bukhārī, *Ṣaḥīḥ*, (1376, 5989); Muslim, *Ṣaḥīḥ*, (1745).
16. Aḥmad, *Musnad,* (2666); Bayhaqī, *Shu'ab al-Īmān*, (1089).

knowledge that God the Exalted only afflicted him with this trial because there is much good for him in it, whether it be raising his degree, increasing his good deeds, or expiating his sins, as many well known *ḥadīths* have stated. He said—may God's blessings and peace be upon him, *The believer suffers no weariness, hardship, anxiety, sorrow, harm, or grief, even* [as little a thing as] *a thorn that pricks him, without God expiating some of his sins.*[17]

A believer will also need much patience when performing his acts of obedience, so as not to neglect them out of indolence and to perform them as God commands him to do, with perfect presence, sincerity, and lack of ostentation or affectation in the presence of others. It is natural for the ego to drag its feet in acts of obedience, so that the servant needs to impose them upon it with gracious patience.

The believer also needs much patience to refrain from sins and forbidden things, for the ego incites to them and thinks about committing them. He thus needs to restrain it with patience and prevent it from outwardly committing sins and inwardly inclining toward and thinking about them.

The believer also needs much patience to refrain from permissible appetites, those that the ego desires for no other reason than to enjoy the pleasures of this world, when to indulge himself to excess and allow himself free rein in doing so will lead him to fall into the suspect and the forbidden, increase one's desire for the world even more, arouse one's greed for it, incite to find comfort and give priority to it, while forgetting the hereafter.

You now know—may God have mercy on you—how the believer needs patience at all times and in all circumstances. Keep to it and you will gain every good and achieve every happiness.

As for gratitude, it is one of the noble stations and lofty degrees. God—Exalted is He—says, *Thank the favor of God if it is Him that you worship.* [16:114] And, *Eat of the provision of your Lord and thank Him.* [34:15] And, *Labor, O House of David, in gratitude, for few indeed among My servants are grateful.* [34:13] And, *We shall reward those who are grateful.* [3:145]

The Messenger of God—may God's blessings and peace be upon him—said, *He who is given and gives thanks, is tried and is patient, is wronged and forgives, wrongs and asks forgiveness*, then he stopped. "What will he deserve O Messenger of God?" They

17. Bukhārī, *Ṣaḥīḥ*, (5210).

asked. He answered, *Those shall have security and those are rightly-guided.* [6:82][18] And he said—may God's blessings and peace be upon him, *Let each of you have a remembering tongue and a grateful heart.*[19] And, *The first to be summoned to the Garden shall be the ever grateful, those who thank God in all circumstances.*[20] Much more has been said concerning gratitude.

The essence of gratitude is for the servant to know that all the favors in his possession, outward as well as inward, are from God—Exalted is He—and by His grace and munificence—Transcendent is He.

It is part of gratitude to rejoice in the presence of favors because they are the means to work in God's obedience and attain to His proximity. It is part of gratitude to thank God in profusion and praise Him verbally. It has been transmitted that should a man who is given the entire world say, '*Al-ḥamdu li'llāh*!' his saying *al-ḥamdu li'llāh* will equal more than it all. He said—may God's blessings and peace be upon him, Al-ḥamdu li'llāh *fills the Scales.*[21] And, *God is well pleased with a servant who eats his meal then thanks Him for it and drinks his beverage then thanks Him for it.*[22]

It is part of gratitude to busy oneself with God's obedience, use His favors as a help in doing so, and use them as God likes them to be used. This is the utmost in gratitude. One should not become arrogant, boast before others of the blessings he has been granted, transgress, wrong others, or overstep the limits in dealing with them. He who does so has not been thankful, but has denied God's favors. Denial leads to dispossession and to one's blessings being changed into afflictions. He says—Exalted is He, *This is because God never changes the blessing He has bestowed on a people until they change what is in themselves, and because God is Hearing, Knowing.* [8:53] Changing what is in themselves means abandoning gratitude for their blessings. He who shows no gratitude exposes himself to dispossession and ruin, while he who is grateful deserves goodness and increase. God—Exalted is He—says, *Your Lord has declared, "If you are thankful, I shall increase you.*" [14:7] It is part of gratitude to see every blessing, even if small, as tremendous, because of

18. Bayhaqī, *Shu'ab al-Īmān*, (4259); Ṭabarānī, *Kabīr*, (6482).
19. Aḥmad, *Musnad,* (21358, 22022); Bayhaqī, *Shu'ab al-Īmān*, (613).
20. Ṭabarānī, *Kabīr*, (12176); *Awsaṭ,* (3151).
21. Muslim, *Ṣaḥīḥ*, (328); Tirmidhī, *Sunan*, (3439).
22. Muslim, *Ṣaḥīḥ*, (4915); Tirmidhī, *Sunan*, (1738).

the immensity of He who has granted it-Blessed and Exalted is He. God's favors upon His servant are innumerable and the servant is incapable of counting them, let alone thank for them. God—Exalted is He—says, *Were you to count the favors of God, you would be incapable of it. God is Forgiving, Compassionate.* [16:18]

A person should never look with envy and resentment at those who have been preferred over him in blessings, for it may lead to his disdaining and belittling God's favors upon him, then neglecting to thank for them. This will lead to his dispossession and their being diverted away from him. Thus he will neither be given as much as his brother whom he has envied, nor retain the little that his Lord has given him, all for failing to thank and observe proper courtesy toward Him. A *ḥadīth* says, *Look at those who are beneath you, not those who are above you, for it is less conducive for you to despise God's favors upon you.*[23] God prefers some of His servants over others for mysterious reasons, a hidden wisdom, to serve interests and attract profits known only to Him. So let each servant be satisfied with God's decisions, thank Him for the favors He has granted him, and ask Him for more. The treasuries of the heavens and earth are in His fist, all good is in His hand, He does what He will and He has power over all things.

As for detachment from this world, it is one of the best saving things and worthy devotions. To induce His servants to renounce the world, God—Exalted is He—says, *We have made all that is on the earth to be an adornment for it, that We may try which of them is more excellent in works, and We shall surely make all that is on it barren dust.* [18:7, 8] And He says—Exalted is He, *Whatever things you have been given are the enjoyments of the life of this world and its ornaments, but that which is with God is better and longer lasting. Will you not understand? Is he to whom We have made a fair promise, and he receives it, as he to whom We have granted enjoyment of the life of this world, then he shall be one of those that are arraigned on Judgment Day*? [28:60, 61] And, *But you prefer the life of this world, when the hereafter is better and longer lasting.* [87:16, 17]

The Messenger of God—may God's blessings and peace be upon him—said, *Renounce the world and God will love you. Renounce*

---

23. Muslim, *Ṣaḥīḥ*, (5264); Tirmidhī, *Sunan*, (2437).

what is in other people's hands and people will love you.[24] And, *Be in this world as a stranger or a passer-by, and count yourself among the people of the graves.*[25] And, *He who loves his hereafter harms his life in this world, and he who loves his life in this world harms his hereafter. So prefer that which is permanent over that which is ephemeral.*[26] And, *He who wakes up in the morning anxious for his life to come, God gathers his affairs for him, preserves his property, and the world comes to him submissively.*[27]

The essence of detachment is for the love and desire for this world to depart from the heart of the servant and it becomes so insignificant in his eyes that for it to withdraw and leave him in scarcity becomes more pleasing to him and preferable than for it to come to him and make him affluent. This is as concerns the inward. As for the outward, the renunciate should keep away from it, shunning it by choice when capable of acquiring it, and restricting himself to the strict necessary in the way of food, clothes, accommodation, or anything else he may need. As he said—may God's blessings and peace be upon him, *Let the provision of each of you from this world be that of a rider.*[28]

He who loves the world, desires it in his heart, and strives to amass it with the intention of enjoying its pleasures is one who loves the world and in whom there is no detachment at all.

He who inclines toward the world and desires it, not to enjoy but to spend it in benevolent and devotional pursuits is doing good if his behavior tallies with his intention. However, he is not safe from danger.

He who desires and pursues the world, but is unable to acquire it, remaining poor and destitute, he is a poor man, not a renunciate. If he is patient and contented in his poverty, he will have great merit and reward.

---

24. Al-Ḥākim, *Mustadrak,* (7985); Bayhaqī, *Shu'ab al-Īmān*, (10132); Ṭabarānī, *Kabīr,* (5839).
25. Bukhārī, *Ṣaḥīḥ*, (5937); Ibn Māja, *Sunan*, (4157); Tirmidhī, *Sunan*, (2255).
26. Aḥmad, *Musnad,* (18866, 18867); Al-Ḥākim, *Mustadrak,* (7964, 8011); Bayhaqī, *Shu'ab al-Īmān*, (9957).
27. Ibn Māja, *Sunan*, (4095); Tirmidhī, *Sunan*, (2389).
28. Aḥmad, *Musnad,* (22597); Al-Ḥākim, *Mustadrak,* (7979); Bayhaqī, *Shu'ab al-Īmān*, (10007).

As for he who takes a large share of the world and enjoys its pleasures freely, then claims he neither desires nor loves it in his heart, he is a presumptuous self deceiver. His claim is groundless and he cannot pretend to be following the example of any of the rightly-guided leaders and virtuous scholars, neither among the ancients nor the latecomers. Know this, may God take over your guidance.

Reliance, Contentment, Love, Good Intentions, and Sincerity

Among noble saving things are reliance on God, love for Him, contentment with Him, good intentions, and outward and inward sincerity.

Reliance (*tawakkul*)

Reliance upon God is one of the most noble stations of the people of certitude and one of certitude's most invaluable consequences. God—Exalted is He—says, *Thus, rely on God.* [27:79] And, *God does indeed love those who rely* [on Him] [3:159] And, *Upon God let the believers rely.* [5:11] And, *And upon God rely if you are beli*evers. [5:23] And, *And rely upon God, and God is sufficient as guardian.* [4:81]

The Prophet—may God's blessings and peace be upon him—said, *If you were to rely upon God as you rightfully should, He would provide for you just as He provides for the birds. They fly off hungry and return satiated.*[29]

Among the best invocations is "God is sufficient for us and the best of guardians." (*Ḥasbuna'llāhu wa ni'ma'l-wakīl*) When he was cast into the blaze, Abraham—may blessings and peace be upon him—said it, as did Muḥammad—may God's blessings and peace be upon him—and the believers when they were told, *the people have mustered for you, so fear them. But it only increased them in faith and they said, 'God is sufficient for us and the best of guardians'*. [3:173]

One of our virtuous predecessors—may God have mercy on him—said, "He who is satisfied with God as his guardian will find a way to every good thing."

The essence of reliance is certainty that all matters are in God's hand, in His fist, that none other than He can cause either harm or benefit, or give or withhold. The heart must be easy; confident in

29. Tirmidhī, *Sunan*, (2266); Ibn Māja, *Sunan*, (4154).

God's promise and His guarantee, so that it neither trembles nor becomes agitated when stricken by hardships or problems, neither is it to seek refuge and assistance with other than God the Exalted whenever afflicted by difficulties and worries. Were one ever to seek any of this with a created being, it should never be inwardly, but only outwardly, and according to the dictates of Divine law.

It is not a condition of reliance to abandon worldly means. On the contrary, one may very well join reliance with making use of secondary causes, so long as one relies on God, not on these causes. The sign of sincerity is that one does not depend on them so as to feel at peace when they are available, but anxious and agitated when they are absent or muddled. A servant may well have no worldly means, yet not be reliant. This is when he is attached to them, attentive to created beings, and desirous of what is in their possession.

Means are of two kinds, religious and worldly. Religious means are the necessary beneficial sciences and good works. Every Muslim must make use of these, but depend on God, not on them. Worldly means are the arts, crafts, and all other manners of making a living. It is not permissible to abandon what one needs of them and cannot do without, unless one is handicapped, unable to move or to exert effort, or else if one is one of those servants of God who are people of gnosis and certainty that God has established in such a state. The rule is that it is not permissible for a man to abandon working for his necessary living unless either he is incapable of working or established in divestment and qualified for it. It is forbidden for a man to leave himself and his dependants in need, begging from others, desiring what is in their possession, when he has said—may God's blessings and peace be upon him, *It is sufficient sin for a man to neglect those for whom he is responsible.*[30]

Love

As for the love of God, it is one of the most noble and elevated stations. God Exalted is He—says, *And those who believe are stronger in their love for God.* [2:165] And, *God will bring people He loves and who love Him.* [5:54] The Prophet—may God's blessings and peace be upon him—said, *Three things will give he who possesses them sweetness in faith: To love God and His Messenger more than*

30. Nasā'ī, *Al-Sunan al-Kubrā*, (9176, 9177); Al-Ḥākim, *Mustadrak*, (8865).

anything else…[31] And, *Love God for the favors He bestows upon you, love me for the love of God, and love the people of my house for my love.*[32]

To love God the Exalted is for the servant to feel inclination in his heart, attachment, and passion for that holiest and loftiest of presences, extreme awareness of its sanctity and transcendence, together with extreme reverence and awe, free from any thoughts of comparability or illusions of limitation, for God is too Exalted. We insist on this because some of the common people who lack insight, when they hear of the states of the men of God and their experiences in loving God, may be subject in their minds and hearts to thoughts and illusions that are exceedingly perilous and harmful.

He who is sincere in loving God the Exalted is driven thereby to prefer Him above all else, move with determination along the road to His proximity and good pleasure, strive in earnest in His obedience, do his utmost in His service, and forsake everything likely to distract him from His remembrance and proper behavior toward Him.

One of the best proofs that one loves God is to follow with excellence the Messenger of God—may God's blessings and peace be upon him. God says—Exalted is He, *Say, 'If you love God, follow me and God will love you and forgive your sins. God is Forgiving, Compassionate'*. [3:31]

Contentment (*riḍā*)

Contentment with God the Exalted is a rare noble state. God—Exalted is He—says, *God is satisfied with them and they are satisfied with Him.* [98:8] The Prophet—may God's blessings and peace be upon him—said, *When God comes to love certain persons He tries them. He who is contented receives contentment in return, while he who is angry receives anger in return.*[33] And, *God in His knowledge and justice, has placed comfort and joy in certainty and contentment, but oppression and anxiety in doubt and anger.*[34]

He who is contented with God is he who is satisfied with His decrees. When He decrees—Transcendent is He—for him that which runs against his desires and displeases him, such as injury to self or

31. Bukhārī, *Ṣaḥīḥ*, (15, 20, 6428); Muslim, *Ṣaḥīḥ*, (60).
32. Tirmidhī, *Sunan*, (3722); Al-Ḥākim, *Mustadrak,* (4699).
33. Tirmidhī, *Sunan*, (2320); Ibn Māja, *Sunan*, (4021).
34. Bayhaqī, *Shu'ab al-Īmān*, (208).

property, or hardship, difficulty, or affliction, he must accept this with contentment, neither being angry with God's decree, nor panicky, nor impatient, for God the Exalted has the right to do as He pleases in His kingdom and none may either dispute or object to His sovereignty.

Let the servant beware of "if only", "why?", or "how?" Let him know that God the Exalted is wise and fair in all His acts and decisions, that He never decrees something for His believing servant, even if detestable to the latter, without there being good in it, for it will be a good choice and have good consequences. Let him think well of his Lord, be contented with His decrees, return to Him with humility and neediness, stand before Him submissive and subdued, thank and praise Him in profusion, whether in times of ease or hardship, difficulty or affluence. All praise belongs to God, Lord of the worlds.

Good Intentions and Sincerity

Good intentions and sincerity are among the greatest and most important of saving things. God—Exalted is He—says, *Among you are those who desire this world and those who desire the hereafter.* [3:152] And, *He who desires the hereafter and strives for it as it should, while being a believer, those their striving shall be thanked.* [17:19] The Prophet—may God's blessings and peace be upon him—said, *Works are valued according to intentions, each person receiving as he intended.*[35] And, *People will be resurrected according to their intentions.*[36] And, *He who fights intending no more than a hobble, he will receive only what he intended.*[37] And, *The intention of the believer is better than his deed.*[38] This is because intention is the act of the heart and because the heart is superior to the members, therefore its acts are superior to theirs; and because the intention is itself profitable, whereas without intention the works of the members are valueless. A *ḥadīth* says, *He who intends a good deed but does not accomplish it, God records it with Him as a complete good deed.*[39]

35. Bukhārī, *Ṣaḥīḥ*, (1).

36. Ibn Māja, *Sunan*, (4219).

37. Nasā'ī, *Sunan*. (3087, 3088); Aḥmad, *Musnad,* (21634, 21669).

38. Bayhaqī, *Shu'ab al-Īmān*, (6596); Al-Shihāb al-Quḍā'ī, *Musnad al-Shihāb*, (141).

39. Bukhārī, *Ṣaḥīḥ*, (6010); Muslim, *Ṣaḥīḥ*, (187).

Persevere in good sincere intentions—may God have mercy on you—and never perform any act of obedience without intending it to be for God's sake, to draw nearer to Him, attain to His good pleasure, and obtain the recompense promised by God—Transcendent is He—in the life to come, out of His favor and grace.

Never initiate a permissible activity, even eating, drinking, or sleeping, without intending it to be of help in obeying God and to give you strength in worshipping Him—Exalted is He. This is how the merely permissible rejoins the devotional, for means have the same legal status as their goals.[40] The deprived is he who is deprived of good intentions.

Make numerous good intentions for each activity; whether devotional or merely permissible, you will thus receive, by the grace of God, a full reward for each of these intentions. Those activities you are incapable of, intend to perform when able to. Say with sincerity, resolution, and good intention, "Had I been able to, I would have done them." You will thus obtain recompense similar to that of he who has actually done them. It has reached us that an Israelite passed by some sand dunes at a time of famine. He said to himself, "Had these been edible and in my possession, I would have distributed them among the people." God revealed to the Prophet of that time, "Inform so and so that God accepts his donation and thanks him for his good intention." It has been handed down that sometimes when the angels raise the servant's record to God—Exalted is He—He will say to them—Transcendent is He, "Record such and such a deed to his credit." They will say, "But he has not done it." He will answer, "He has intended it."

God-exalted is He—says about sincerity, *They were commanded only to worship God, making the religion His sincerely, pure in faith, and to perform the ritual prayer and pay the* zakāt. *That is the worthy religion.* [98:5] And, *Indeed sincere religion is all God's.* [39:3] The Prophet—may God's blessings and peace be upon him—said, *Be sincere in your religion and a few works will suffice you.*[41] When he was asked about faith, he replied that it was sincerity with

40. Means are judged according to their ends. If the end is an obligatory devotion, then the means to it attract a reward similar to that of an obligatory activity. The same applies for supererogatory, merely permissible, discouraged, and forbidden acts.

41. Al-Ḥākim, *Mustadrak,* (7955); Bayhaqī, *Shu'ab al-Īmān*, (6593, 6594).

God. And he said, *God only accepts those works that are sincerely His and purely for His sake.*[42] And, *He who is sincere with God for forty mornings, the fountains of wisdom flow from his heart to his tongue.*[43]

Sincerity is for a human being to have no purpose in his devotions, nor in his other works other than to draw nearer to God and seek His proximity and good pleasure. No other purpose should exist, such as showing off, seeking the approval of others, or desiring what can be obtained from them. Sahl ibn 'Abdallāh al-Tustarī—may God the Exalted have mercy on him—said, "Sagacious people have searched for the definition of sincerity and found nothing but this: That both one's movements and standstills, private or public, should be for God the Exalted, unadulterated by anything else, whether ego, passion, or this world." He who works for the purpose of drawing nearer to God and seeking His good pleasure and recompense, he is the sincere person. He who works both for this and to show off, he is ostentatious and his works are unacceptable. He who works just to show off and would have done nothing at all were it not for the people observing him, he is in formidable danger and his kind of ostentation is that of the hypocrites. We ask God for protection from such things and safety from all afflictions.

Veracity, Vigilance, Reflection, Short Hopes, Remembering Death and Preparing for it

Among the best of saving things are also veracity with God, vigilance, reflection, short hopes, remembering death in abundance and preparing for it.

Veracity (*ṣidq*)

God—Exalted is He—says concerning veracity, *O believers! Fear God and be with the veracious.* [9:119] And, *This is a day when the veracious shall profit from their veracity.* [5:119] And, *Among the believers are men who were true in what they promised God.* [33:23] And, *That God may reward the veracious for their veracity.* [33:24] The Prophet—may God's blessings and peace be upon him—said, *Veracity leads to benevolence and benevolence leads to the Garden. A servant is veracious and perseveres in veracity until*

42. Nasā'ī, *Sunan*. (3089).

43. Al-Shihāb al-Quḍā'ī, *Musnad al-Shihāb*, (446); Ibn Abī Shayba, *Muṣannaf*, vol. 8, p. 131.

he is recorded with God as truly veracious. Lying leads to corruption and corruption leads to the Fire. A servant will lie and persevere in lying until he is recorded with God as a liar.[44]

The beginning of veracity is to avoid lying in all speech, following which veracity must have a share in all works, intentions, states, and stations. Veracity here means steadfastness in all these and performing them in the best and most cautious manner, doing one's very best, being serious and resolute to the extreme, both outwardly and inwardly.

Vigilance (*murāqaba*)

As for vigilance, it means feeling God's permanent nearness to the servant, His encompassing him, being with him, aware of him, and gazing at him. God—Exalted is He—says, *God is ever watchful over everything*. [33:52] And, *I am with you both, hearing and seeing*. [20:46] And, *And We have created man and know what his ego whispers to him, and we are nearer to him than his jugular vein.* [50:16] And, *He is with you wherever you are, and God sees well what you do*. [57:4] The Prophet said—may God's blessings and peace be upon him, *Excellence is to worship God as if you saw Him, for if you see Him not, He sees you.*[45] Thus, vigilance belongs to the station of excellence and he who realizes it achieves awe of God—Exalted is He, shyness lest God sees him where He has forbidden him or misses him where He has enjoined him to be, or sees him lazy in obedience, dragging his feet in worship, distracted from His service, forgetful of His remembrance or of proper conduct toward Him.

Reflection (*tafakkur*)

As for excellent and upright reflection, it has numerous benefits and great profits. God—Exalted is He—says, *Thus does God make clear the signs for you, that you may reflect on this world and the next.* [2:219, 220] And, *In this are signs for people who reflect*. [30:21] And, *Say, 'Observe what is in the heavens and earth'*. [10:101] The Prophet—may God's blessings and peace be upon him—once said that an hour's reflection was better than sixty years of worship-

44. Bukhārī, *Ṣaḥīḥ*, (5629); Muslim, *Ṣaḥīḥ*, (4719).
45. Bukhārī, *Ṣaḥīḥ*, (48, 4404); Muslim, *Ṣaḥīḥ*, (9, 10).

ping[46]; and 'Alī—may God honor his countenance—said, "There is no devotion better than reflection."[47]

There are many kinds of reflection. The best and most noble is to reflect on Divine acts and signs and the wonders of His making in His earth and heavens. He who reflects deeply on these gains an increase in his knowledge of God, which thing is the greatest elixir.

Another kind of reflection is to reflect on the favors and blessings that God bestows upon you, both religious and worldly. Reflecting deeply on these leads to an increase in one's love for God and induces one to thank Him.

Another kind is to reflect on the immensity of God's rights upon you and your numerous shortcomings in fulfilling His rights of Lordship. Reflecting deeply on these leads to fear, awe, and shyness of God the exalted and induces one to strive resolutely and in earnest to obey Him and fulfill His rights.

Another kind is to reflect on this world and how evanescent it is, how full of preoccupations and vexations. Reflecting deeply on this leads to detachment from it, forsaking and losing desire for it.

Yet another is to reflect on the hereafter, how unending it is, how unadulterated its bliss, and how permanent its pleasures and joys. Reflecting deeply on these leads to preferring the hereafter, desiring it, and striving for it with determination.

There are many more avenues for reflection. The sharper a servant's insight and the broader and more abundant his knowledge, the vaster and more abundant his reflection.

Short Hopes, Remembering Death, and Preparing for It

As for short hopes, frequent remembrance of death, and preparing for it, their benefits are immense and their merits great. He whose hopes are short and his remembrance of death abundant will be resolute in good works, not subject to procrastination or laziness, detached from this world and desirous of the hereafter, swift to repent and return to God the Exalted, distant from whatever may distract him from obedience to God the Exalted and from following the path leading to His good pleasure. He whose hopes are long and remembrance of death scarce will be the opposite of all this.

46. Abul-Shaykh al-Aṣbahānī, *Kitāb al-'Aẓama*, (42).

47. Bayhaqī, *Shu'ab al-Īmān*, (4469); Al-Shihāb al-Quḍā'ī, *Musnad al-Shihāb*, (779); Ṭabarānī, *Kabīr*, (2622).

Early in this work when discussing knowledge we have already had a useful discussion of the merits of short hopes and feeling the nearness of death, and everything that follows upon these. Thus there is no need for lengthy elaboration here.

Al-Ḥasan al-Baṣrī—may God have mercy on him—said, "The Messenger of God—may God's blessings and peace be upon him—asked, 'Do you all wish to be admitted to the Garden?' They answered, 'Yes, O Messenger of God.' He said, 'Shorten your hopes, place your appointed time before your eyes, and feel shy from God as you rightfully should.'"[48] The Messenger of God—may God's blessings and peace be upon him—used to say in his prayers, "O God! I seek Your protection from a world that bars the good of the hereafter, and I seek Your protection from a life that bars the good of death, and I seek Your protection from hopes that bar the good of works." Once 'Ā'isha—may God be pleased with her—asked, "O Messenger of God! Are other than the martyrs mustered with them?" He answered, "Yes, those who remember death more than twenty times every day and night." He also said—may God's blessings and peace be upon him, *Remember in abundance the Defeater of Pleasures,*[49] (the reason for remembering death being that) this will expiate sins and detach you from the world. When he was asked—may God's blessings and peace be upon him—about the meaning of the expansion mentioned in His saying—Exalted is He, *Is he whose breast God expands for Islam, so that he is upon a light from his Lord…*[39:22] He answered, *When light penetrates the heart, the breast expands for it.* They asked, "Is there a sign for this?" He answered, *Yes, to shun the abode of illusion, concentrate on the abode of immortality, and prepare for death before it comes.*[50] Imām al-Ghazālī—may God have mercy on him—says in *Bidāyat al-Hidāya*, "Reflect on the brevity of your life, even were you to live a hundred years, compared to your life in the hereafter which is for eternity. Consider how you endure hardships and humiliations in the pursuit of this world for a month or a year, in the hope of gaining rest for twenty years. Will you not endure this for a few days in the hope of gaining rest for eternity? Do not lengthen your hopes so much that you come to find works too laborious. Assume that death

48. Ibn al-Mubārak, *Al-Zuhd wa'l-Raqā'iq*, (318).

49. Tirmidhī, *Sunan*, (2229); Nasā'ī, *Sunan* (1801); Ibn Māja, *Sunan* (4248).

50. Al-Ḥākim, *Mustadrak,* (7974); Bayhaqī, *Shu'ab al-Īmān*, (10156).

is imminent. Say to yourself, 'I shall endure hardship today, for I may die tonight,' or 'I shall endure patiently tonight, for I may die tomorrow.' For death does not pounce predictably, whether as concerns time, situation, or age; but inevitably it will pounce. Therefore, preparing for it must take precedence over preparing for this world, in which you know you will live only a short while. It may be that only a single breath or a single day remains in your life. Think about this daily and impose upon yourself, day by day, patience in obeying God. But if you estimate you are to live fifty years and impose upon your ego patience in obeying God, it will bolt and rebel. If you heed the above advice you will be endlessly happy when death comes, but if you procrastinate and neglect, death will come unexpectedly and you will be endlessly remorseful. When morning comes, people are grateful for having traveled by night. When death comes, certain news come with it; and you shall learn about it in due course."

Chapter Thirteen: The Creed of *Ahl al-Sunna wa'l-Jamā'a*

A concise comprehensive creed, beneficial-God the exalted willing-according to the manner of the Group that is to be Saved, who are the People of *Sunna* and *Jamā'a*, the majority of Muslims.

Praise belongs to God alone. May God bless our master Muḥammad, his Family and Companions, and grant them peace. We know, assent, believe, confess with certainty, and testify that there is no god but God, Alone without partner. He is a Mighty God, a Great King. There is no lord besides Him, and we worship none other than He. He is ancient and Pre—Existent, Eternal and Everlasting. His firstness has no beginning, neither has His lastness any end. He is Solitary, Self-Subsistent, neither begetting, nor begotten, matchless, without partner or peer. '*There is nothing that resembles Him, and He is the Hearer, the Seer.*' [42:11]

"And we confess that His holiness (Exalted is He!) renders Him beyond time and space, beyond resembling anything in existence, so that He cannot be encompassed by directions, nor be subject to contingent events. And that He is established on His Throne in the manner which He has described, and in the sense which He has intended, in a manner befitting the might of His Majesty, and the exaltation of His glory and magnificence. And that He (Exalted is He!) is Near to everything in existence, being "*closer to man than his jugular vein.*" [50:16] He is Watchful and Seeing over all things. He is *the Living, the Self-Subsistent, slumber overtakes Him not, nor sleep*; [2:255] He is *the Originator of the heavens and earth; when He decrees a thing He only says to it Be! And it is* [2:117] *God is Creator of all things, and He is Guardian over everything.* [39:62]

"And that He (Exalted be He!) is over all things Powerful, and of all things knower; His knowledge is all-embracing and He keeps count of all things. *Not an atom's weight in the earth or in the sky escapes your Lord.* [10:61] *He knows what goes down into the earth and that which comes forth from it, and what descends from heaven and what ascends into it. He is with you wherever you may be, and God is Seer of what you do.* [57:4] *He knows what is in the land and the sea. A leaf cannot fall but that He knows it, nor is there a grain amid the darkness of the earth, nor a wet or dry thing, but that is recorded in a clear Book.* [6:59]

"And that he (Exalted be He!) wills existent things, and directs events. And that nothing may exist, whether good or evil, beneficial or harmful, except by His decree and will. Whatever He wills is, whatever He does not, is not. Should all creatures unite to move or halt a single atom in the universe, in the absence of His will, they would be unable to do so.

"And that He (Exalted be He!) is Hearer, Seer, Speaker of a Speech that is pre-existent and does not resemble the speech of creatures. And that the Mighty Qur'ān is His ancient speech, His Book which He sent down upon His Messenger and Prophet Muḥammad (may His blessings and peace be upon him).

"And that He (Transcendent be He!) is Creator of all things and their Provider, Who disposes them as He wills; neither rival nor opponent is there in His realm. He gives to whomsoever He wills and withholds from whomsoever He wills. *He is not questioned about His actions, rather they are questioned.* [21:23]

"And that He (Exalted be He!) is Wise in His acts; Just in His decrees, so that no injustice or tyranny can be imaginable on His part, and that no one has any rights over Him. Should He (Transcendent be He!) destroy all His creatures in the blink of an eye, He would be neither unjust nor tyrannous to them, for they are His dominion and His slaves. He has the right to do as He pleases in His dominion, *and your Lord is not a tyrant to His slave.* [41:46] He rewards His slaves for obeying Him, out of grace and generosity, and punishes them when they rebel, out of His wisdom and justice.

"And that to obey Him is an obligation binding upon His bondsmen, as was made clear through the speech of His messengers (upon them be peace). We believe in every Book sent down by God, and in all of His messengers, His angels, and in destiny, whether good or bad.

"And we testify that Muḥammad is His slave and Messenger, whom He sent to jinn and to mankind, to the Arabs and the non-Arabs, *with guidance and the religion of truth, that he may cause it to prevail over all religion, though the polytheists are averse.* [9:33] And that he delivered the Message, was faithful to his trust, advised the community, did away with grief, and strove for God's sake as is His due, being truthful and trustworthy, supported by authentic proofs and norm-breaking miracles. And that God has made it incumbent upon His slaves to believe, obey, and follow him, and that a man's faith is not acceptable—even should he believe in Him—

until he believes in Muḥammad (may God's blessings and peace be upon him and his Family) and in everything that he brought and informed us of, whether of the affairs of this world or the next. This includes faith in the questioning of the dead by Munkar and Nakīr about religion, *Tawḥīd* and Prophethood, and in the bliss which is in the grave for those who were obedient, and the torment which it contains for the rebellious.

"And that one should believe in the Resurrection after Death, the gathering of bodies and spirits to stand in the presence of God the Exalted, and in the Reckoning; and that His slaves will be at that time in different states, some being called to account, some being exempted, while others shall enter the Garden without reckoning.

"One should believe in the Scales in which good and evil deeds will be weighed; and in the *Ṣirāt*, which is a bridge stretched over the depths of Hell; and in the Pool [*Ḥawḍ]* of our Prophet Muḥammad, may God's blessings and peace be upon him and his Family, the water of which is from the Garden, and from which the believers shall drink before entering the Garden. And in the intercession of the Prophets, followed by the Veracious Saints [*ṣiddīqūn*], and then the scholars, the virtuous [*ṣāliḥūn*] and the other believers. And that the Greatest Intercession is the prerogative of Muḥammad (may God's blessings and peace be upon him and his Family). And that the people of *Tawḥīd* who have entered the fire shall be taken out of it until not one person in whose heart there lies an atom's weight of faith shall remain in it eternally. And that the people of polytheism and disbelief shall abide in the Fire eternally and for evermore, *their suffering shall not be diminished; neither shall they be reprieved.* [2:162] And that the believers shall abide in the Garden eternally and without end, *wherein no tiredness shall befall them, and from which they shall not be expelled.* [15:48] And that the believers shall see their Lord with their eyes, in a way befitting His Majesty and the Holiness of His Perfection.

"And that the Companions of the Messenger of God (may God's blessings and peace be upon him and his family) were virtuous, that their status was of various ranks, and that they were just, good, and trustworthy. It is not lawful to insult or denigrate any of them. And that the rightful successor [*khalīfa*] to the Messenger of God (may God's blessings and peace be upon him and his Family) was Abū Bakr al-Ṣiddīq, followed by 'Umar al-Fārūq, then 'Uthmān al Shahīd, then 'Alī al-Murtaḍā, may God be pleased with them and with all his other Companions, and with those who follow them with excellence until the Day of Judgment, and with us also, by Your mercy, O Most Merciful!"

Conclusion

A conclusion constituted of seven *ḥadīths* including comprehensive wisdom and profitable counsels from the traditions of the Messenger of God—may God's blessings and peace be upon him.

First *ḥadīth*: Jābir ibn 'Abdallāh—may God be pleased with them both—said, I heard the Messenger of God—may God's blessings and peace be upon him—say, *The Son of Adam is indeed forgetful of what he was created for. When God wishes to create him, He says to the angel, 'Write down his provision, write down his traces, write down his appointed time, and write down whether he is wretched or fortunate.' The angel then ascends back and God appoints two other angels to record his good and evil deeds. When death comes, these two angels ascend and the Angel of Death arrives to take his spirit. When he is placed in the grave, his spirit is returned to his body and the two Angels of the Grave come to try him. Then they ascend back. When the Hour comes, the Angel of Good Deeds and the Angel of Evil Deeds descend toward him. They untie the record that is wound around his neck, then accompany him, one leading him, the other a witness*. Then the Messenger of God—may God's blessings and peace be upon him—said, *Ahead of you is a formidable thing that you underestimate, so seek help from God the Immense.*[1]

Second *ḥadīth*: 'Abdal-Raḥmān ibn Samura—may God be pleased with him—said, The Messenger of God—may God's blessings and peace be upon him—came out to us, saying, *Last night I saw wonders. I saw a man from my community to whom the Angel of Death had come to take his spirit. His loyalty to his parents came and drove him away from him. And I saw a man from my community around whom the torment of the grave had been spread. His ritual ablutions came and saved him from it. And I saw a man from my community surrounded by the devils. The remembrance of God came and rescued him from them. And I saw a man from my community surrounded by the Angels of Torment. His ritual prayers came and saved him from them. And I saw a man from my community panting from thirst. Whenever he approached a basin he was driven away from it. His fasts came and gave him to drink until his thirst was quenched. And I saw a man from my community as the*

1. Abū Nu'aym al-Aṣbahānī, *Ḥilyat al-Awliyā'*, vol. 1, p. 478.

Prophets were sitting in circles, whenever he approached a circle he was sent away. His purification from major impurity (ghusl) came, took him by the hand, and sat him next to me. And I saw a man from my community before whom was darkness, behind whom was darkness, on the right of whom was darkness, on the left of whom was darkness, above whom was darkness, and below whom was darkness. As he was perplexed therein, there came his Ḥajj and 'Umra, and they brought him out of the darkness and into the light. And I saw a man from my community who spoke to the believers, but they did not answer him. His preservation of kinship bonds came, saying, 'O believers! Speak to him.' So they spoke to him. And I saw a man from my community protecting his face from the heat and sparks of the Fire. His charity came and became a veil before his face to shade it. And I saw a man from my community surrounded on all sides by the Guardians of Hell. His enjoining good and forbidding evil saved it from their hands and handed him over to the Angels of Mercy. And I saw a man from my community on his knees, a veil standing between him and God. His good character came to take him by the hand and admit him to the presence of God the Exalted. And I saw a man from my community being dragged down by his record which was in his left hand. His fear of God came, took the record and placed it in his right hand. And I saw a man from my community whose scales were light. His little children who had died before him came and made them heavier. And I saw a man from my community standing on the edge of Hell. His awe of God came, saved him from this, and sent him on his way. And I saw a man from my community who had fallen into the Fire. The tears he had shed for the fear of God came and took him out of the Fire. And I saw a man from my community standing on the Bridge, shaking like a palm leaf. His thinking well of God the Exalted came, his shaking subsided and he went on his way. And I saw a man from my community on the Bridge, crawling at times, going on all four at others. His invocation of prayers upon me came, took him by the hand, steadied him up, and he started walking on the Bridge. And I saw a man from my community who had reached the gates of the Garden, but they were shut before him. His testimony that there is no god other than God came, opened the gates and admitted him to the Garden.[2] *And I saw people from my community whose lips were*

2. Ṭabarānī, *Al-Aḥādīth al-Ṭuwāl*, (41); Ibn Shāhīn, *Faḍā'il al-A'māl wa Thawābu Dhālik*, (526); Ibn Bishrān, *Amālī*, (249).

being clipped. I said, 'O Gabriel! Who are these?' He said, 'Those who circulate talebearing among the people.' And I saw men from my community hanging by their tongues. I said, 'Who are these, O Gabriel?' He answered, 'Those who slander men and women believers for nothing they have committed.' [33:58]

Third *ḥadīth*: Rakb al-Miṣrī—may God be pleased with him—said, The Messenger of God—may God's blessings and peace be upon him—said, *Blessed is he who is humble without servility, keeps his abasement to himself and does not beg, spends the money he has amassed but not sinfully, is compassionate to the humble and indigent, and keeps company with the people of knowledge and wisdom. Blessed is he whose earnings are lawful, his inward good, his outward noble, and from whose evil people are safe. Blessed is he who acts according to his knowledge, gives away the excess of his money, and withholds the excess of his speech.*[3]

Fourth *ḥadīth*: Asmā' bint 'Umays—may God be pleased with her—said, I heard the Messenger of God—may God's blessings and peace be upon him—say, *Evil is the servant who is miserly, yet proud, forgetful of the Great, the Most High. Evil is the servant who is overbearing and aggressive, forgetful of the Compeller, the Lofty. Evil is the servant who is distracted and frivolous, forgetful of the graves and of decay. Evil is the servant who is tyrannical and transgressing, forgetful of the beginning and the end. Evil is the servant who seeks the world with acts of religion. Evil is the servant who sells his religion for lusts. Evil is the servant who is led by his greed. Evil is the servant who is led astray by his whims. Evil is the servant who abases himself to obtain his desires.*[4]

Fifth *ḥadīth*: 'Alī—may God be pleased with him—said, The Messenger of God—may God's blessings and peace be upon him—said, *When my community commits fifteen things, afflictions will befall it.* They asked, "What are they, O Messenger of God?" He answered, *When turns are taken in appropriating spoils, when things in trust are treated as booty, zakāt is considered a burdensome expenditure, a man obeys his wife, while rebelling against his mother, treats his friends well, but not his father, when voices are raised in the mosques, the leader of the community is the worst*

3. Bayhaqī, *Shu'ab al-Īmān*, (3237); Bayhaqī, *Al-Sunan al-Kubrā*, vol. 4, p. 182; Ṭabarānī, *Kabīr*, (4480), Al-Shihāb al-Quḍā'ī, *Musnad al-Shihāb*, (580).

4. Tirmidhī, *Sunan*, (2372).

among them, a man is honored for fear of his evil, alcohol is drunk, silk is worn, girl singers and concerts abound, and the last among this community curses the first, let them expect tempestuous winds, sinking into the ground, or disfiguring mutations.[5]

Sixth *ḥadīth*: Abū Dharr—may God be pleased with him—said, I said, "O Messenger of God! What did the leaves of Abraham—may peace be upon him—consist of?" He said, "*They consisted entirely of precepts:*

> *O king empowered and being tested, subject to illusions! I have not raised you to accumulate the things of this world one on top of the other, but I raised you to prevent the prayers of those who are wronged from reaching Me, for I never reject them, even from a disbeliever.*
>
> *A man of reason, unless he loses his reason, must divide his time into periods: A period when he communes with his Lord, a period when he brings himself to account, a period when he reflects on God's creation, and a period devoted to his food and beverage. A man of reason must move only for three reasons: To acquire provision for the hereafter, earn a living, or find pleasure but in no unlawful manner. A man of reason must be aware of his times, concentrated on his purpose, and in control of his tongue. He who counts his words as deeds will speak little of what concerns him not.*

I said, "O Messenger of God! What did the leaves of Moses consist of?" He said, *They were all lessons of wisdom:*

> *I wonder at he who is certain of death yet rejoices!*
>
> *I wonder at he who is certain of the Fire yet laughs!*
>
> *I wonder at he who is certain of predestination yet toils!*
>
> *I wonder at he who sees the world and how it turns its people about, yet trusts it!*
>
> *I wonder at he who is certain of the morrow's reckoning yet does not work."*

I said, "O Messenger of God! Counsel me." He said, "*I counsel you to fear God, for it is the most important thing*." I said, "O Mes-

5. Ṭabarānī, *Awsaṭ*, (476); Abū 'Amr al-Dānī, *Al-Sunan al-Wārida fi'l-Fitan*, (322).

senger of God! Give me more." He said, "*Recite the Qur'ān, for it is a light for you on earth and a remembrance for you in heaven.*" I said, "O Messenger of God! Give me more." He said, "*Beware of laughing excessively, for it deadens the heart and removes the light of one's face.*" I said, "O Messenger of God! Give me more." He said, "*Maintain silence except for good words, for it repels the devil from you and helps you in your religious affairs.*" I said, "O Messenger of God! Give me more." He said, *Go to* Jihād, *for it is the monasticism of my community*. I said, "O Messenger of God! Give me more." He said, *Love the poor and sit with them*. I said, "O Messenger of God! Give me more." He said, *Look at those beneath you, not those above you, you will thus be less likely to belittle God's favor upon you*. I said, "O Messenger of God! Give me more." He said, *Speak the truth even when it is bitter*. I said, "O Messenger of God! Give me more." He said, *Let what you know of yourself prevent you from criticizing others. Do not be angry with them for things you commit yourself. It is enough of a fault to notice in others what you fail to recognize in yourself and become irritated with them for things you do yourself*. Then he patted me on the chest saying, *There is no intelligence better than considering consequences, no circumspection better than abstention, and no honor better than good character*.[6]

Seventh *ḥadīth*: Abū Dharr—may God be pleased with him—also said that the Prophet—may God's blessings and peace be upon him—said that his Lord—August and Majestic- said, *"O My servants! I have forbidden Myself injustice and made it forbidden amongst you, so wrong not one another. O My servants! You are all astray save those whom I guide, so ask Me for guidance and I shall guide you. O My servants! You are all hungry save those whom I feed, so ask Me to feed you and I shall. O My servants! You are all naked save those whom I clothe, so ask Me to clothe you and I shall. O My servants! You commit faults night and day and I am the one who forgives all sins, so ask Me for forgiveness and I shall forgive you. O My servants! You will never be able to cause Me harm, nor will you ever be able to bring Me benefit. O My servants! Were the first and the last among you, the humans and the jinns, to have hearts similar to that of the most God-fearing man among you, it would increase nothing to My kingdom. O My servants! Were the first and the last among you, the humans and the*

6. Ibn Ḥibbān, *Ṣaḥīḥ*, (362).

jinns, to have hearts similar to that of the most corrupt man among you, it would detract nothing from My kingdom. O My servants! Were the first and the last among you, the humans and the jinns, to stand all together and ask Me, and were I to grant each one of them his requests, it would diminish what I possess as much as a needle dipped into the ocean diminishes it. O My servants! It is but your deeds which I reckon for you, then repay you in full. He who meets with good, let him thank God, and he who meets with other than that, let him blame only himself.[7]

We have concluded the book, as we have begun it, with *ḥadīth*s of the Messenger of God—may God's blessings and peace be upon him—for the *baraka* and auspiciousness of the words of the Messenger of God—may God's blessings and peace be upon him. We hope that by this God shall make what we have compiled in between acceptable to Him, conducive to His good pleasure, and intended purely for His obedience and proximity. We hope He will forgive us and overlook whatever errors or confusion it may contain, as well as whatever ostentatious feelings, pride, or conceit may have affected us. We ask God to forgive us all these, as well as all other sins, and we repent to Him from them. *And who may forgive sins save God*? [3:135]

Our Lord! Accept from us, You are the Hearing, the Knowing. Relent toward us, You are the Relenter, the Compassionate. [2: 127, 128]] *Our Lord! Condemn us not whenever we forget or err. Our Lord! Lay not upon us a burden similar to that You have laid on those before us. Our Lord! Impose not on us what we cannot bear. And pardon us, and forgive us, and have mercy on us, for You are our Ally, so give us victory over the disbelieving people.* [2:286] There is no god other than You—Transcendent are You. O God! I ask you forgiveness for my sin and I ask you for your mercy. O God! Increase me in knowledge and allow not my heart to swerve after You have guided me. Bestow upon me mercy from You, for You are the Bestower.

This book has now been completed—may God be praised—with His help and His gracious granting of success. *May God be praised who has guided us to this. We would never have been guided had not God guided us. The Messengers of our Lord have come with the truth.*[7:43] *Transcendent is your Lord, the Lord of Might, beyond that they describe. May peace be upon the Messengers, and*

7. Muslim, *Ṣaḥīḥ*, (4674).

praise belongs to God, Lord of the worlds. [37:180-182] There is neither power nor ability save by God, the High, the Immense. And may God's blessings and peace be upon our master Muḥammad, his family, and Companions.

Dictation was concluded on Sunday the twenty second of the blessed month of Sha'bān of the year 1089 of his emigration—blessings and peace be upon him.

May God's blessings and peace be upon our master Muḥammad, his family, and Companions.

Dedication

To Zaid, Karim, Ali, and Bilal–Love God with all your heart so He too may love you. Then nothing is impossible.

A.M.U.

Nour Akhras and Syed Mohammed Amjad Quadri would like to dedicate this book to their parents, Fayha and Abdul-Bari Akhras, and Syed Ahmedullah Quadri and UmmulAsfia al-Aidroos, and to the people of the generation before them who took great care in raising them according to the Sunnah of our Beloved Prophet Muhammad—peace be upon him. We would also like anyone who benefits from this book to keep us, our parents, and our children, Syed Hamza al-Ahdal Quadri and his siblings-to-come, in his/her prayers.